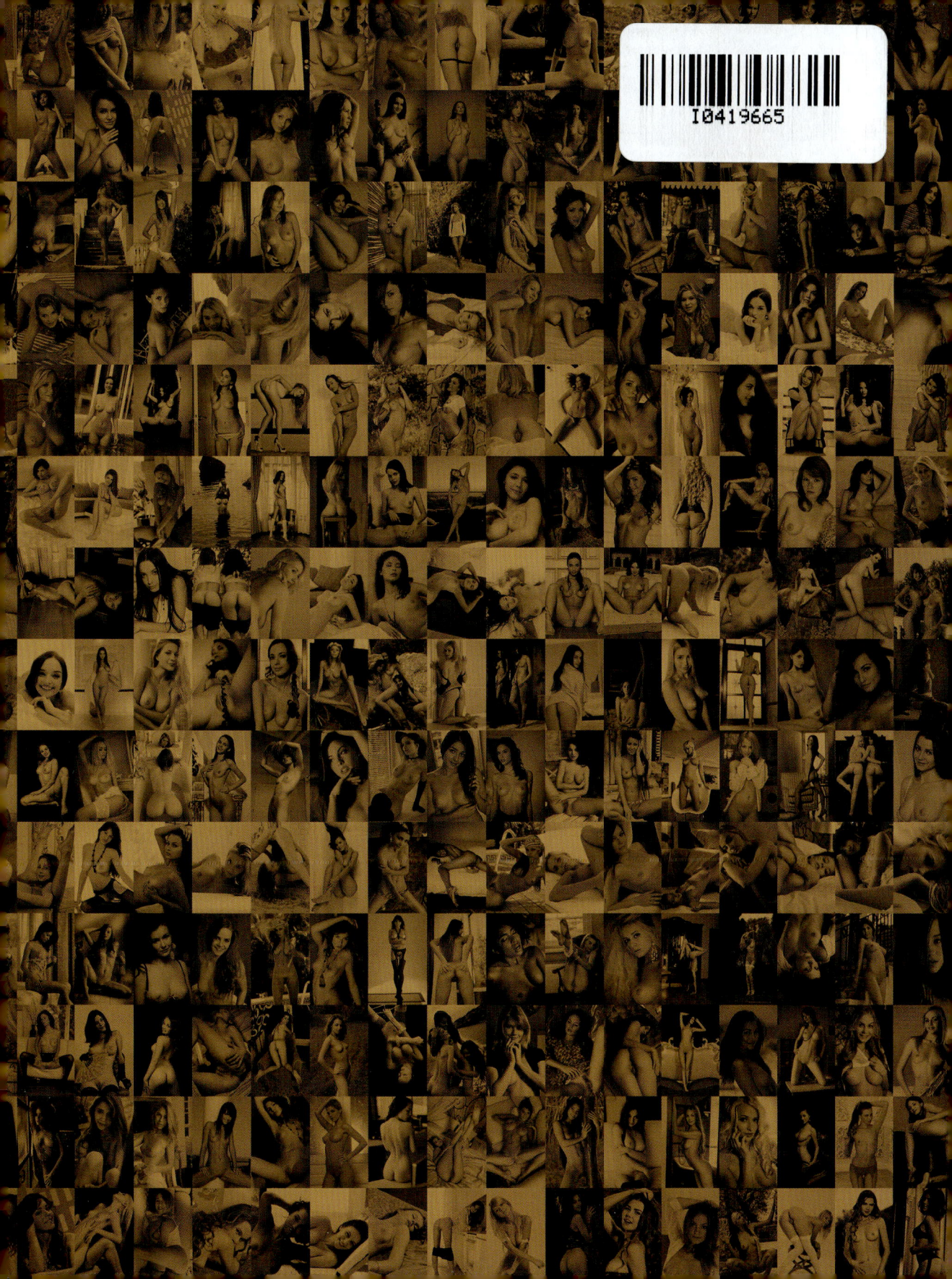

I0419665

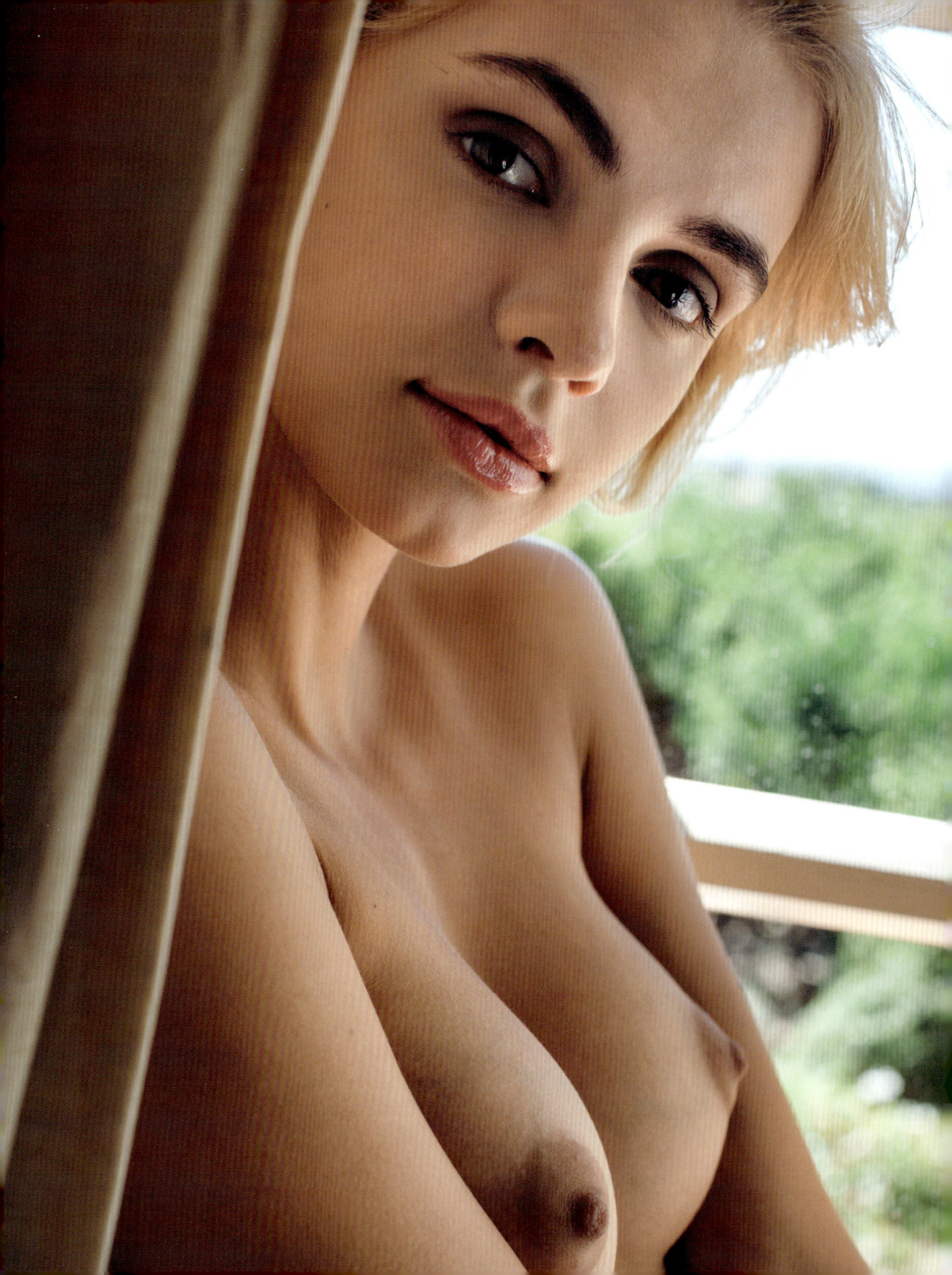

TOP MODELS OF
MetArt.com
WHERE FLAWLESS BEAUTY MEETS ART

LILIT A

COLLECTED AND EDITED BY ISABELLA CATALINA

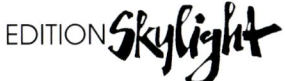
EDITION Skylight

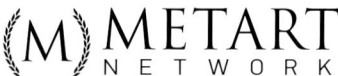

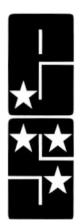

First edition 2023
Copyright © 2023 by Edition Skylight

EDITION SKYLIGHT
Rosengartenstrasse 13B
CH-8608 Bubikon / Zürich
Switzerland
info@edition-skylight.com
www.edition-skylight.com

ISBN 978-3-03766-693-7

Bibliographic information published by Die Deutsche Bibliothek
Die Deutsche Bibliothek lists this publication in the
Deutsche Nationalbibliografie; detailed bibliographic data
are available in the Internet at http://dnb.ddb.de.

Printed in Slovenia

LILIT A IS THE KIND OF HOT GIRL YOU DESIRE AT FIRST SIGHT

Of herself she says "I am a very peaceful, quiet girl. I love discreet recreation outdoors, but don't like big cities. My hobbies are romantic music, movies, and reading French poetry in the park, which is my favorite pastime. I'm posing for Met-Art to try something new. Although I was very shy at first, I now find it interesting and revealing." Lilit's beauty is classic and timeless. Her slim frame is alluring and captivating, but it's her incredible facial features that will leave you spellbound and craving for more. She has an innocent, pure look with an angelic face and a superb, lean nubile body. This girl is impossible to resist ... Prepare to be captivated by Lilit A from Ukraine, she's a true explorer, not just of the world, but of her mind and body. She walks down unknown, sometimes explicit paths, searching not just for pleasure, but also for her true self. She has not yet satisfied her many desires but is still hungry. So, take our word for it, this is a girl you won't be able to get enough of! Lilit A is simply stunning. Her features are so divine that you would think she was sculpted from clay by a Greek god. Lucky for you, she loves to show off her perfect assets and doe-like eyes for us to appreciate. You won't be disappointed by her awesome curves and youthful face. Lilit A began her nude modeling career in 2015, and is presented in 26 portfolios on Metart, 11 portfolios on SexArt and 8 portfolios on MetartX.

„Ich bin ein sehr friedliches und ruhiges Girl. Ich liebe Erholung in der Natur und mag keine großen Städte. Meine Hobbys sind romantische Musik und Filme. Französische Gedichte im Park zu lesen ist meine Lieblingsbeschäftigung. Ich posiere für Metart, um etwas Neues auszuprobieren. Obwohl ich anfangs sehr schüchtern war, finde ich es jetzt interessant und aufschlussreich." Lilits Schönheit ist zeitlos und klassisch. Ihr schlanker Körper ist verführerisch und fesselnd, aber es sind ihre unglaublichen Gesichtszüge, die den Betrachter in den Bann ziehen. Sie hat diesen unschuldig reinen Blick mit einem engelhaften Gesicht und einen strammen schlanken, jugendlichen Körper. Diesem Wunder der Natur wird unmöglich zu widerstehen sein. Lilit A stammt aus der Ukraine und betört uns alle. Sie ist eine wahre Entdeckerin, nicht nur von der Welt, sondern auch von ihrem Geist und Körper. Sie wandert auf unbekannten und expliziten Wegen und sucht nicht nur nach Vergnügen, sondern auch nach ihrem wahren Ich. Bisher hat sie ihre vielen Wünsche noch nicht erfüllt; sie ist immer noch hungrig nach mehr. Lilit A ist einfach atemberaubend. Ihre Züge sind so göttlich, dass man meinen könnte, sie wurde von einem griechischen Gott aus Ton geformt. Glücklicherweise liebt sie es, ihre perfekten Kurven zu zeigen, damit jeder sie bewundern kann. Sie begann ihre Karriere als Aktmodell im Jahr 2015 und wird in 26 Portfolios auf Metart, 11 Portfolios auf SexArt und 8 Portfolios auf MetartX präsentiert.

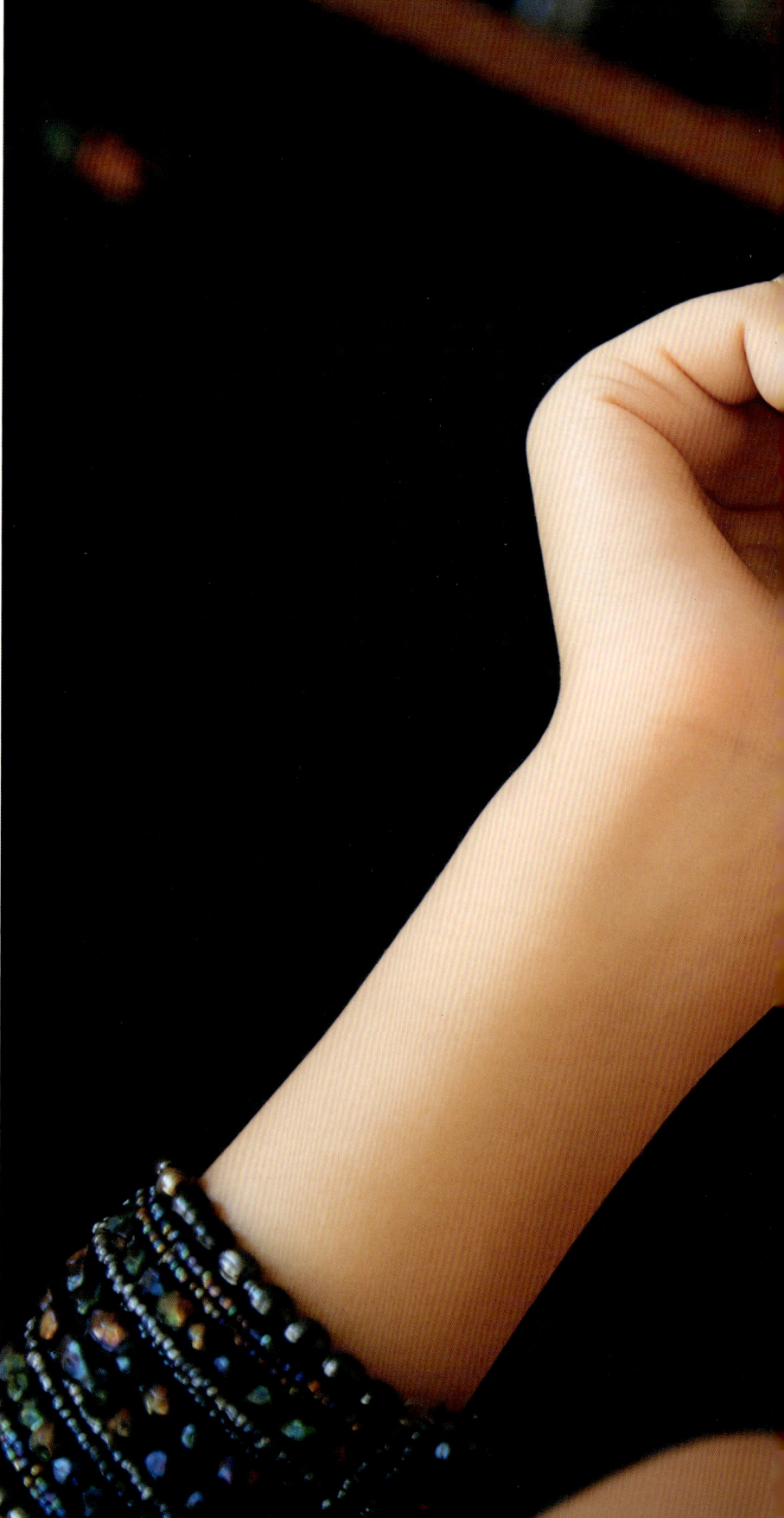

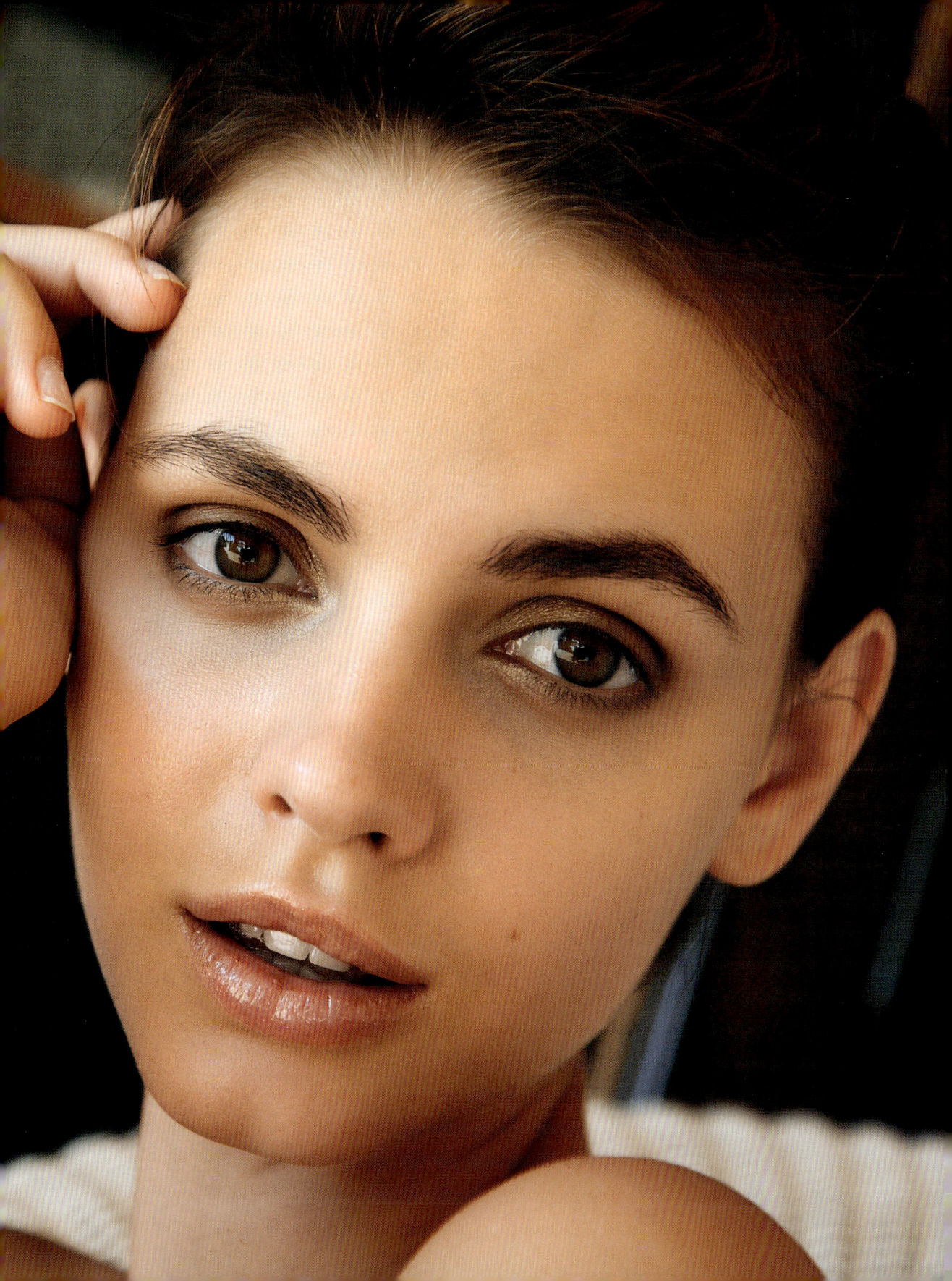

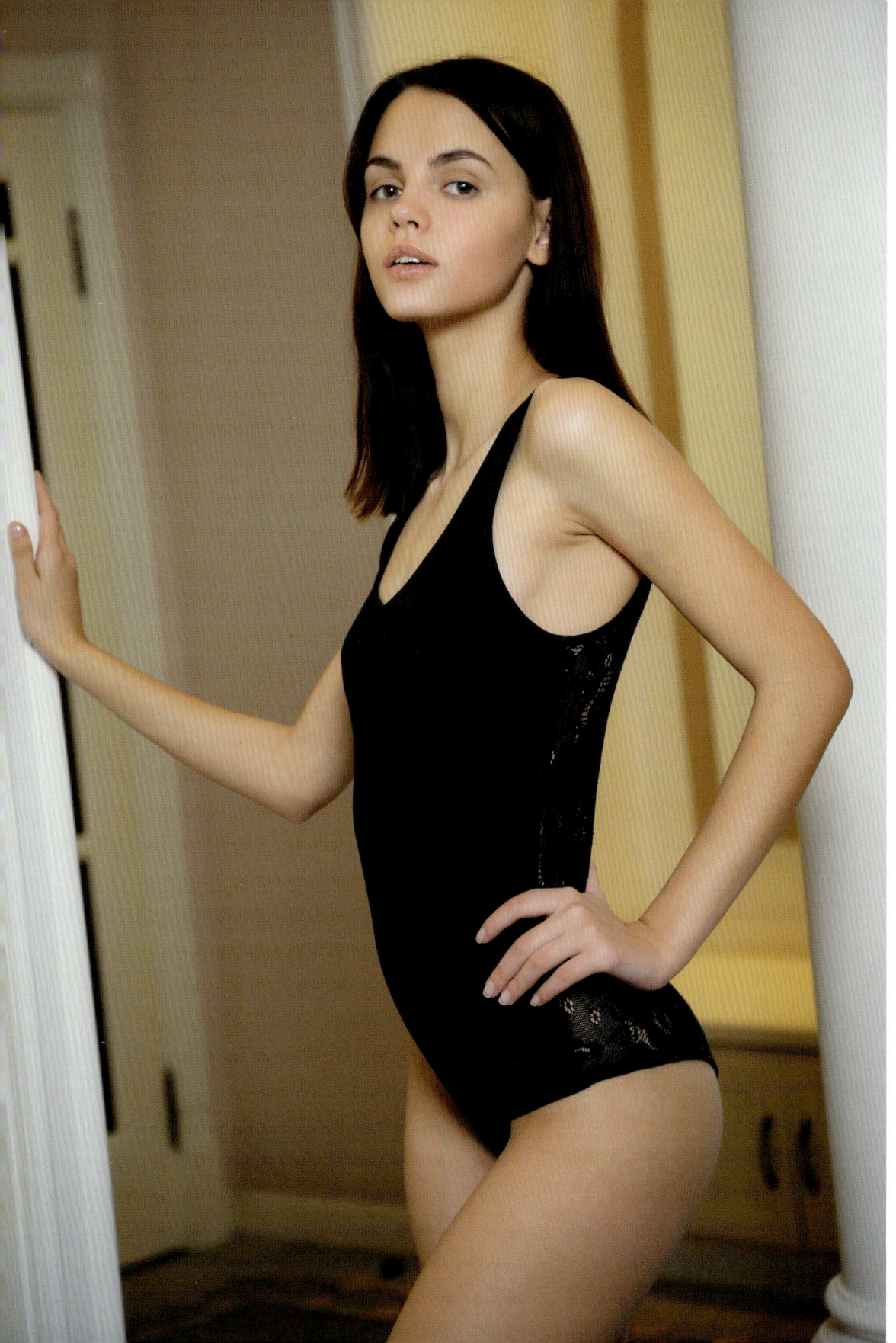

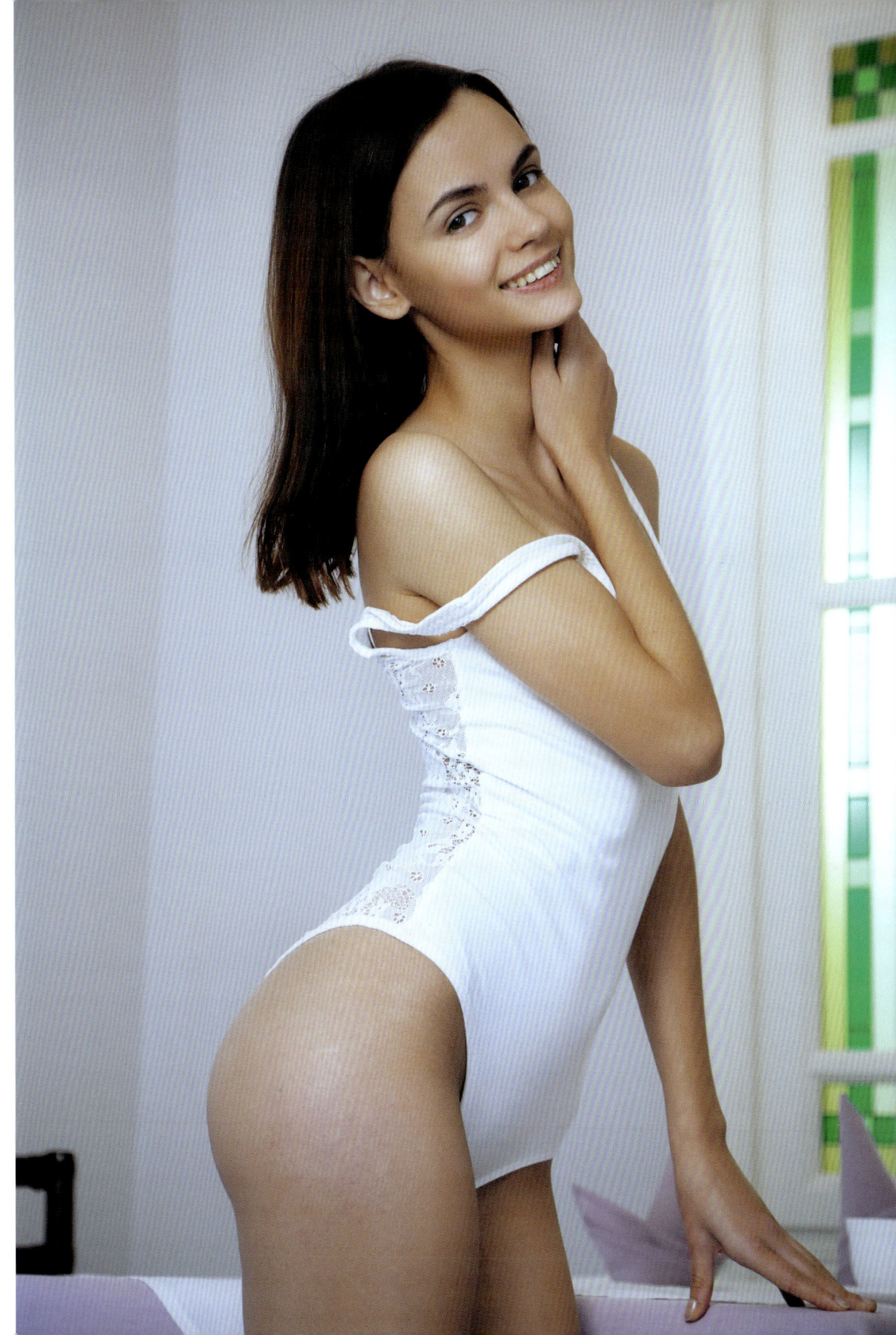

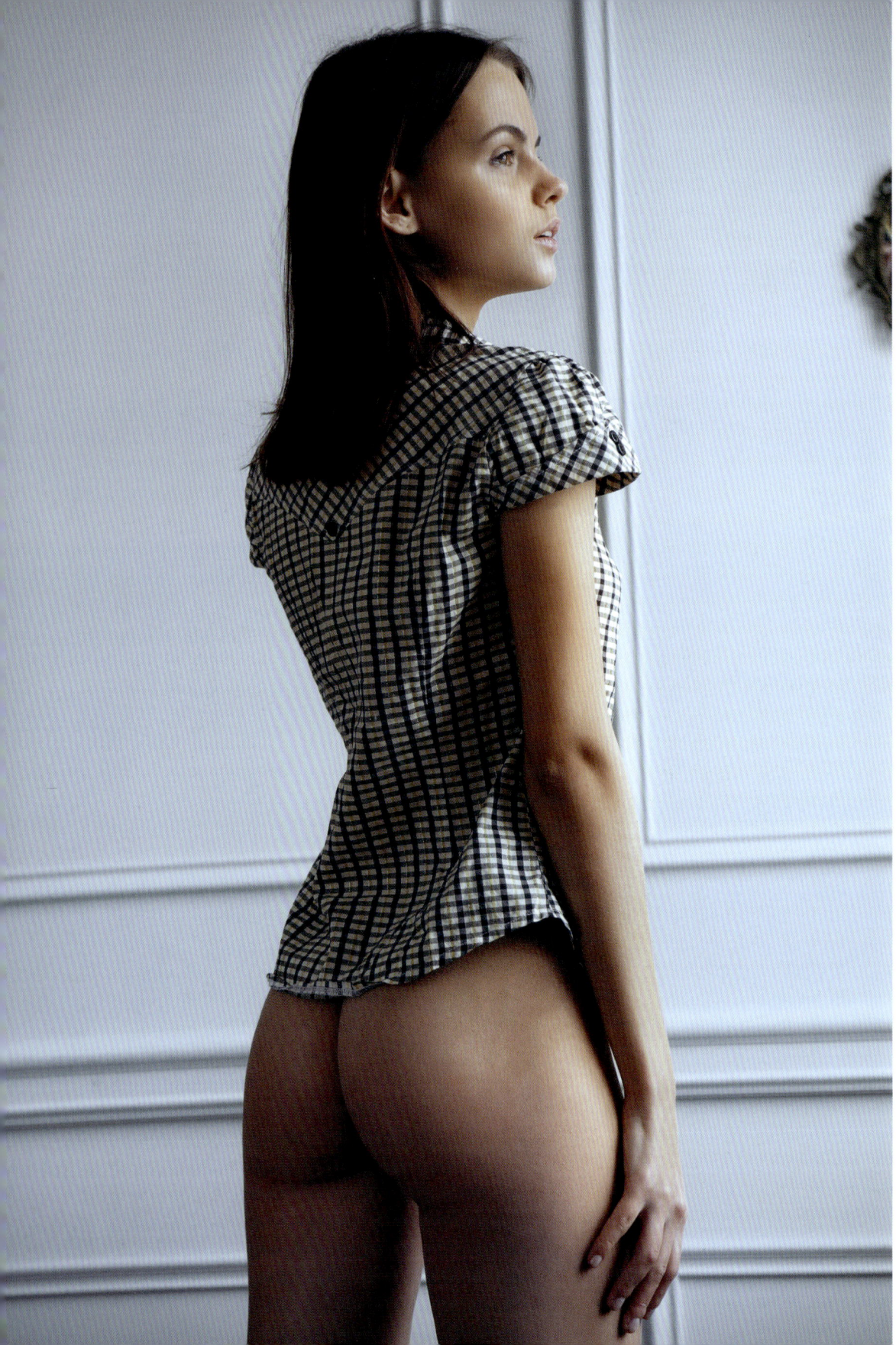

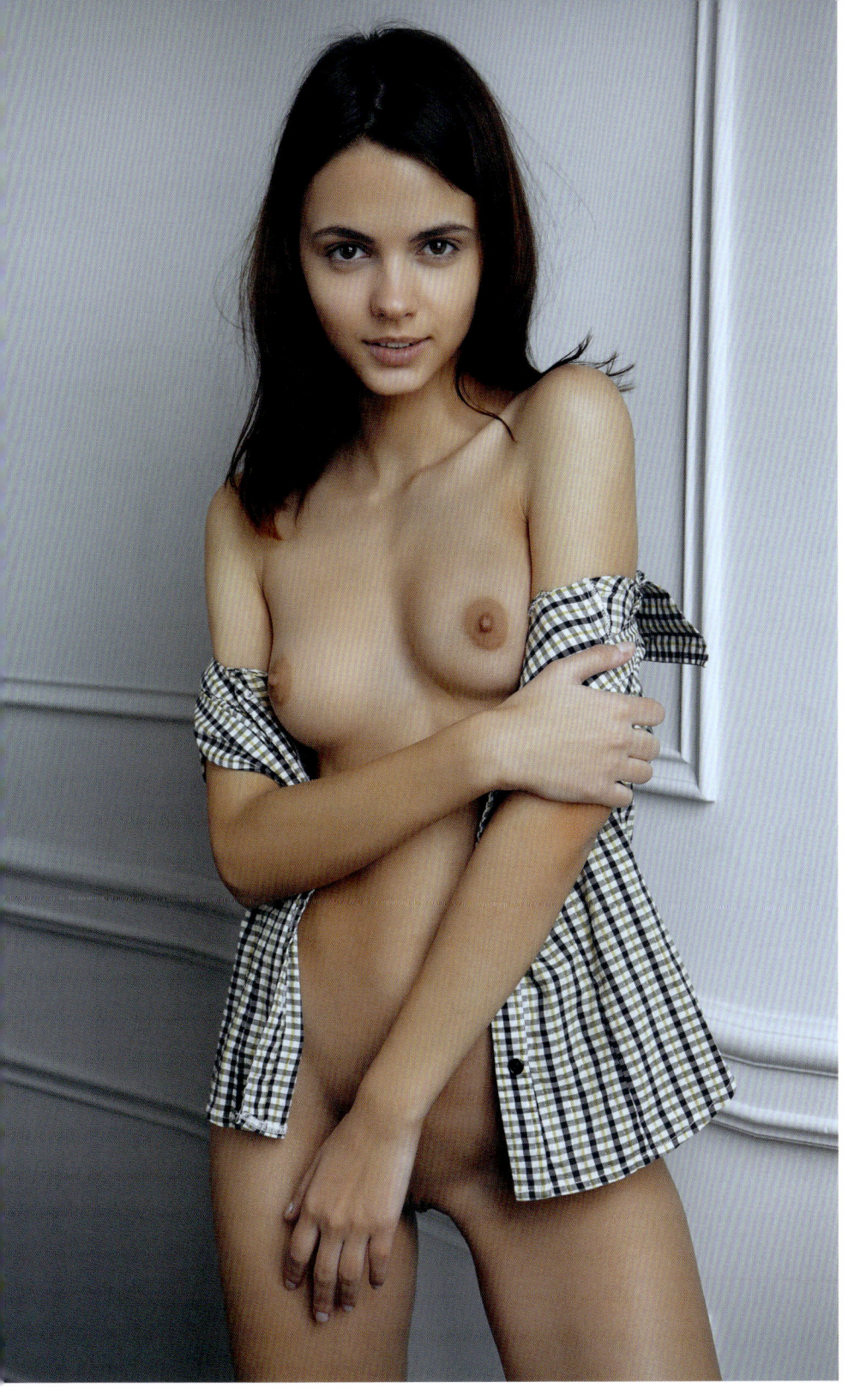

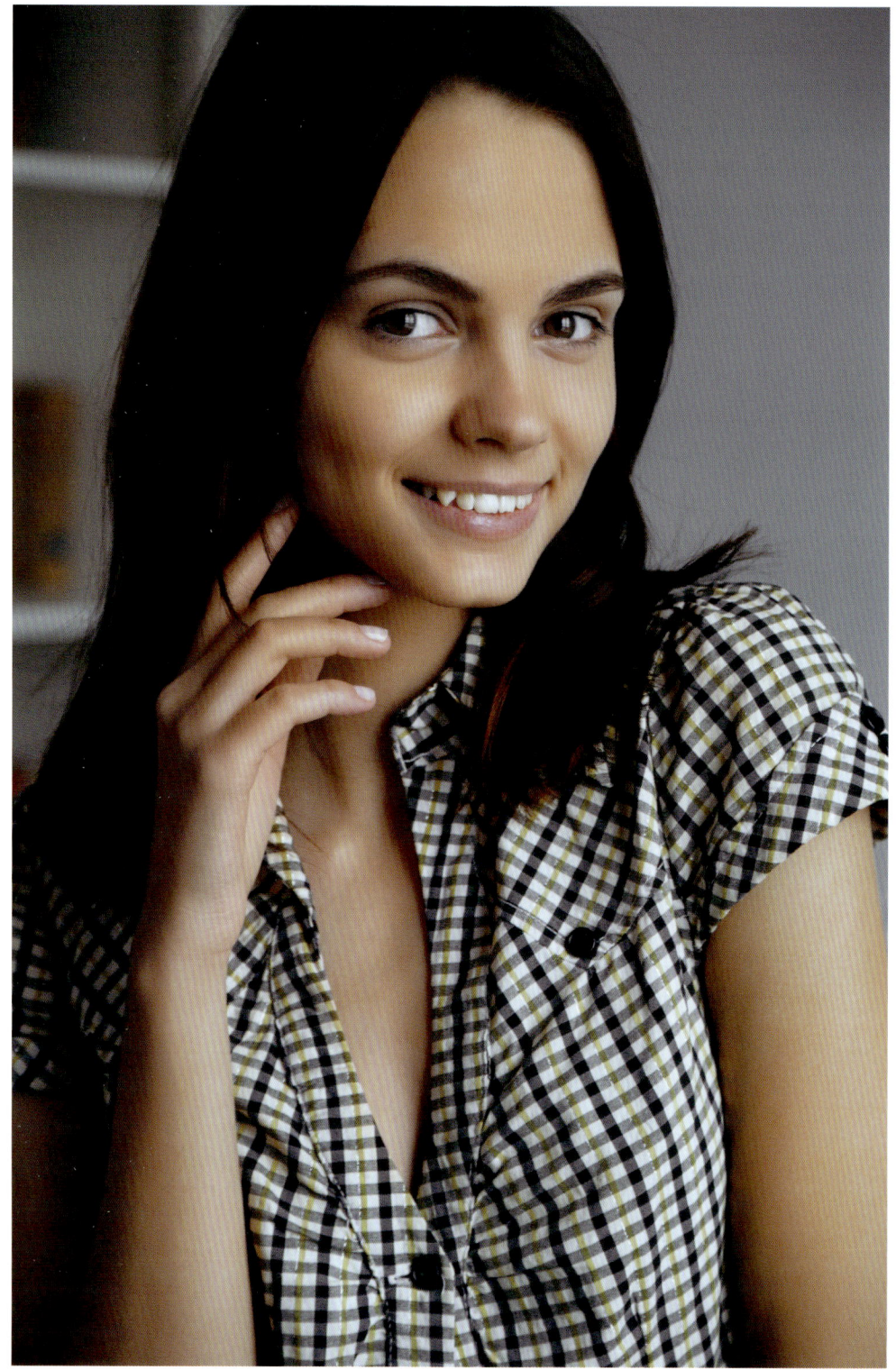

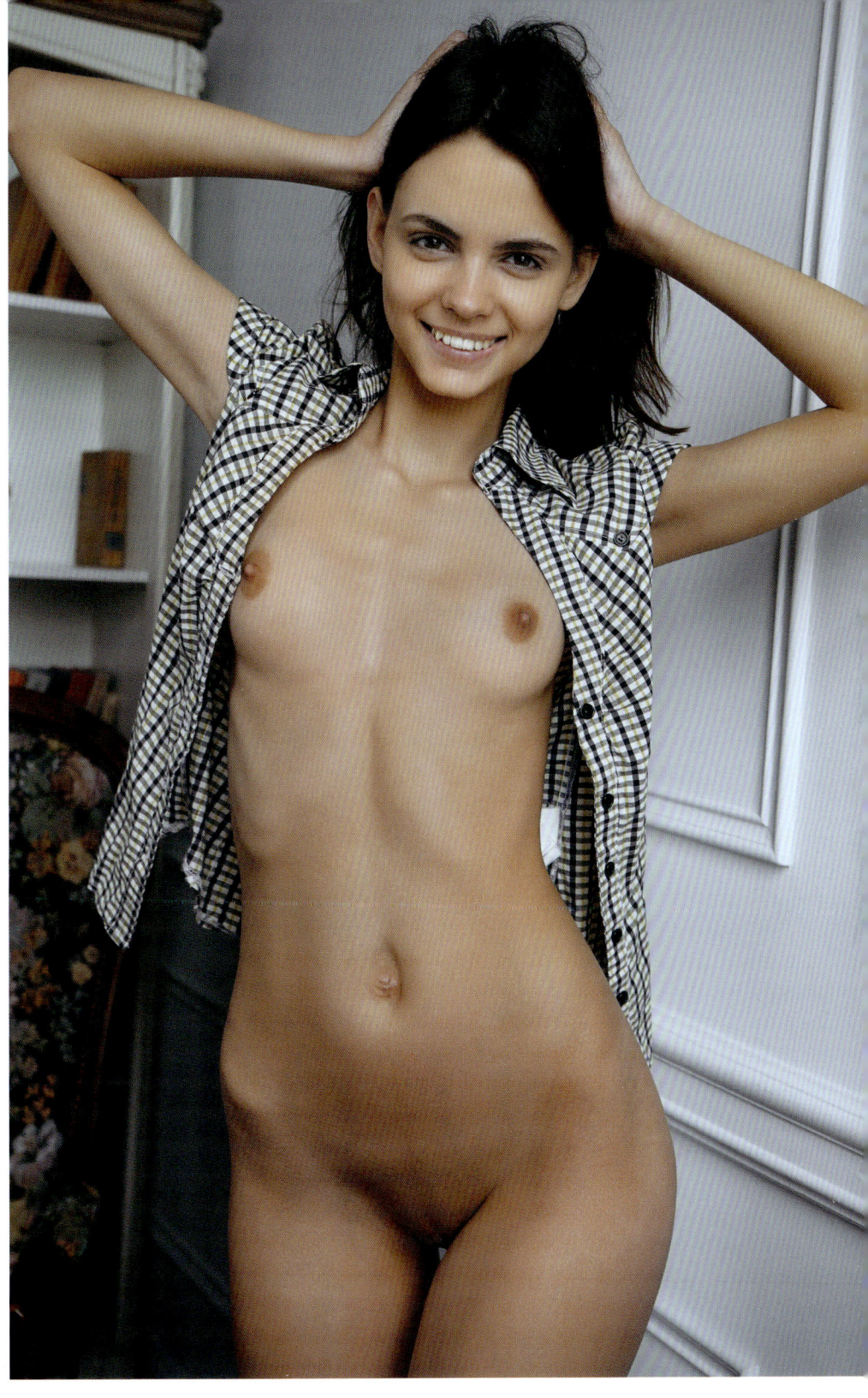

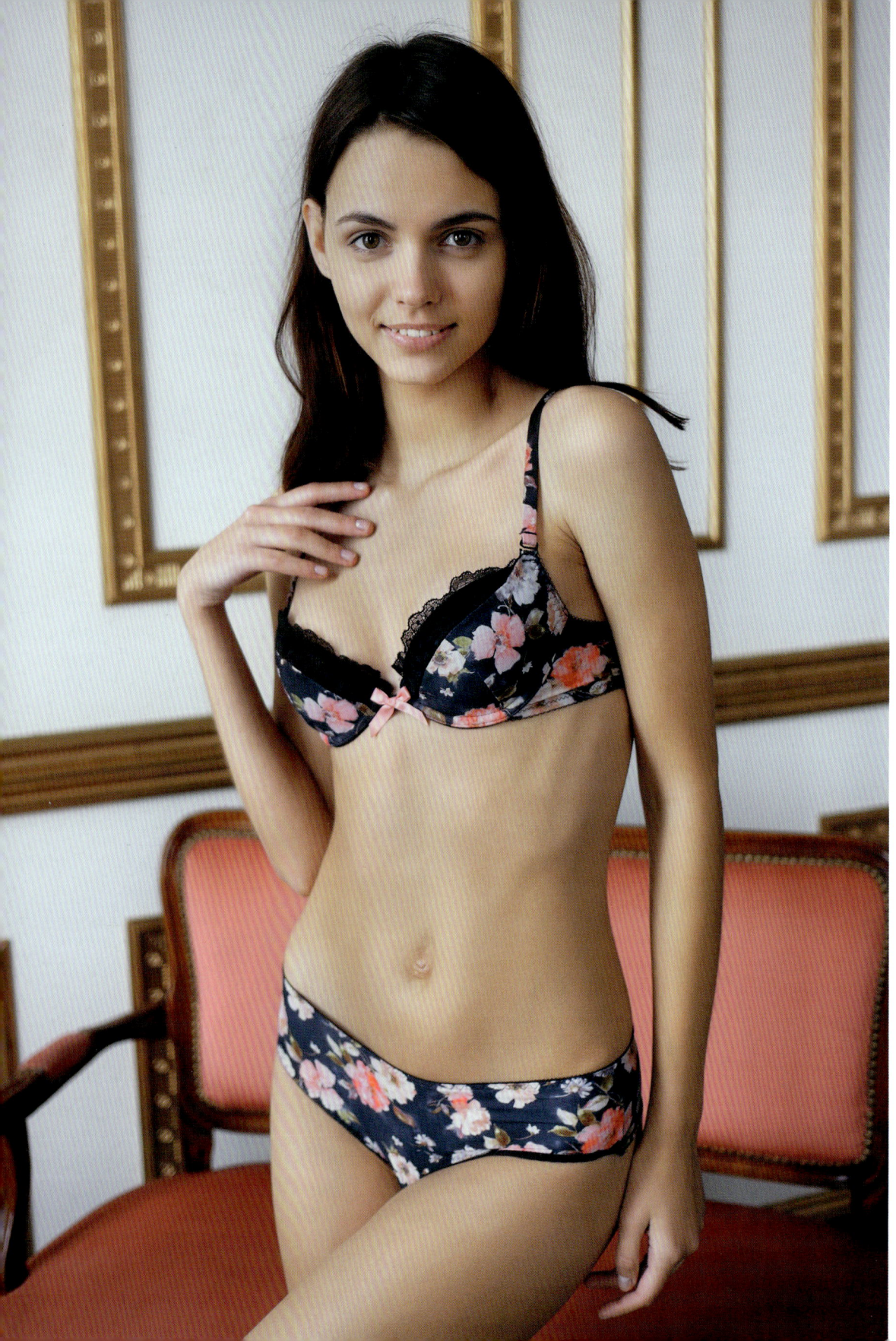

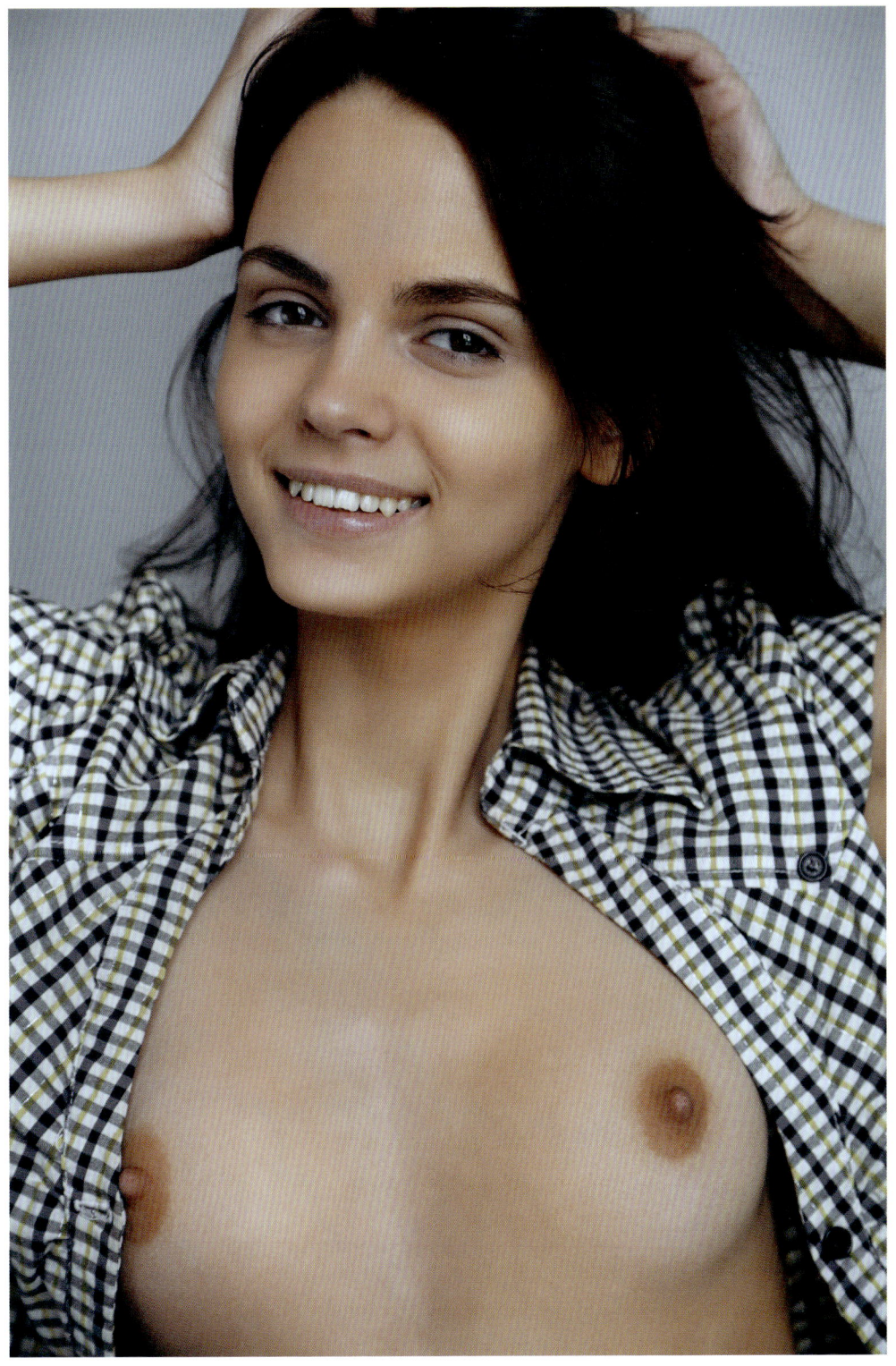

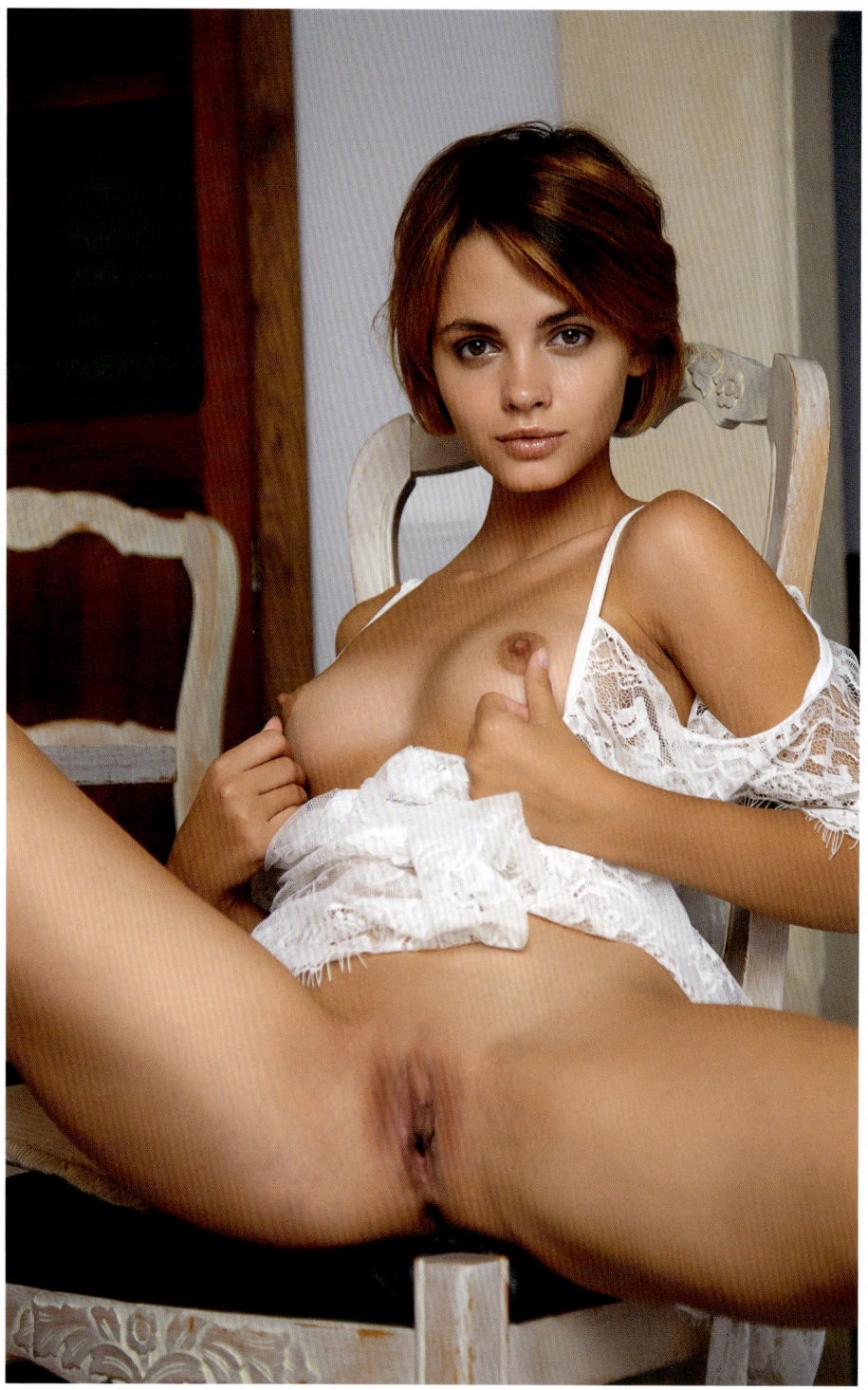

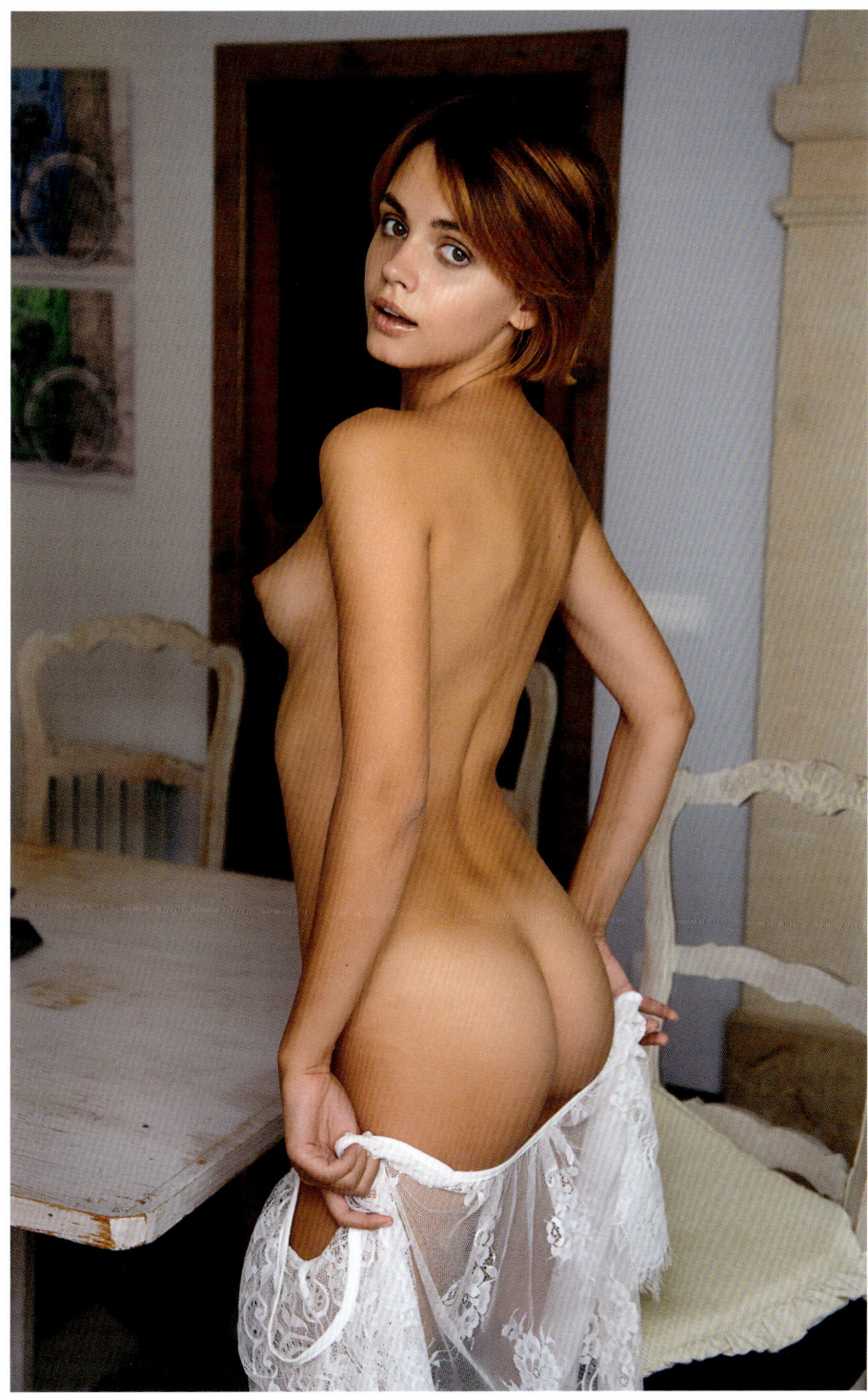

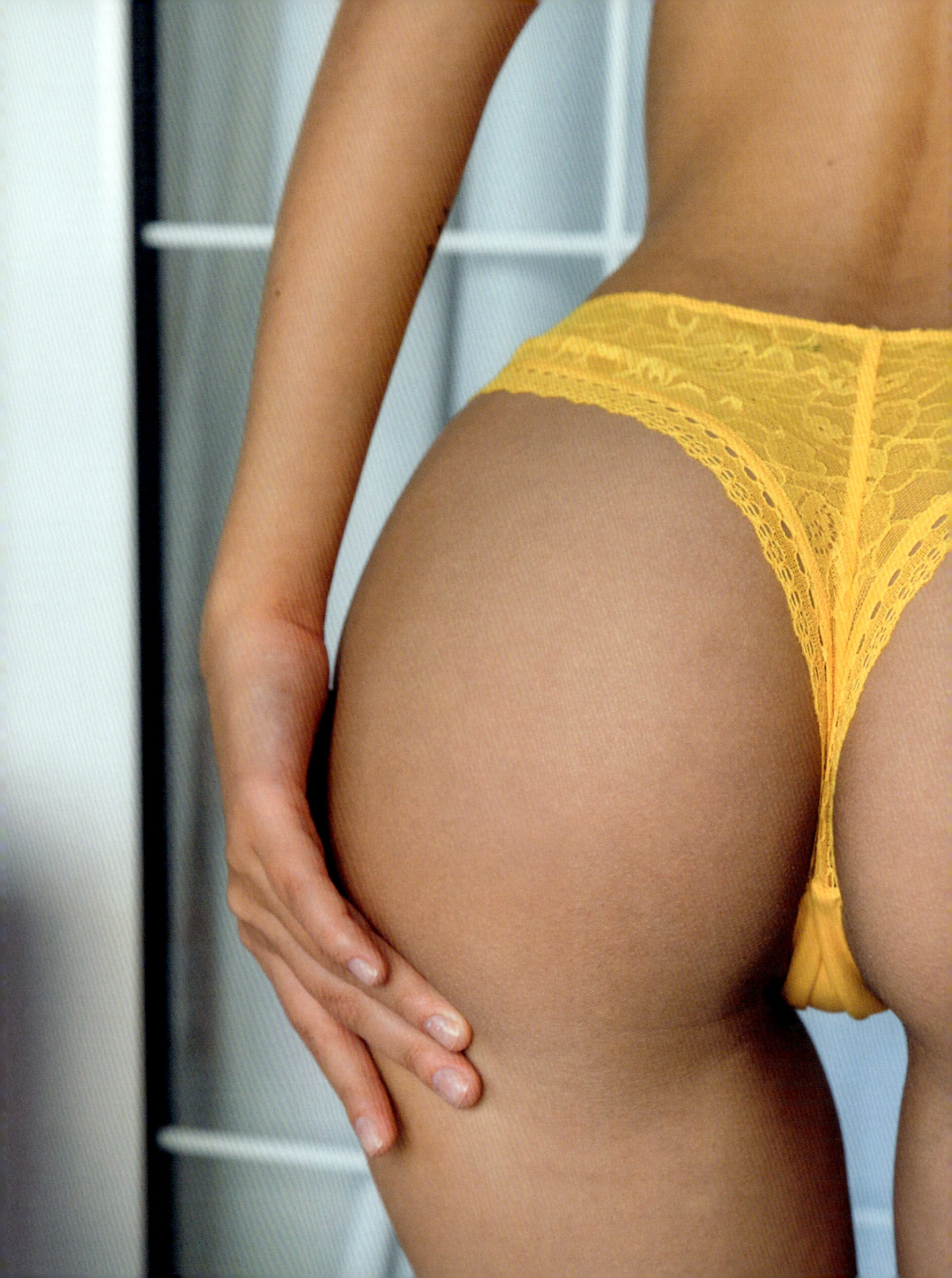

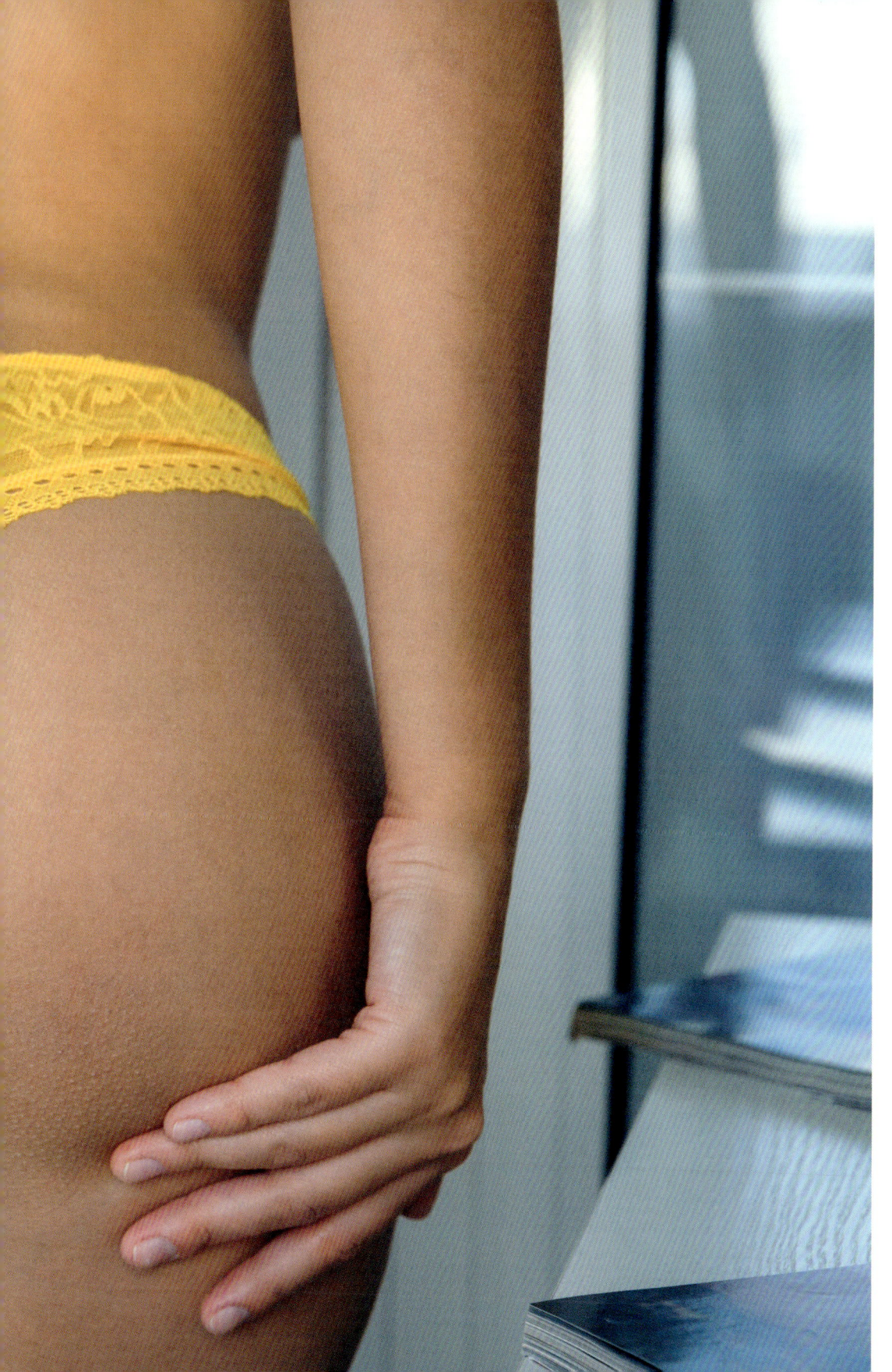

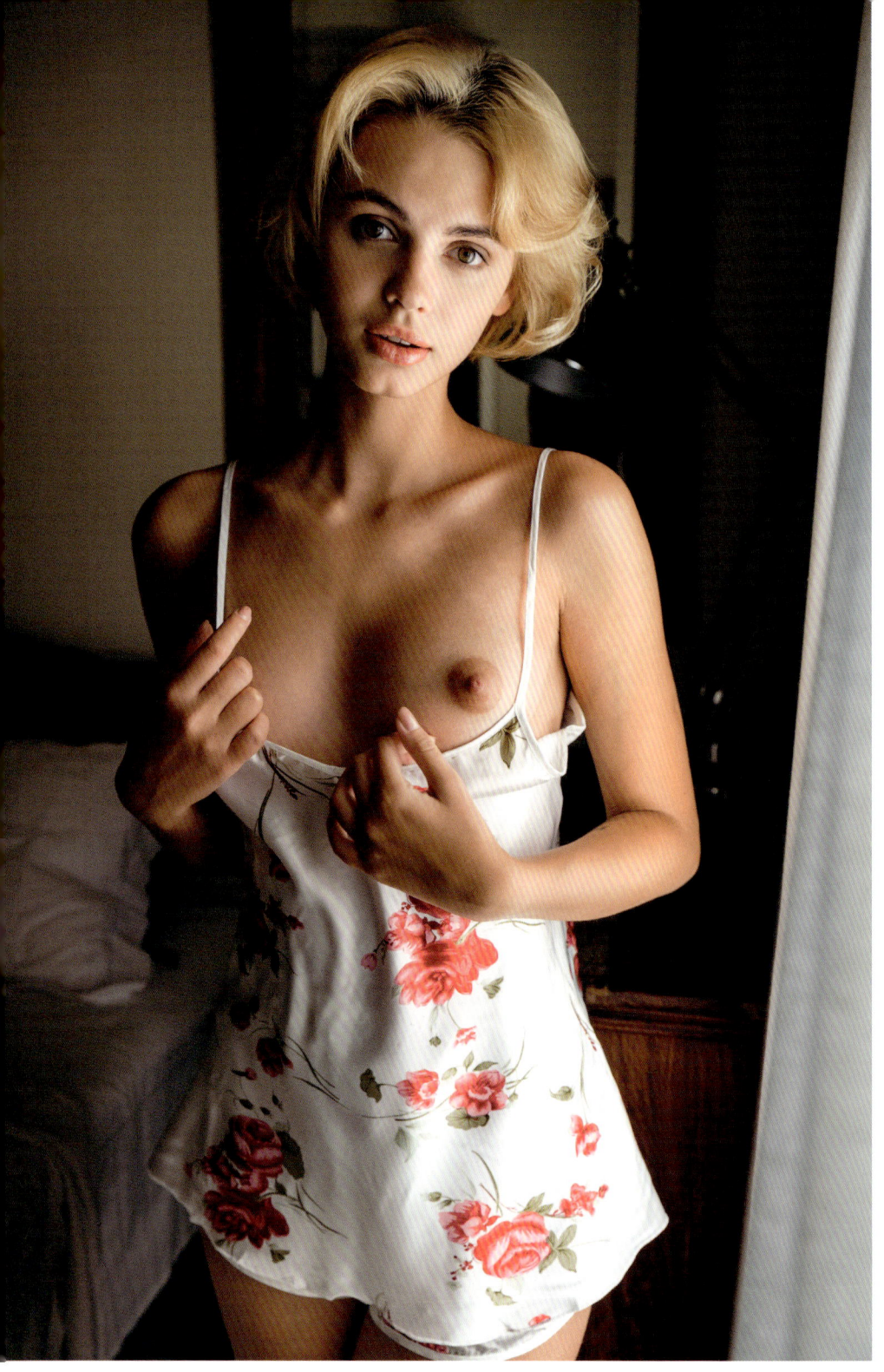

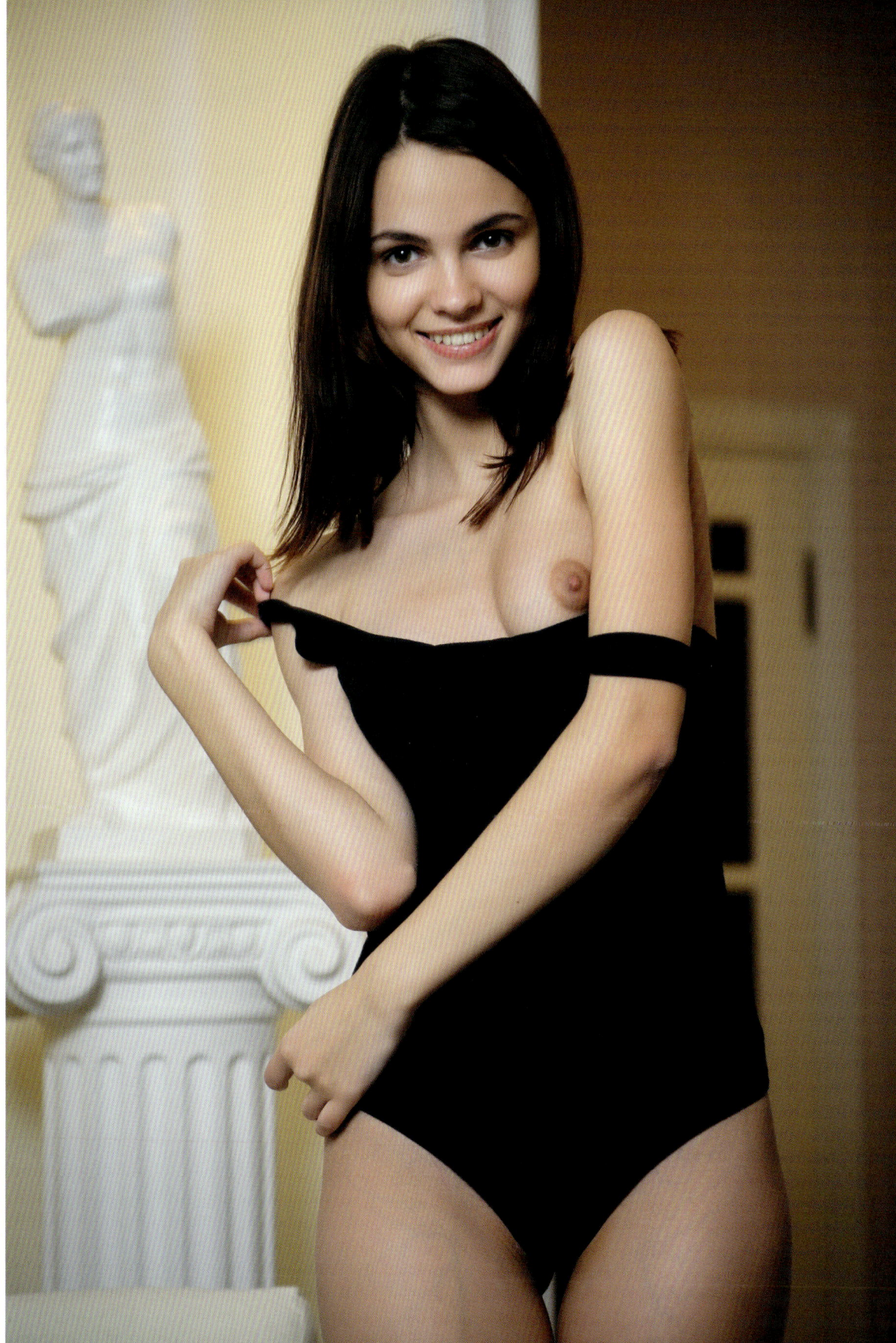

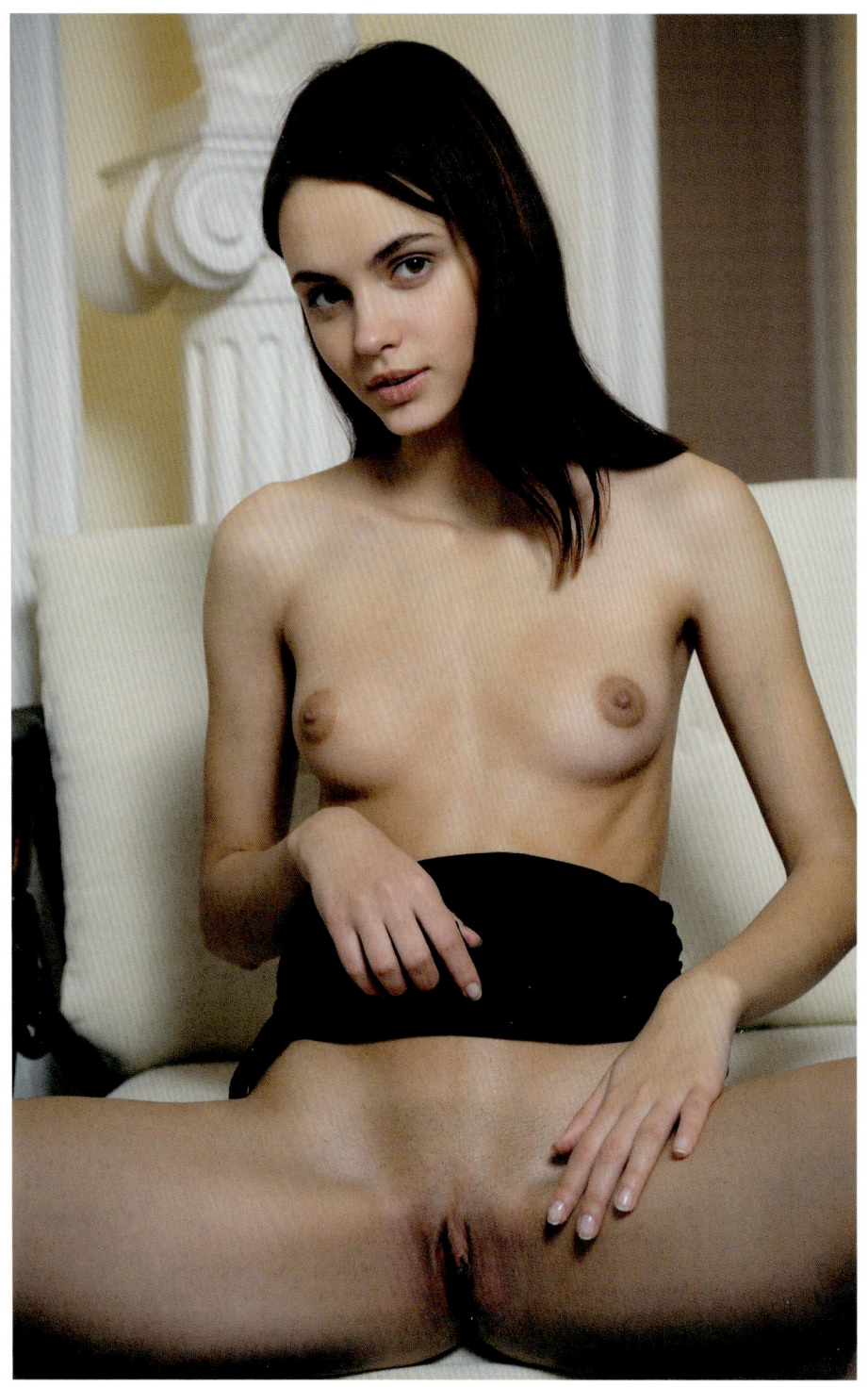

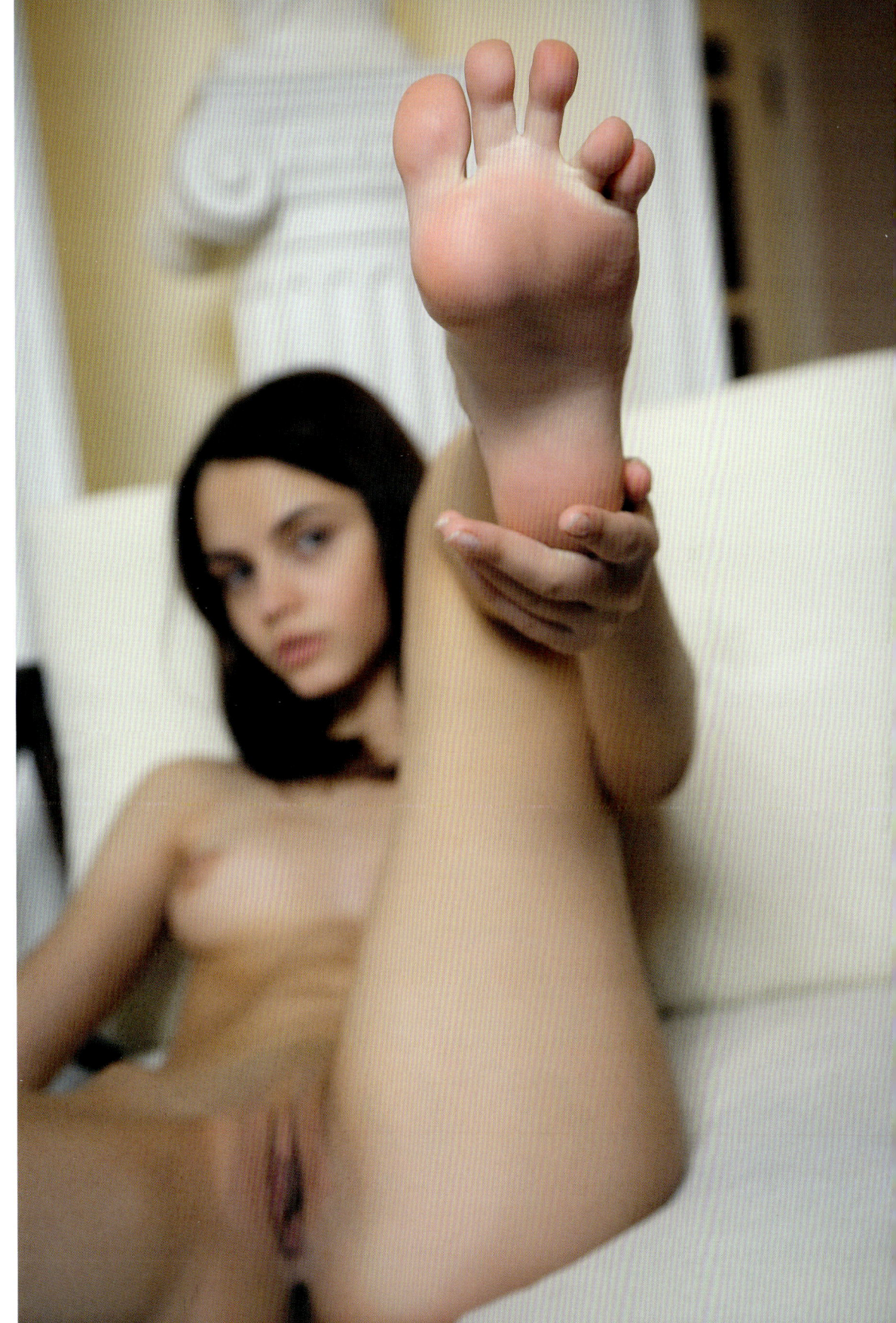

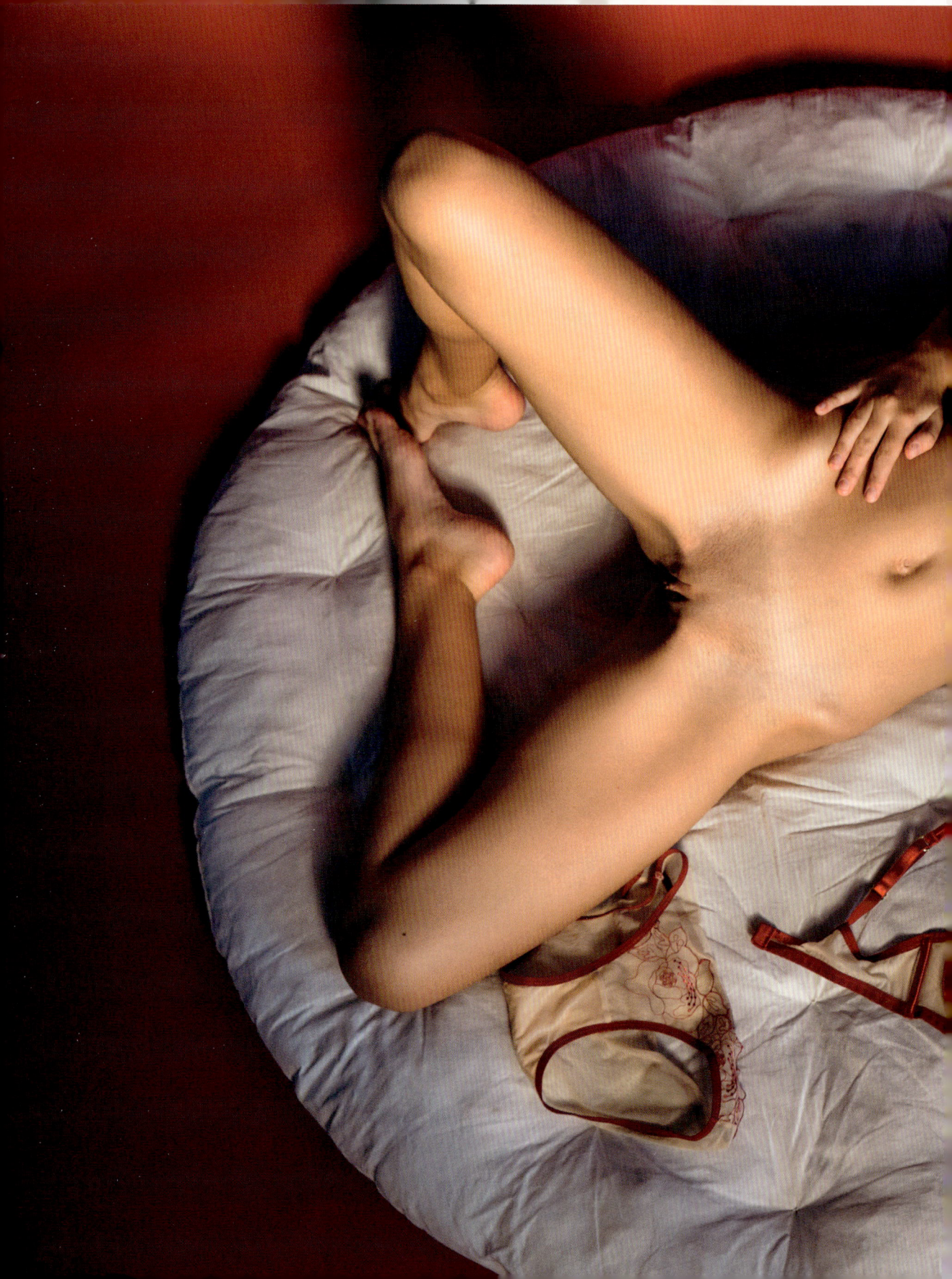

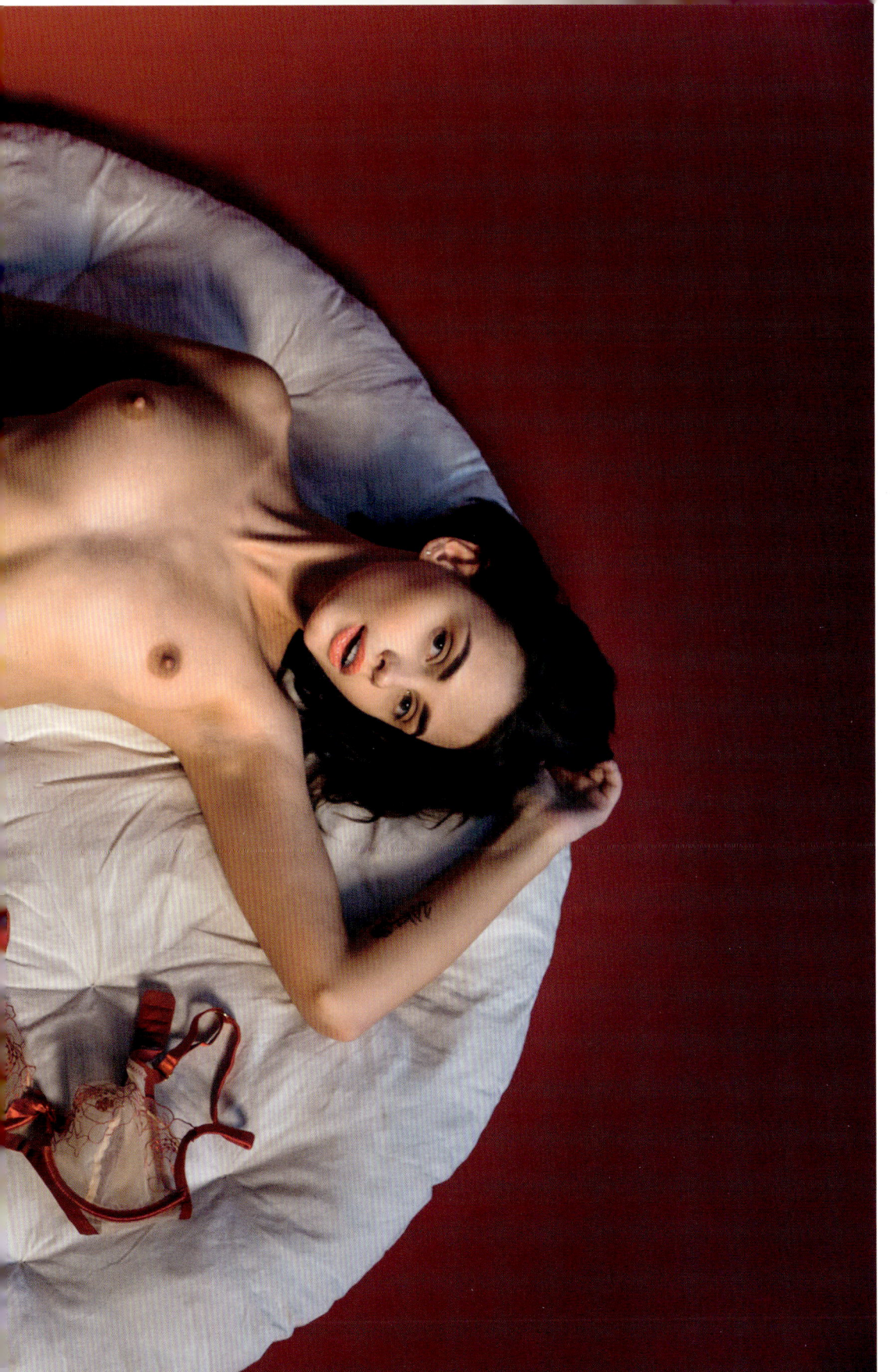

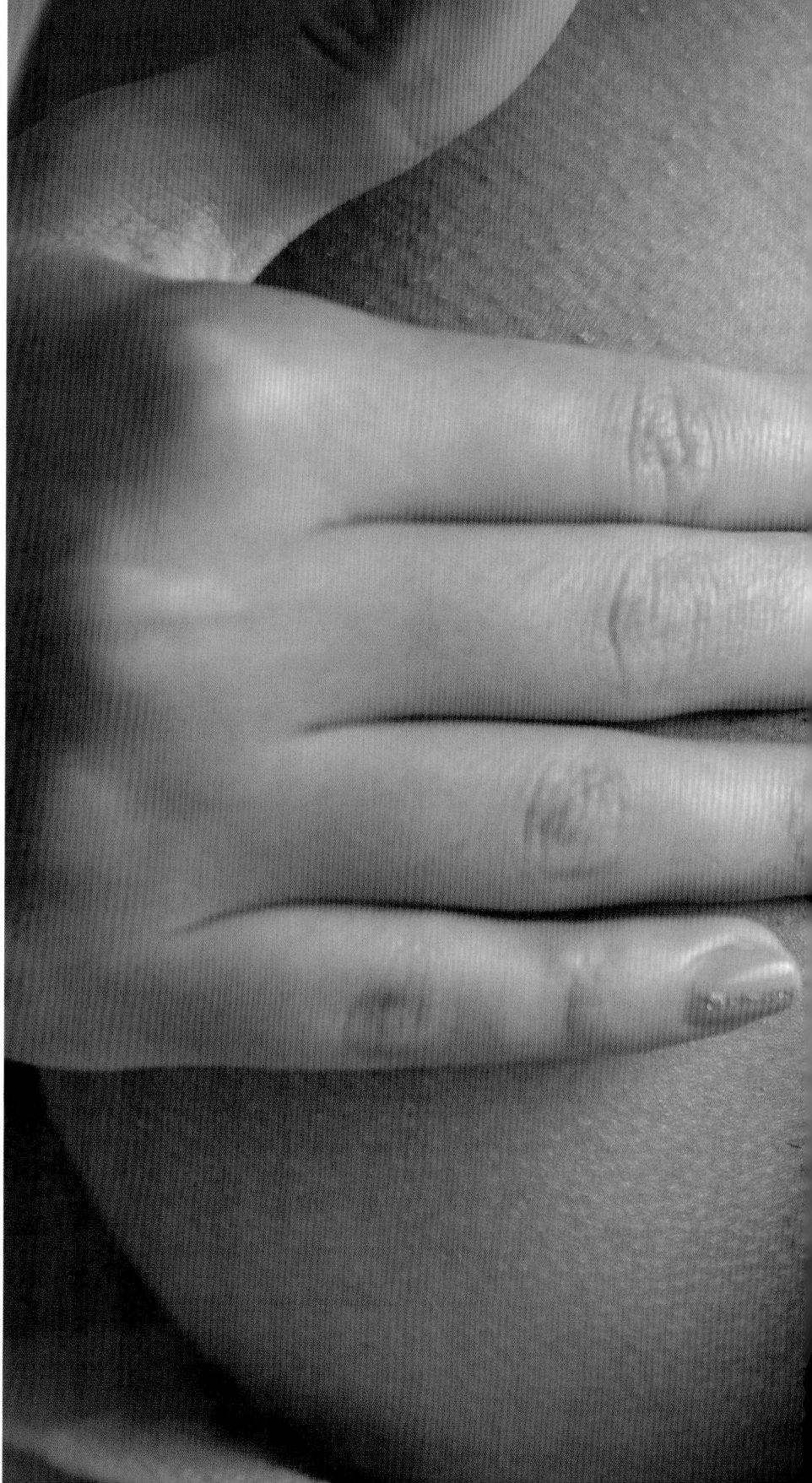

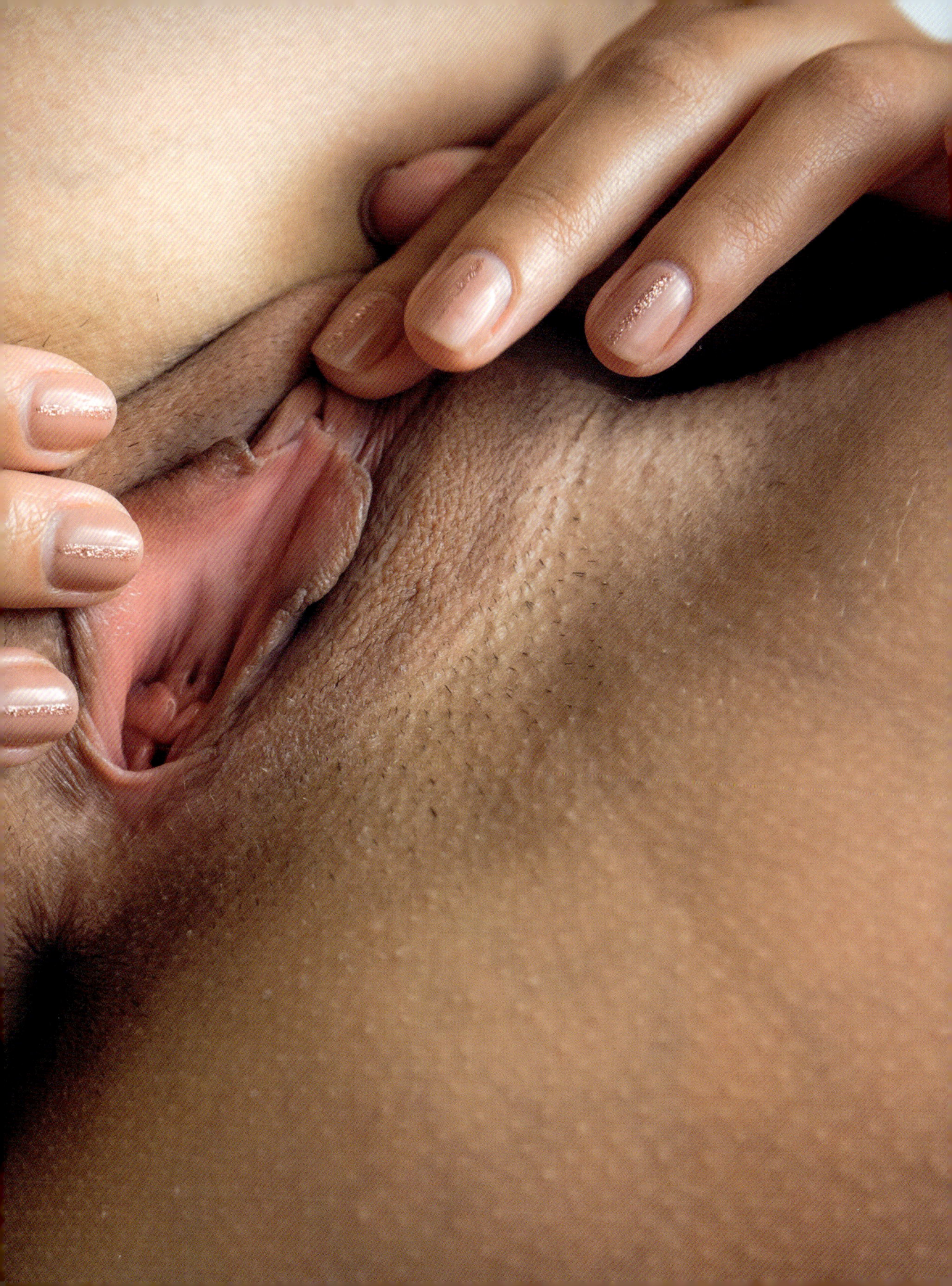

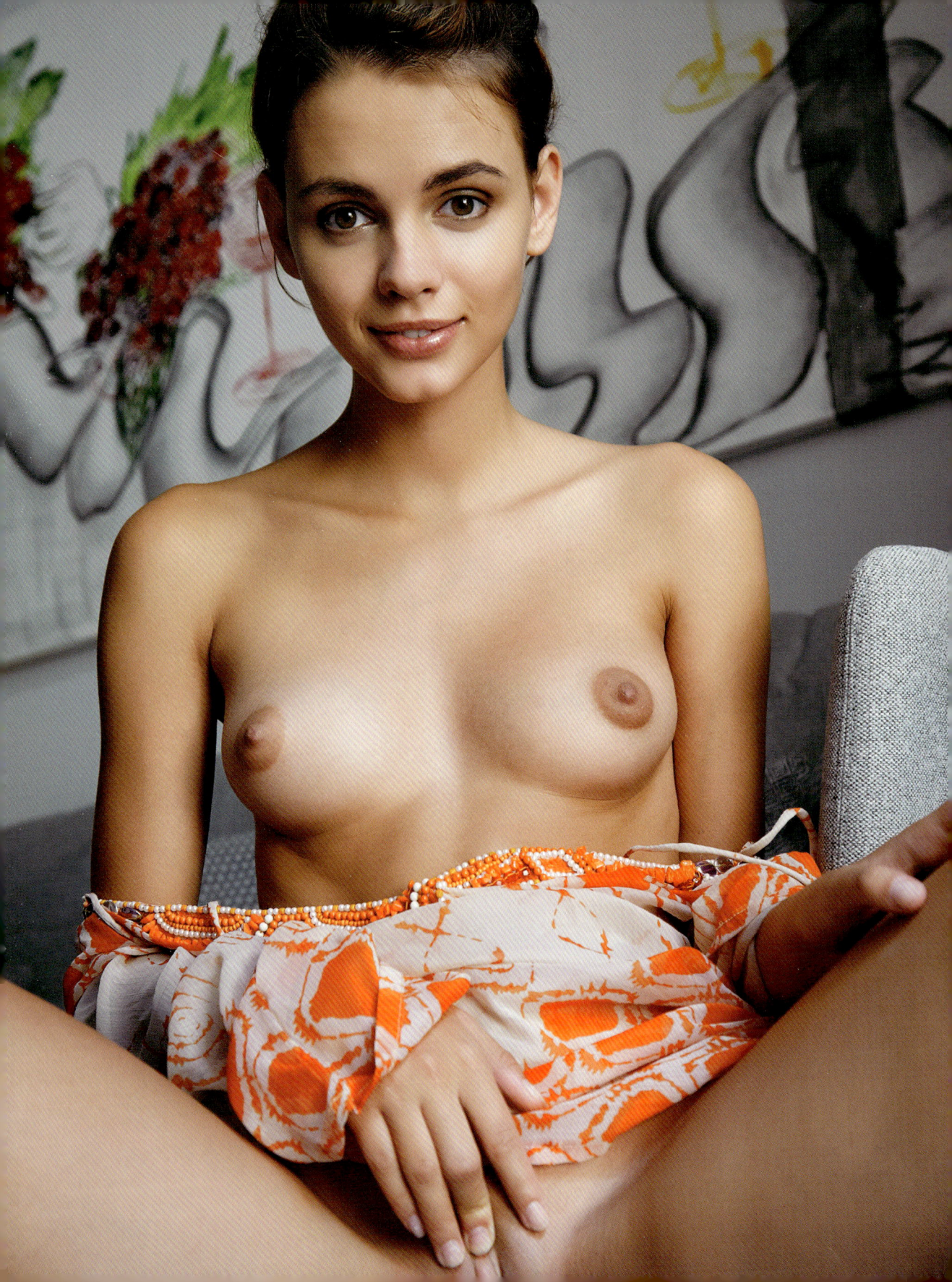

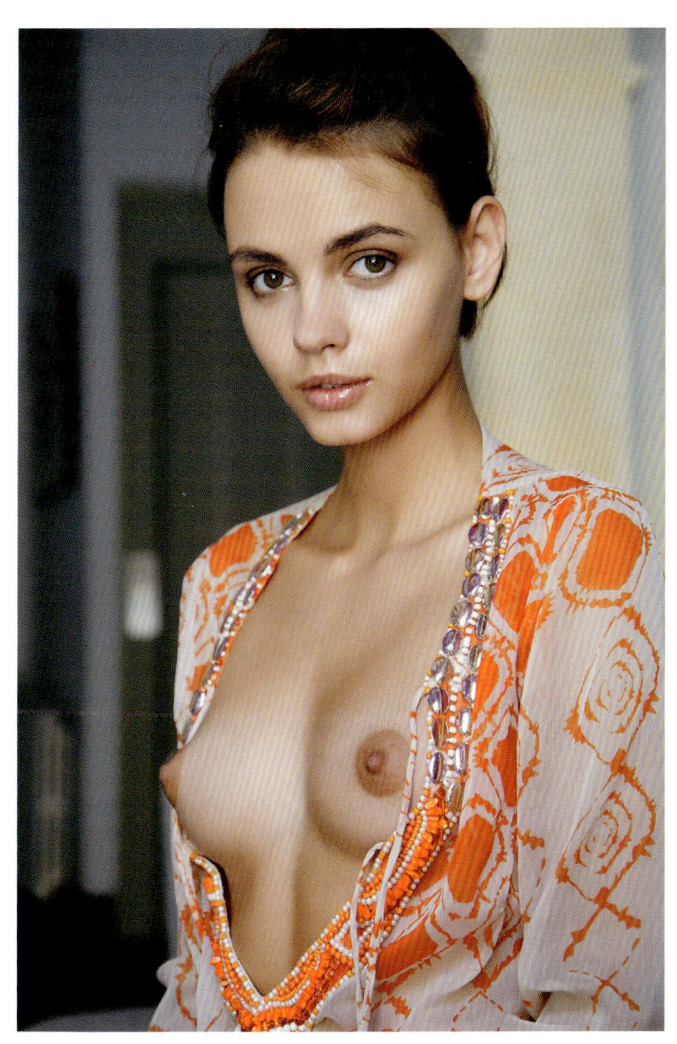

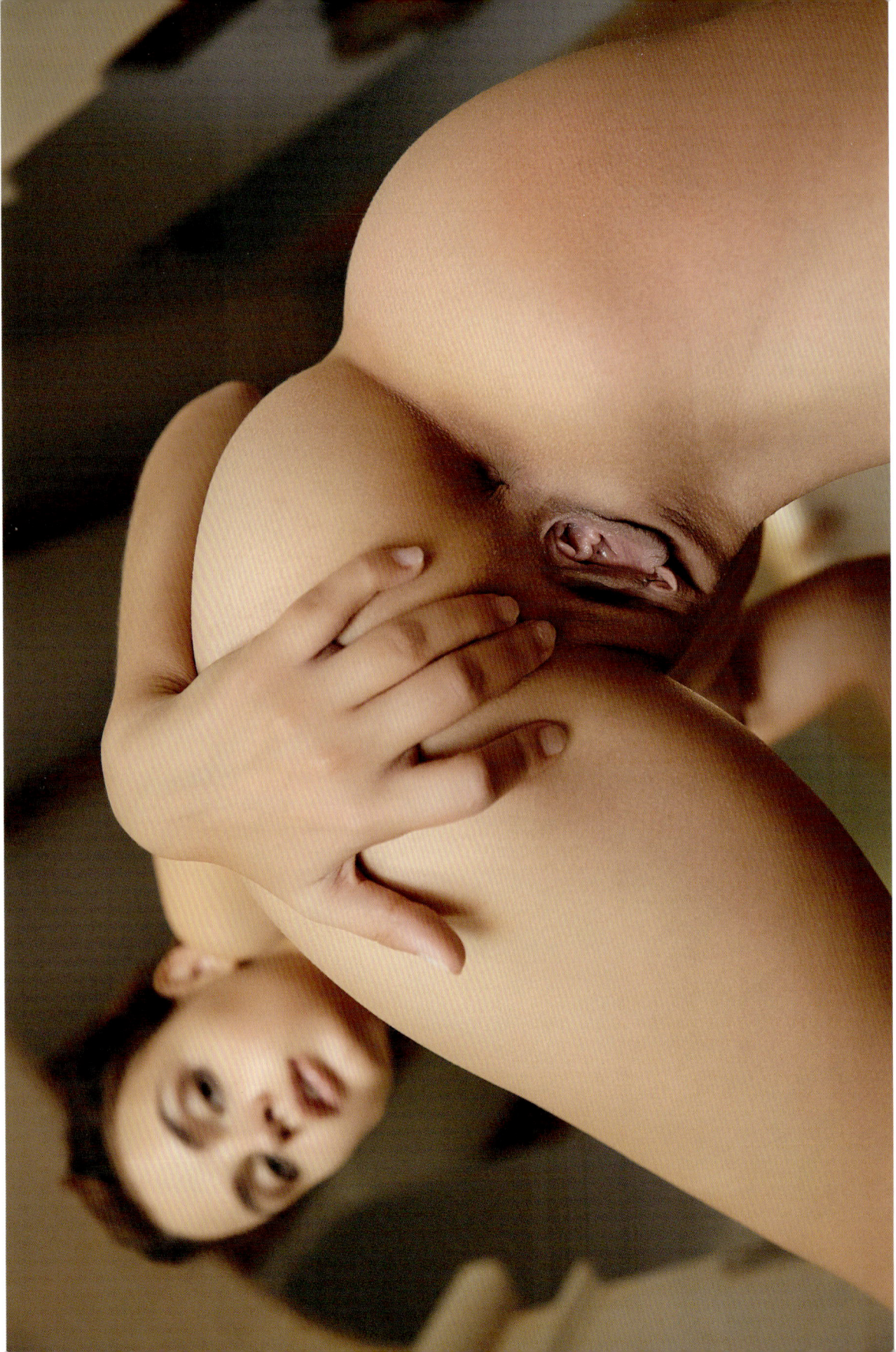

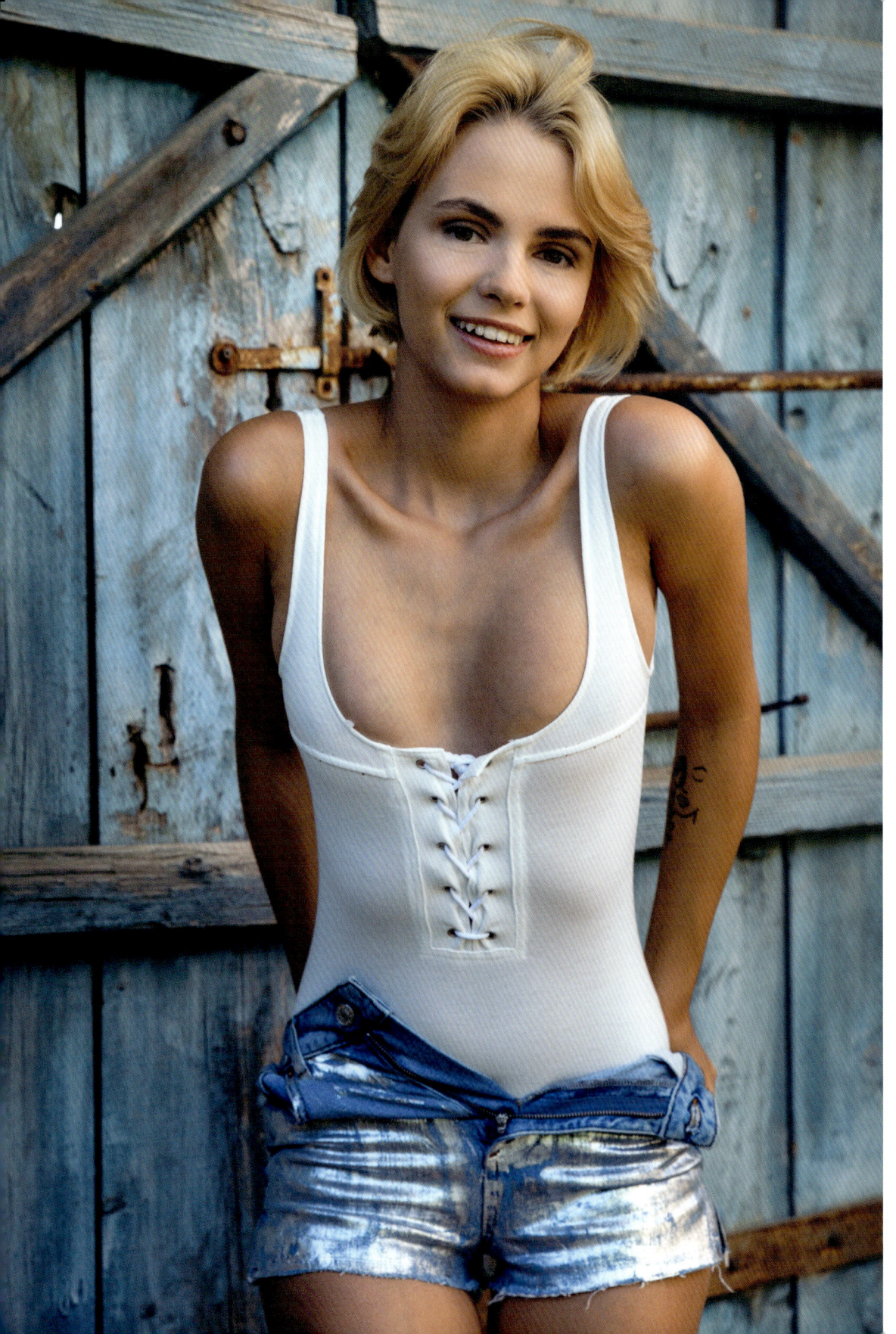

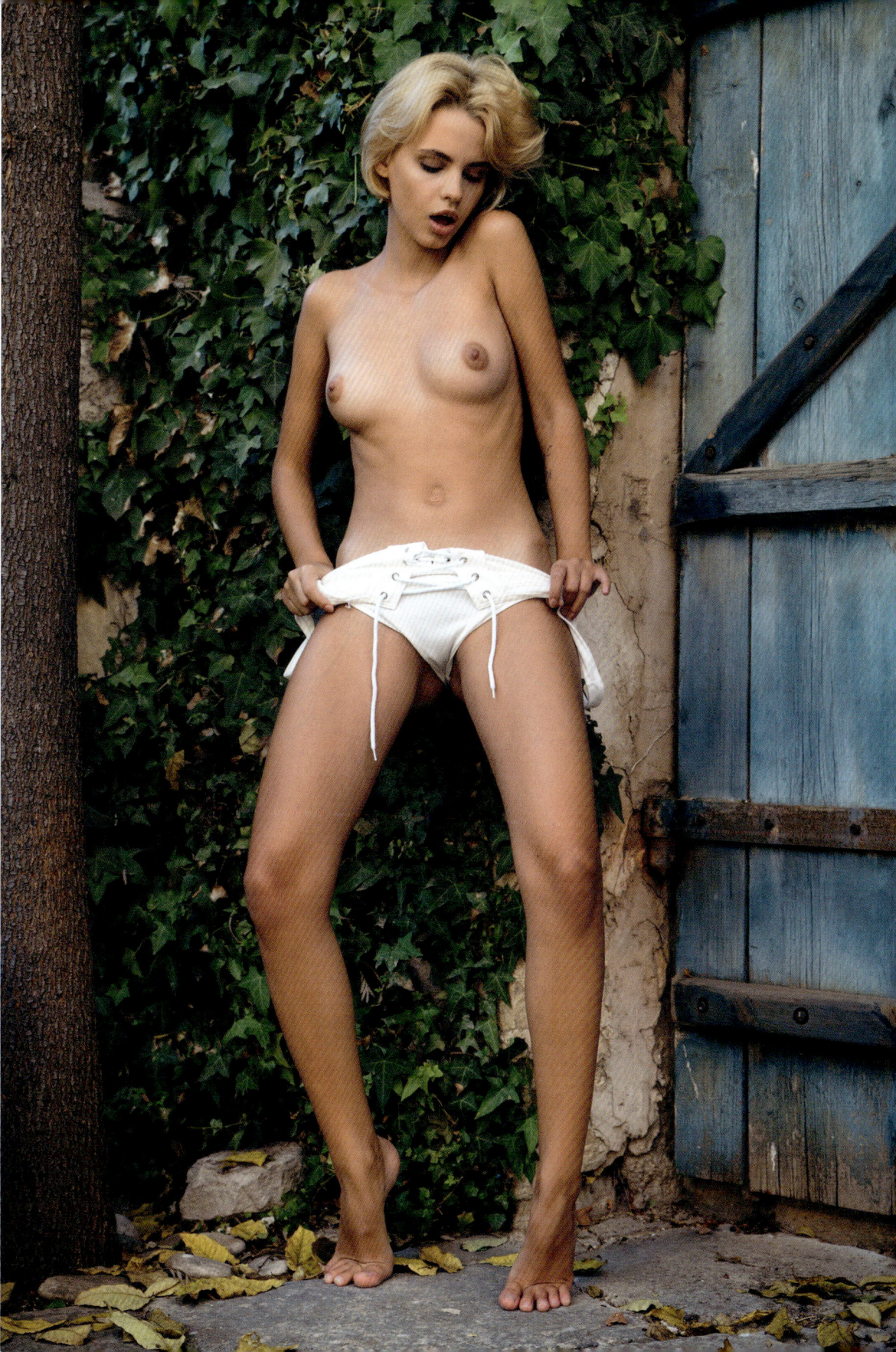

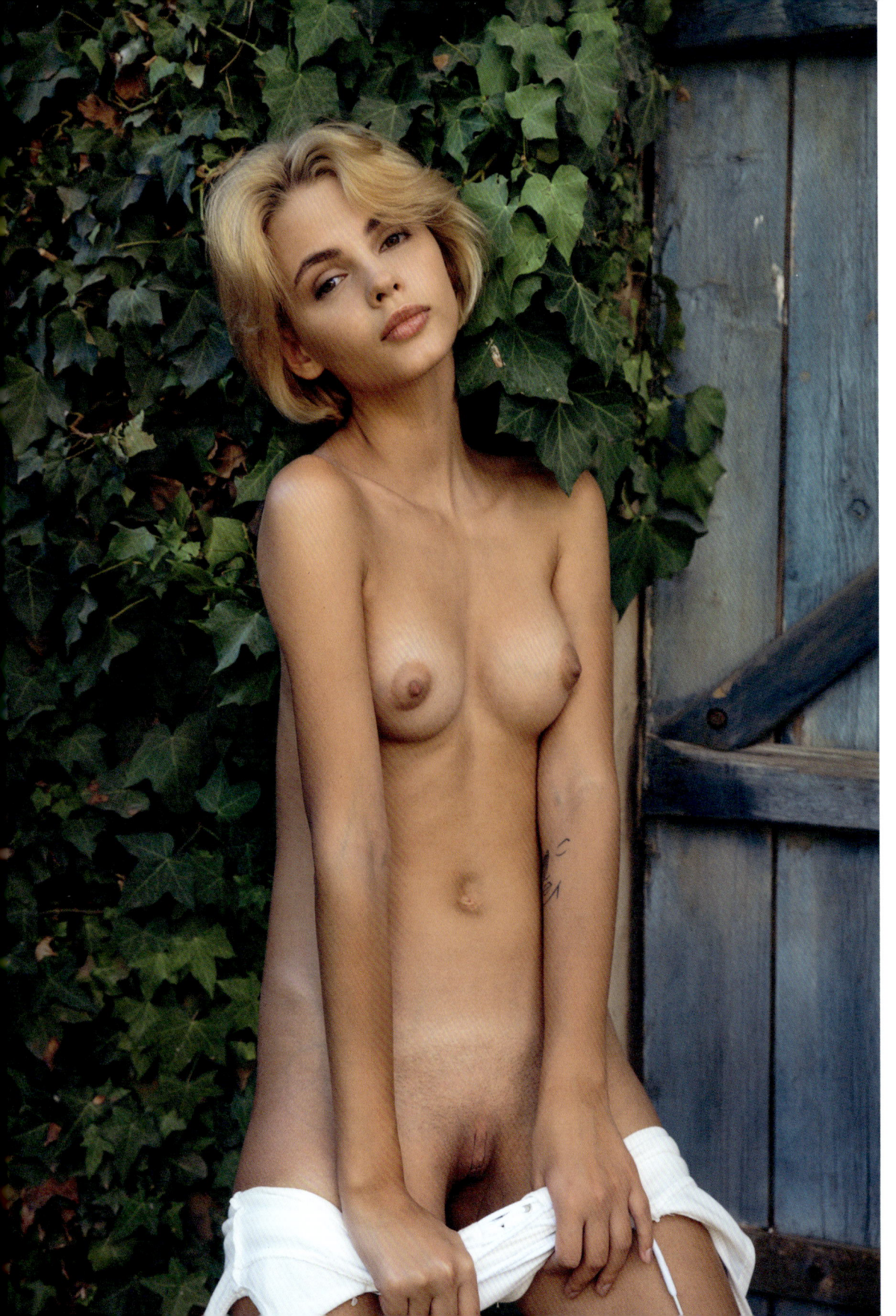

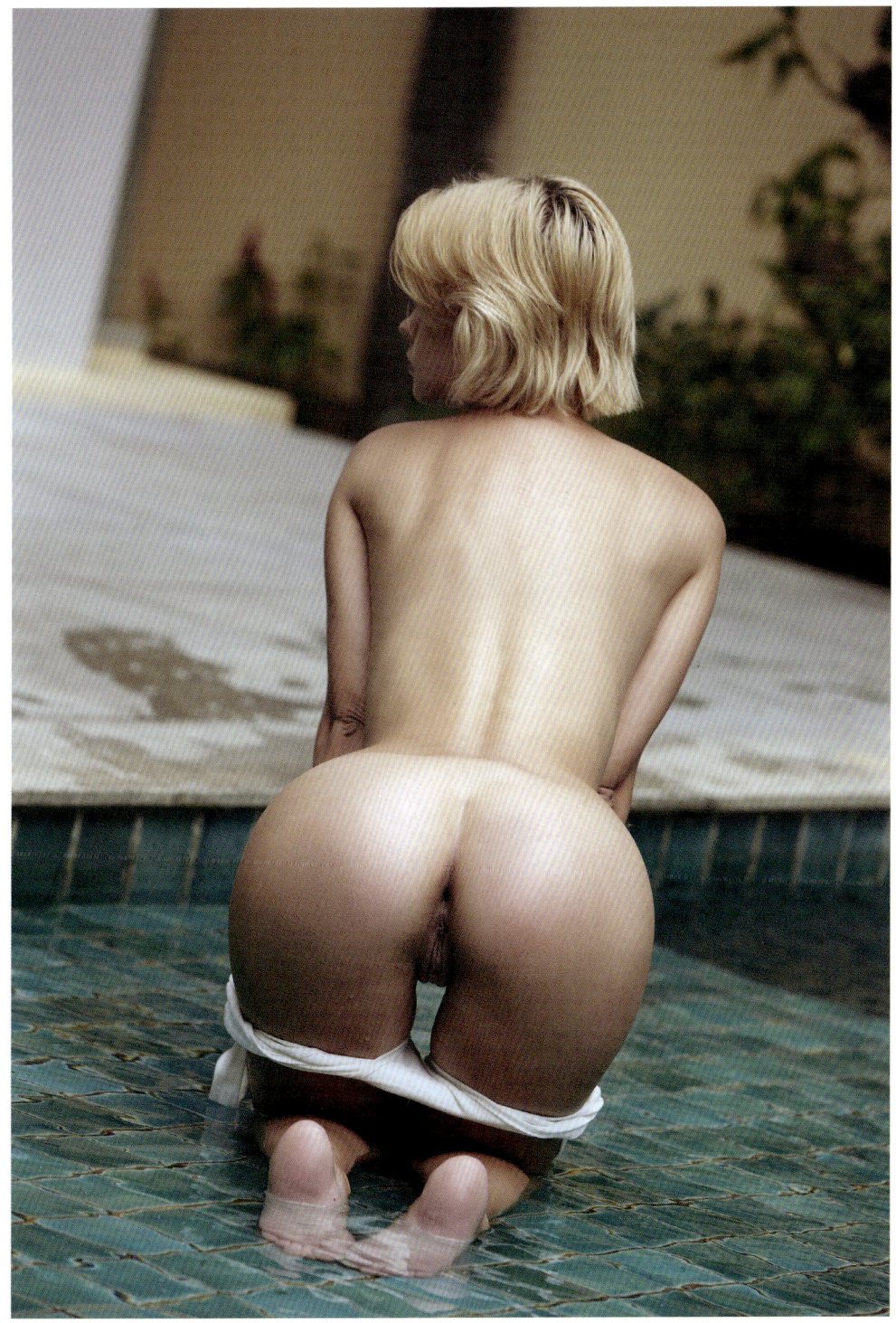

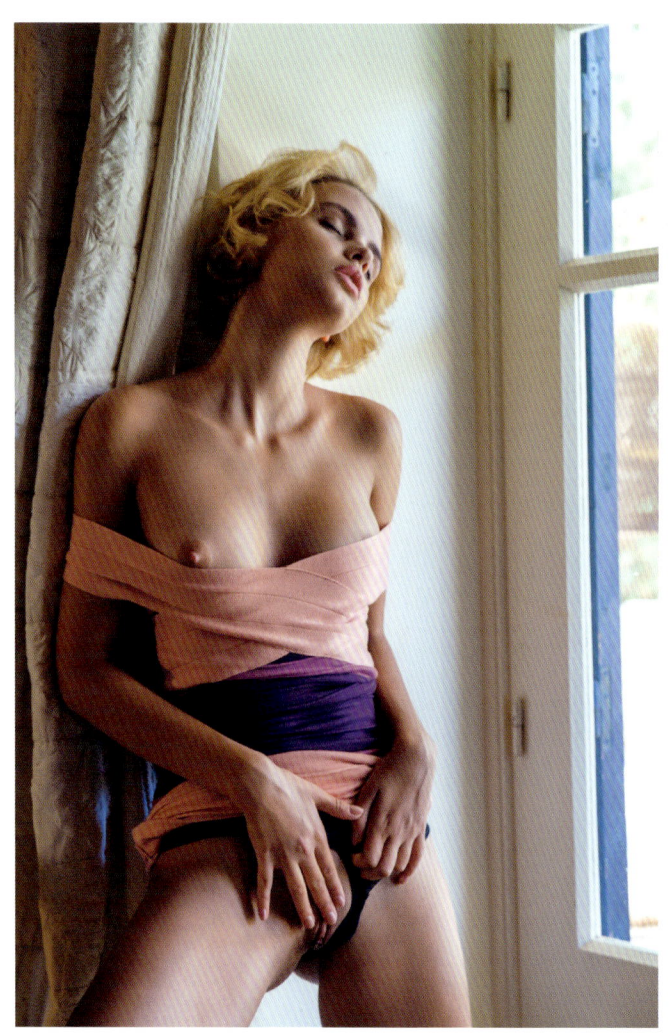

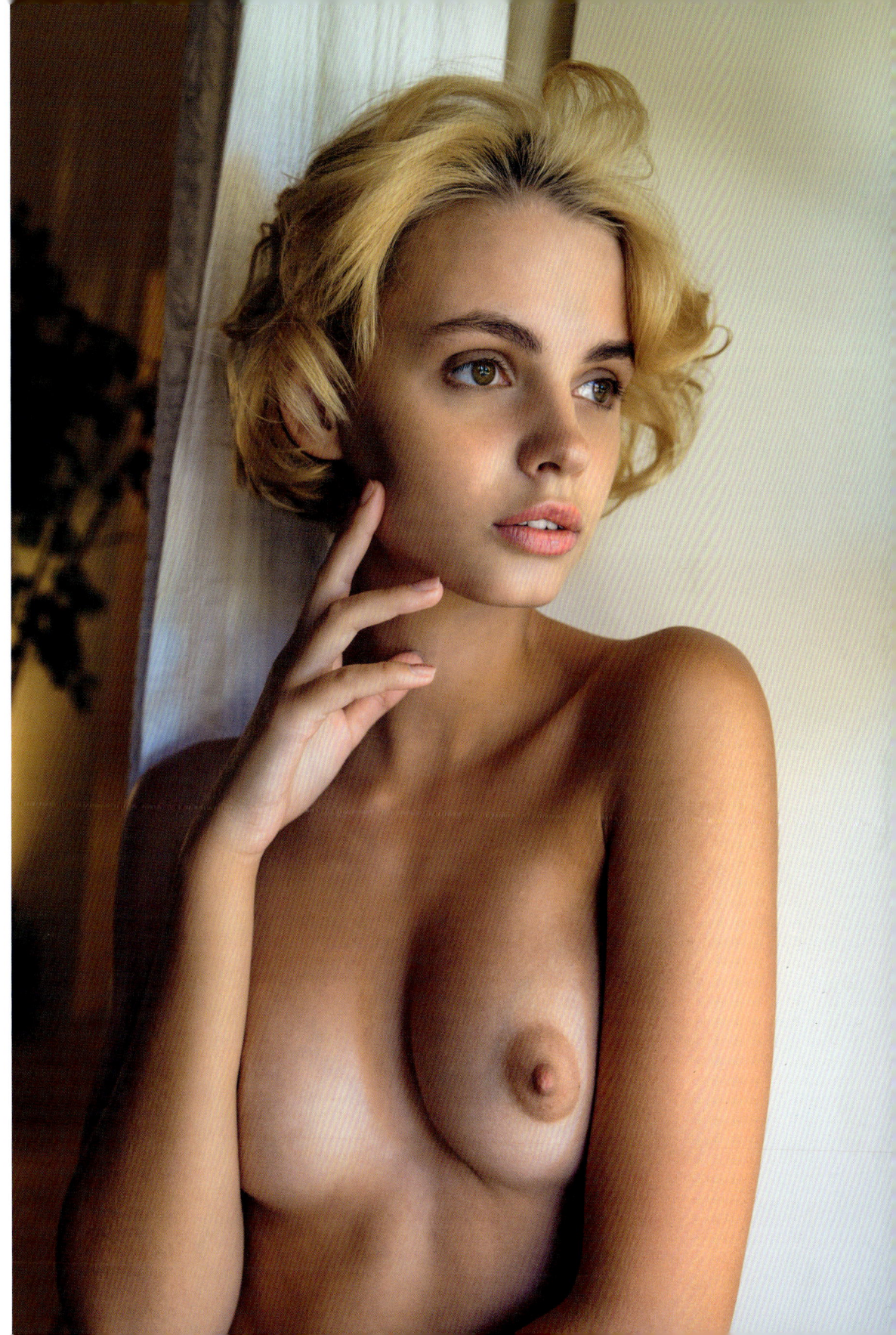

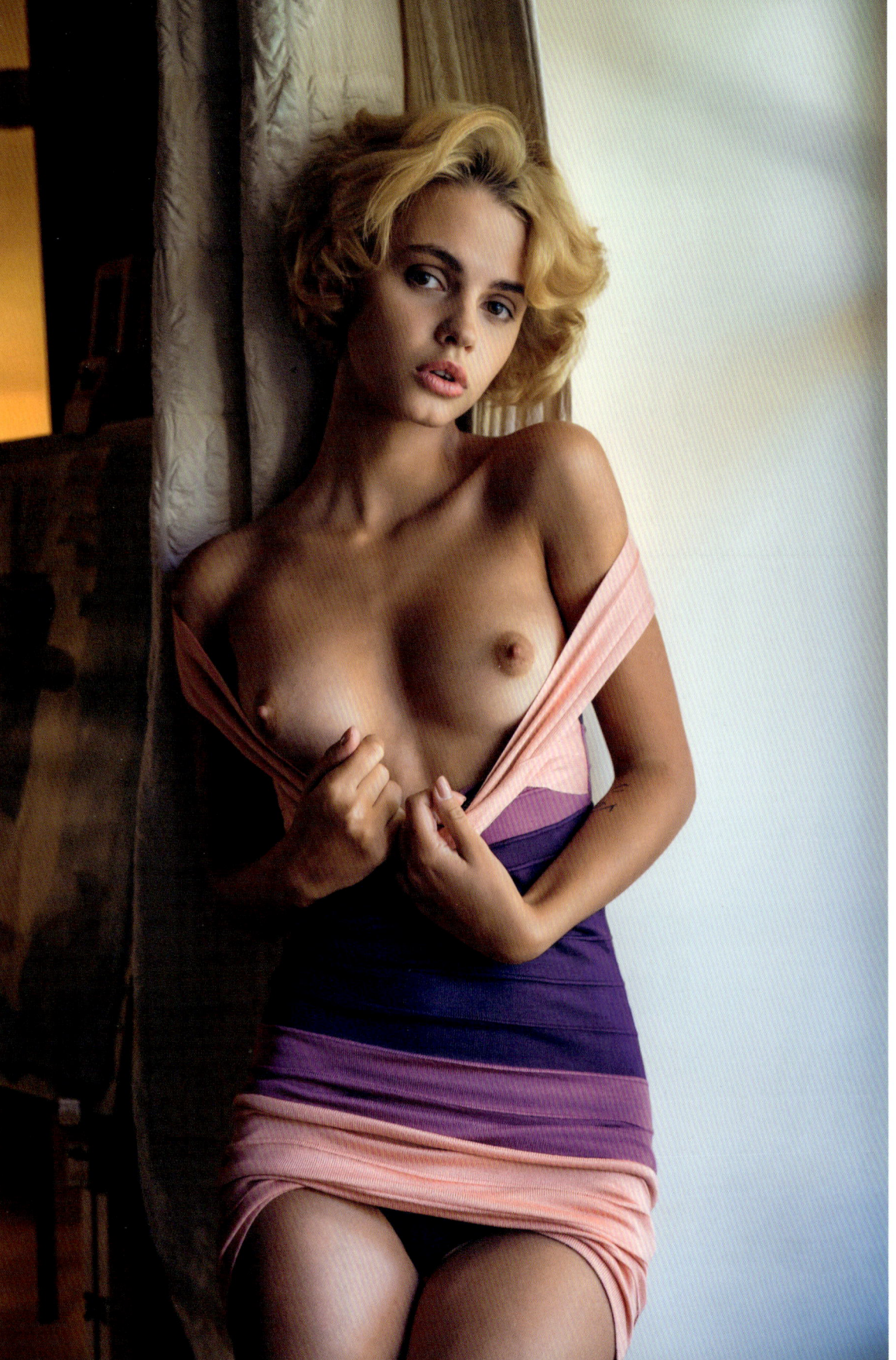

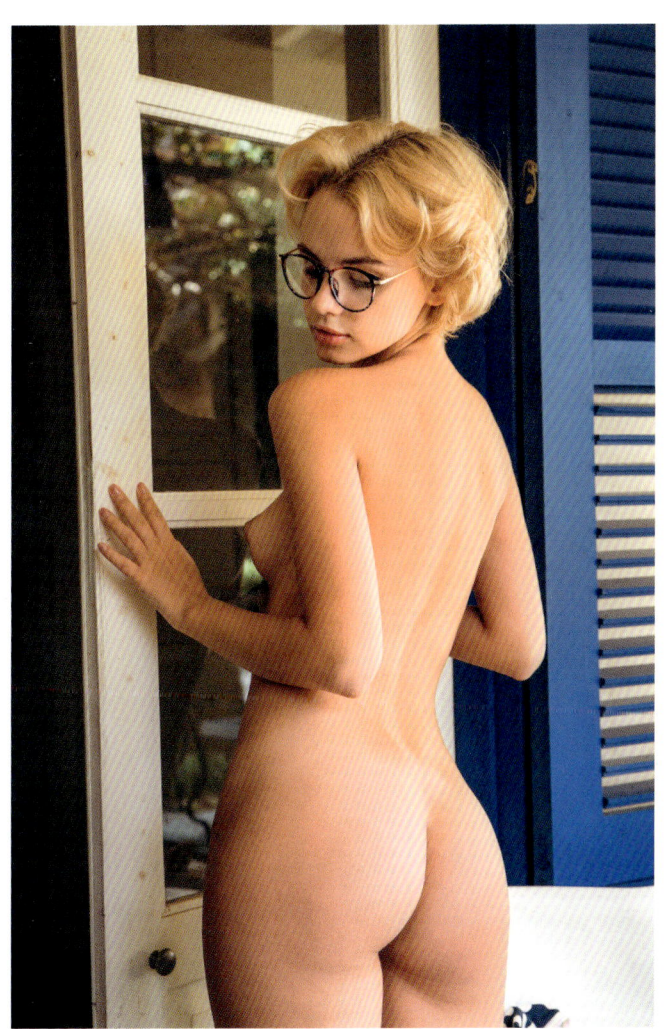

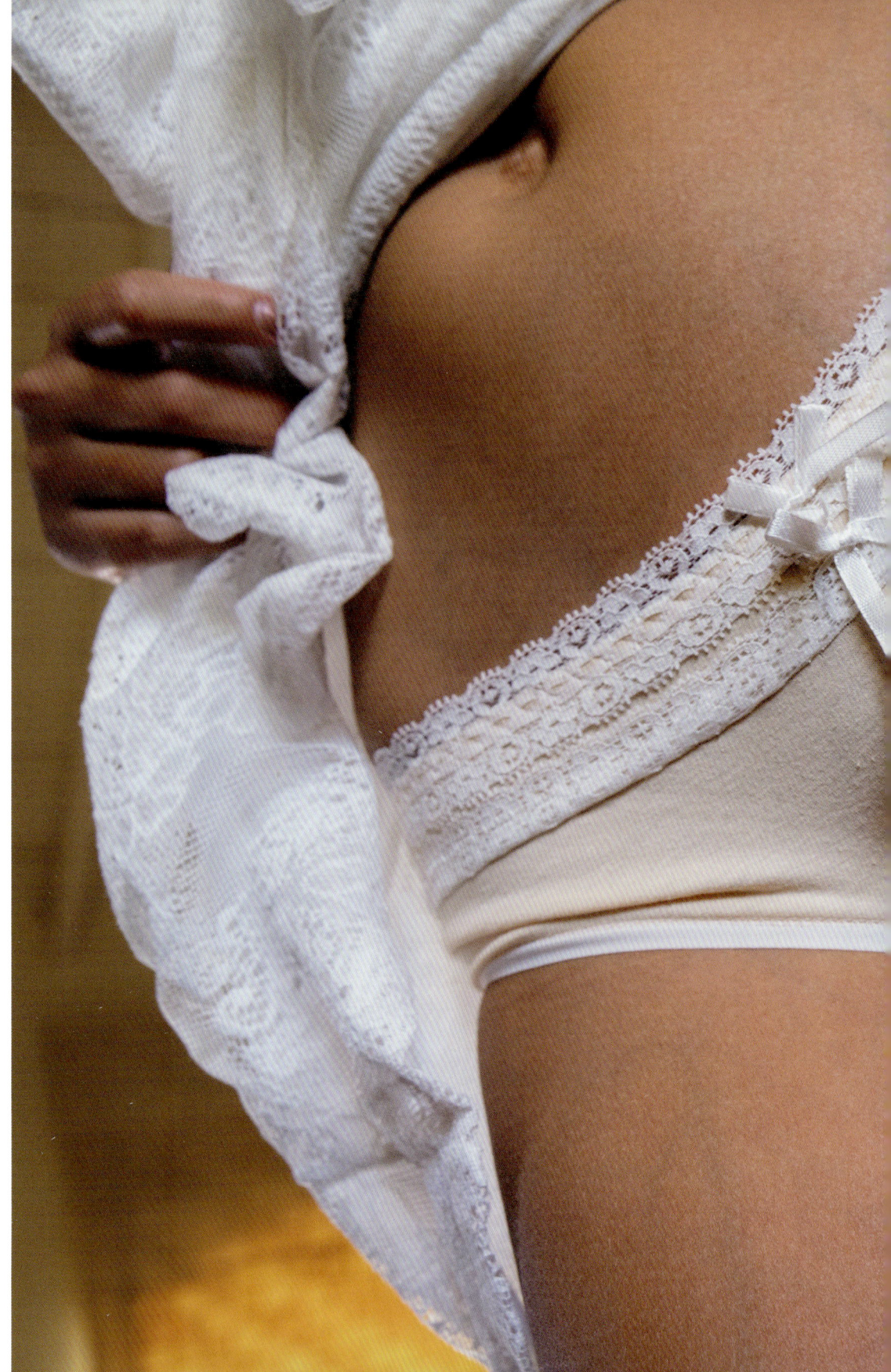

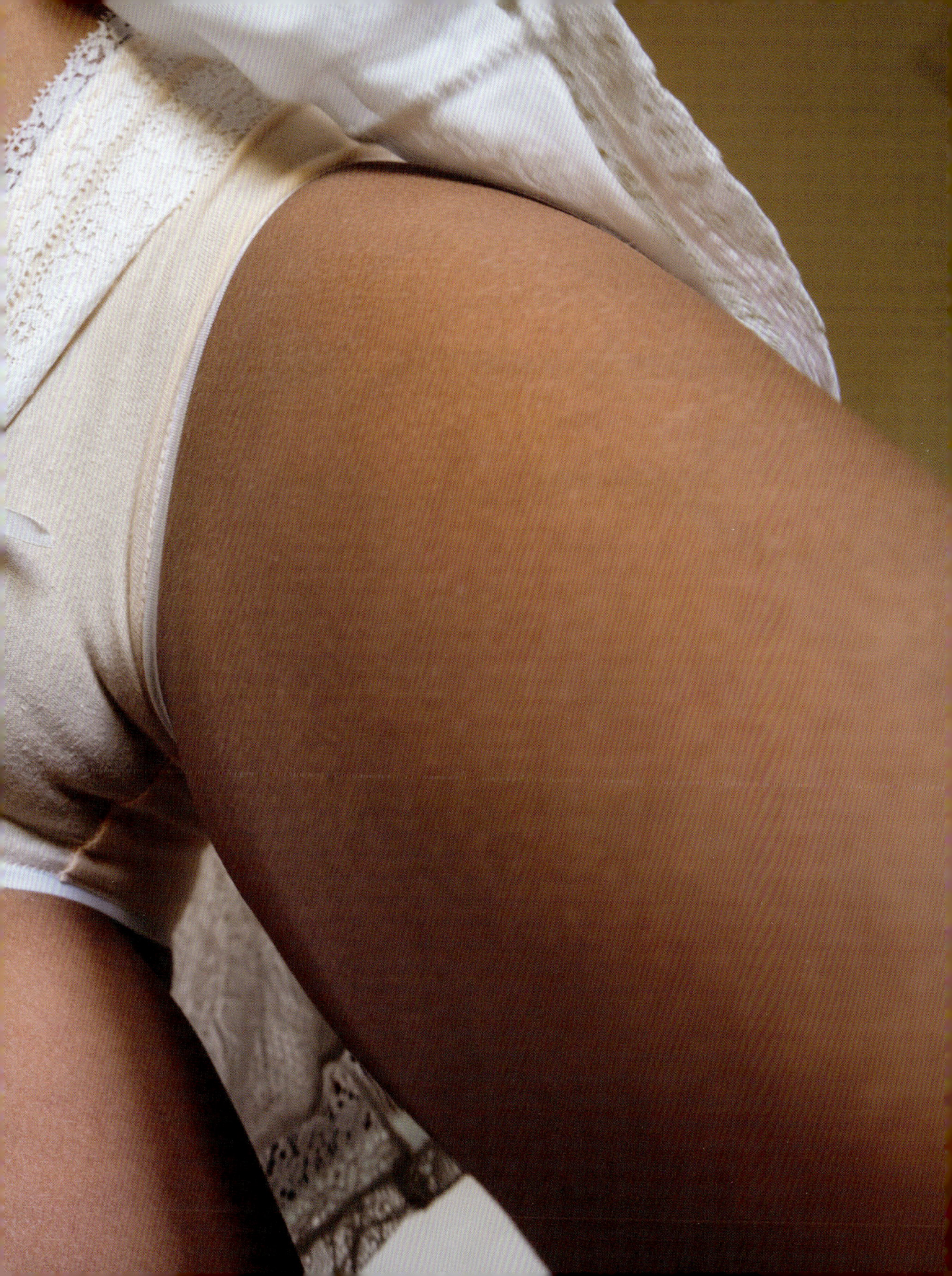

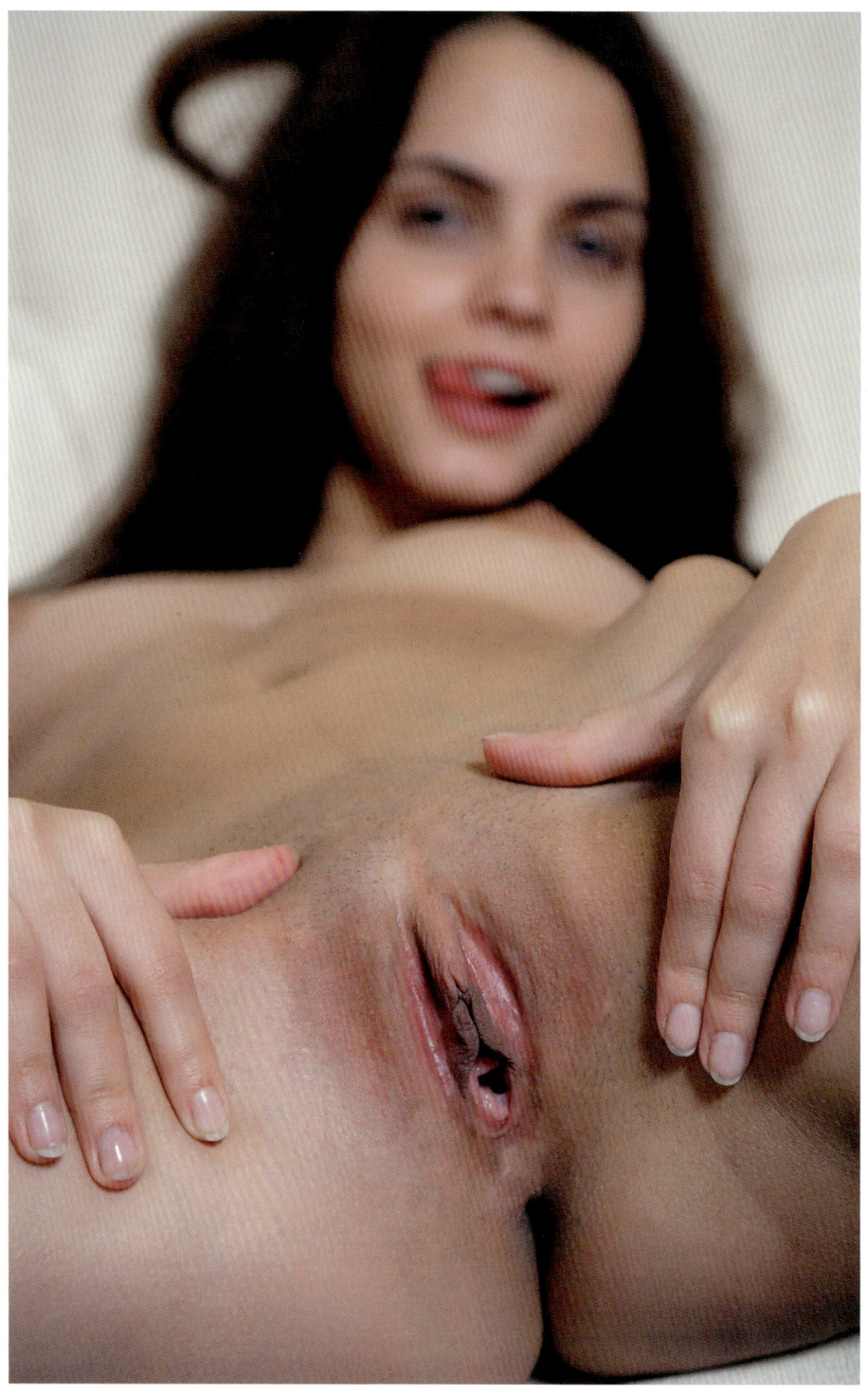

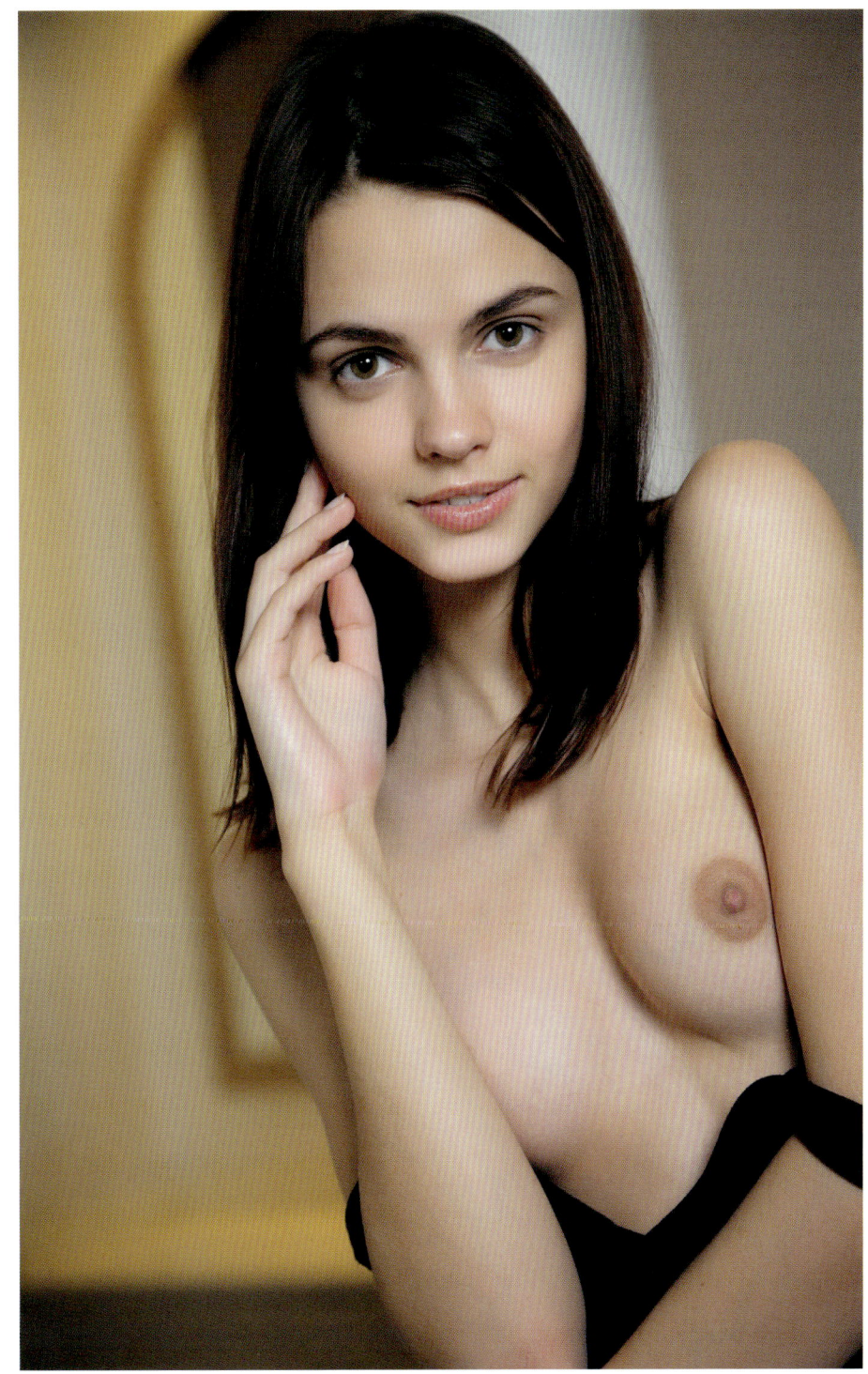

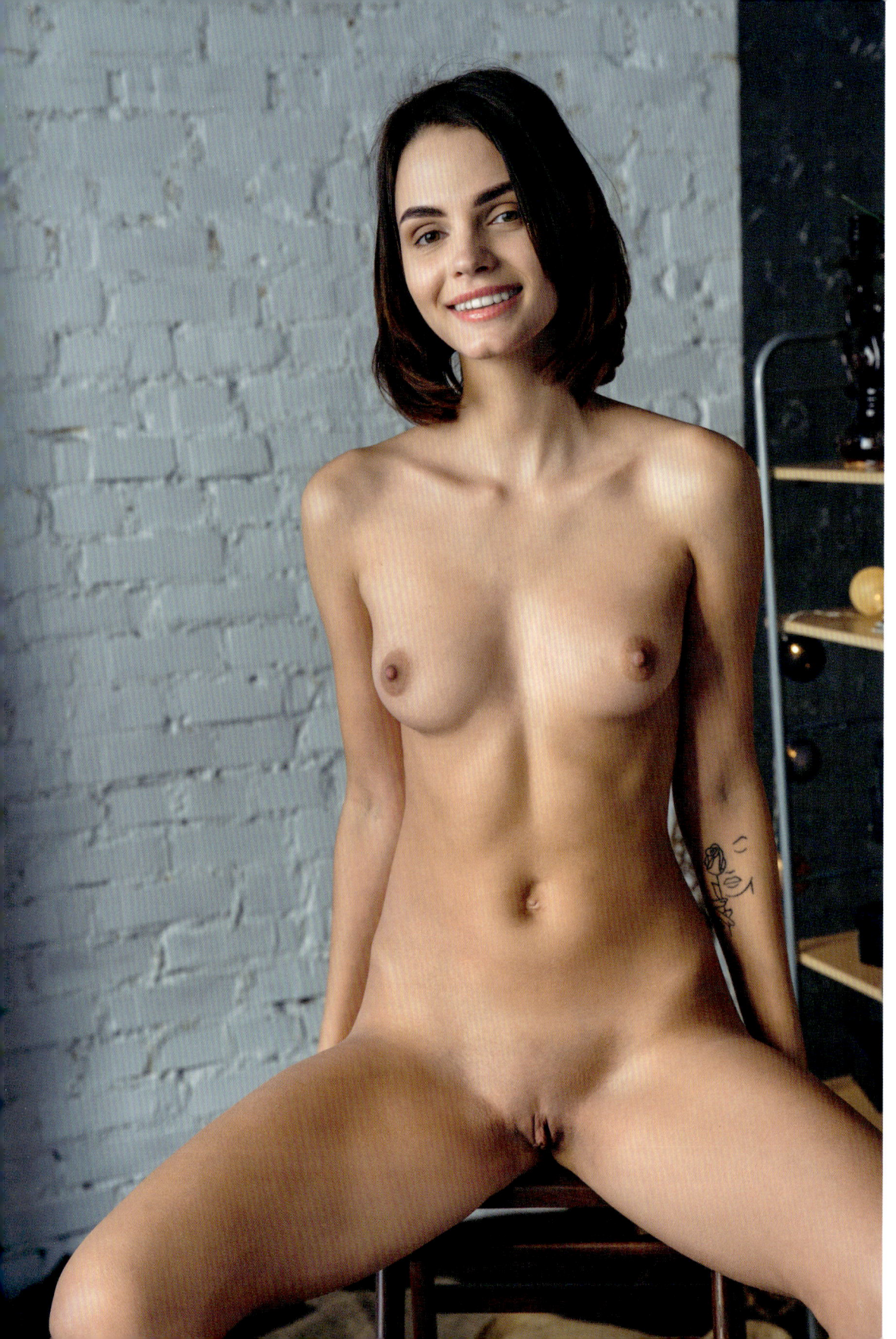

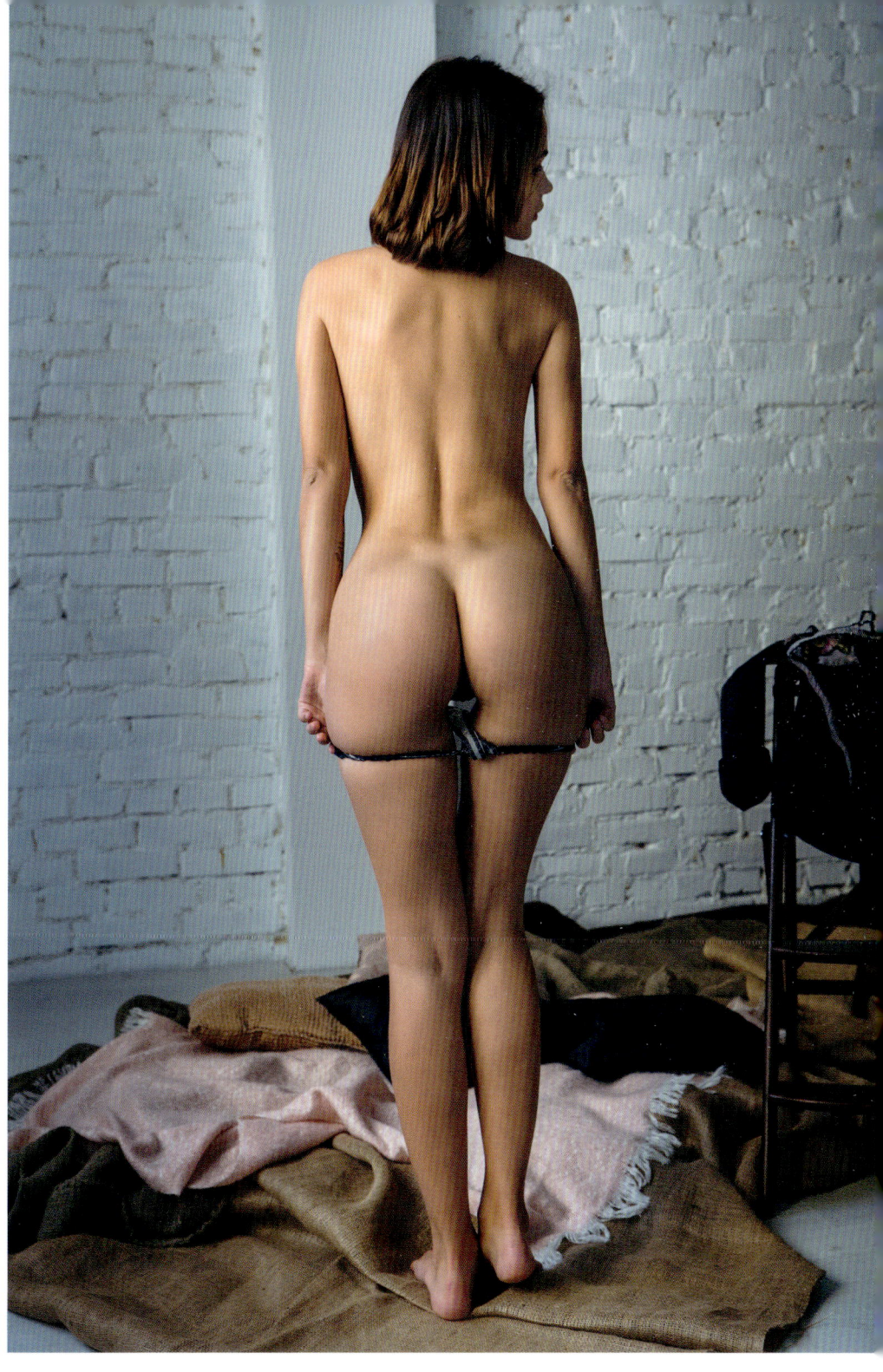

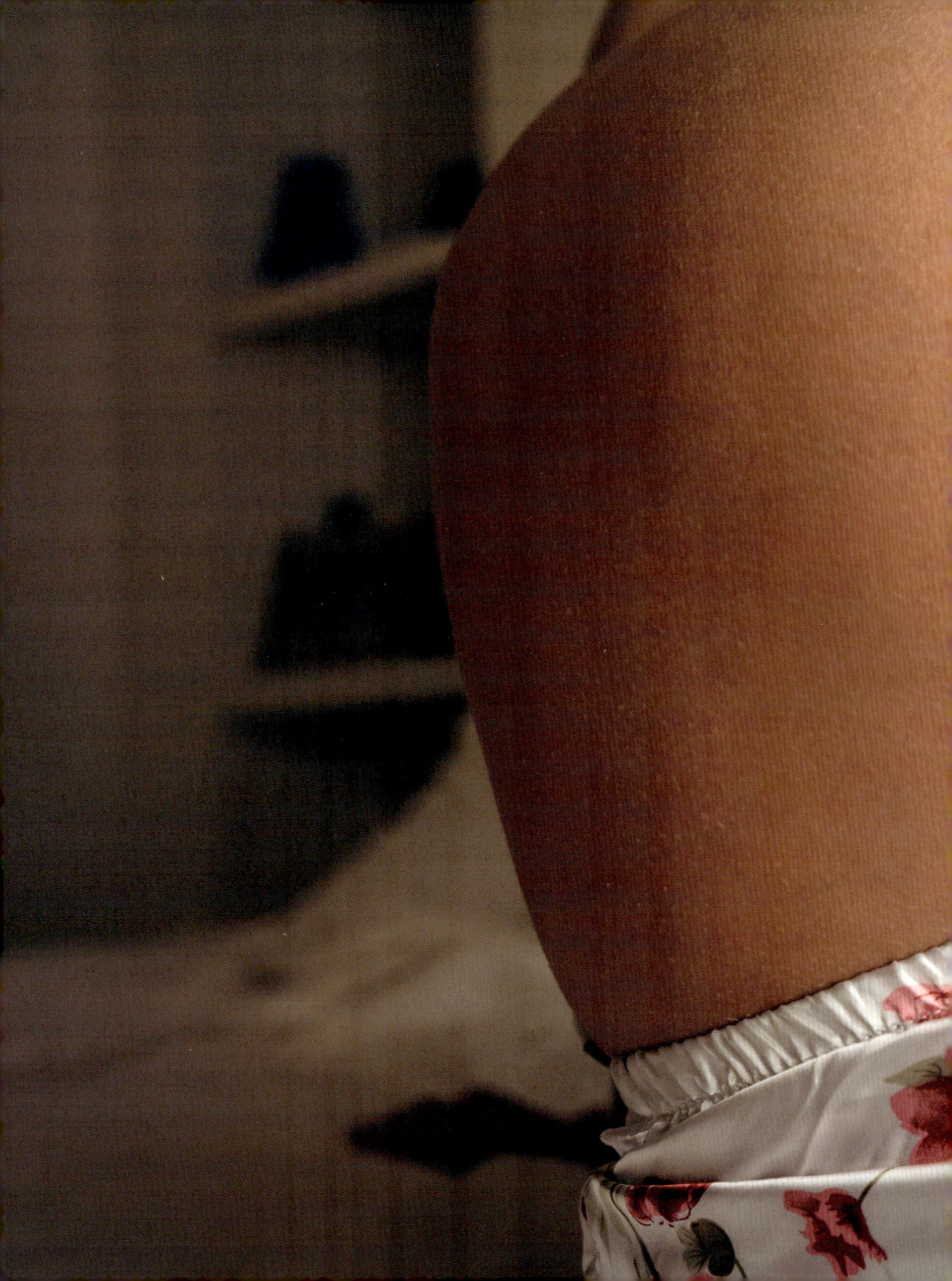

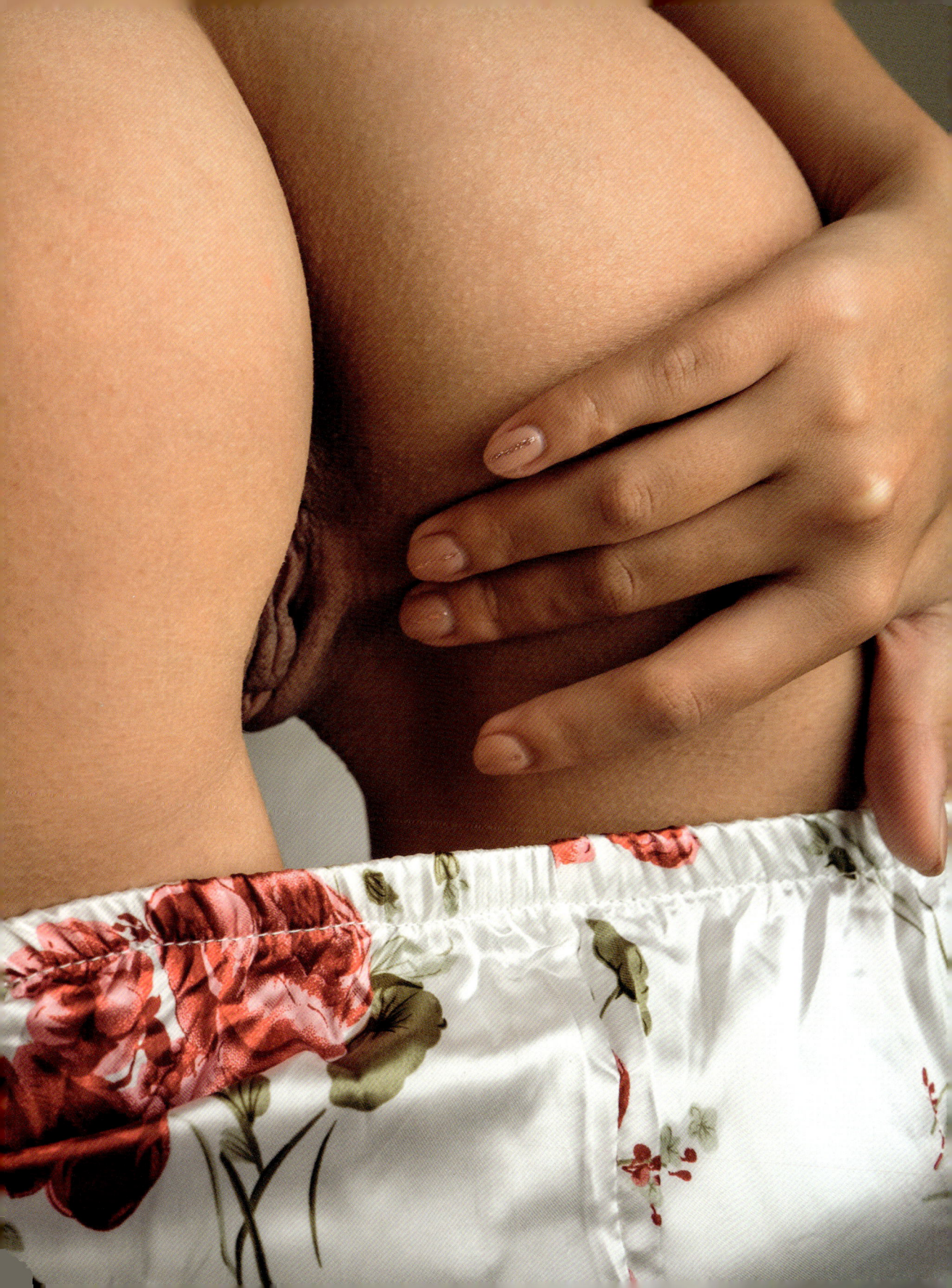

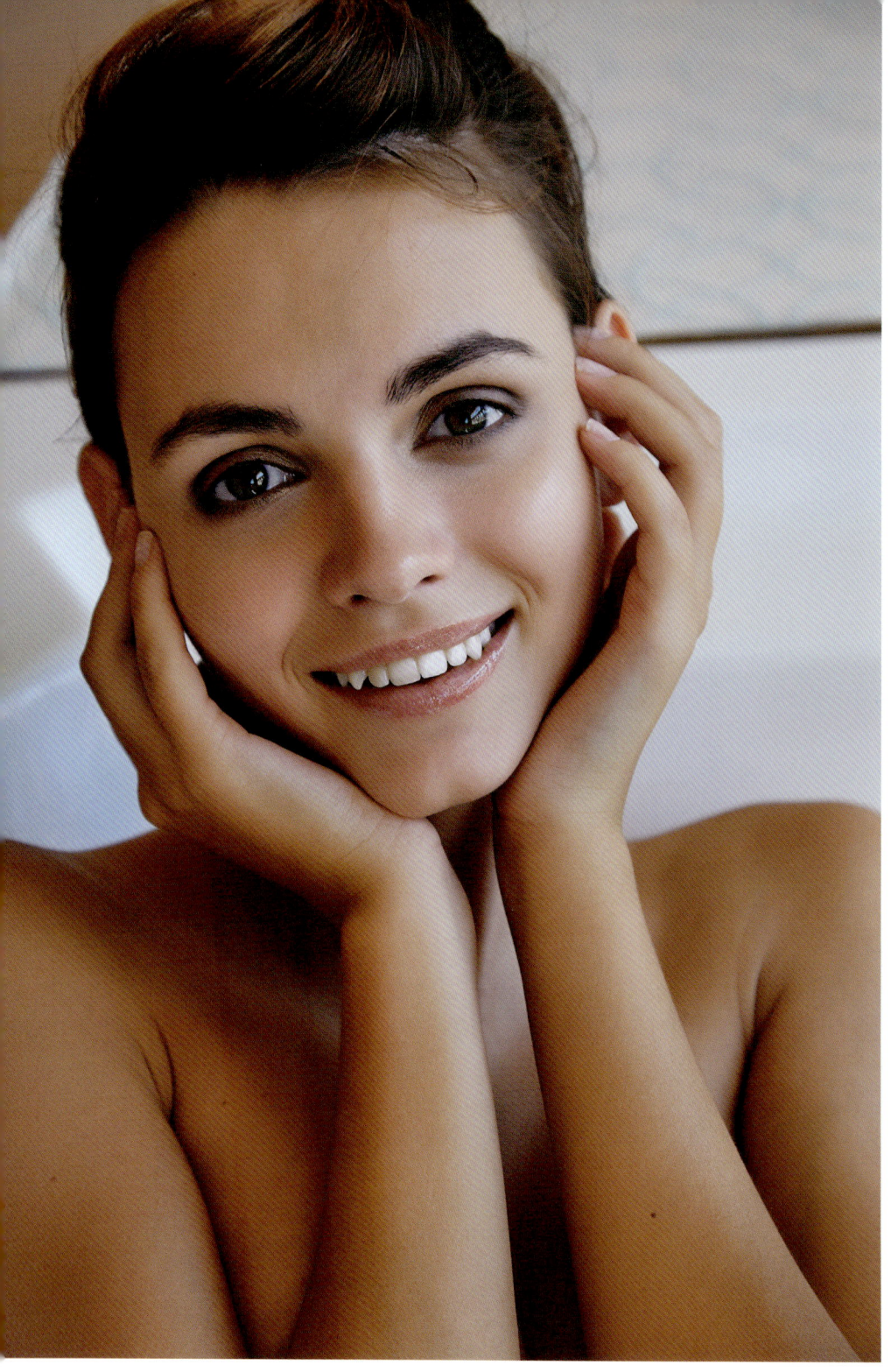

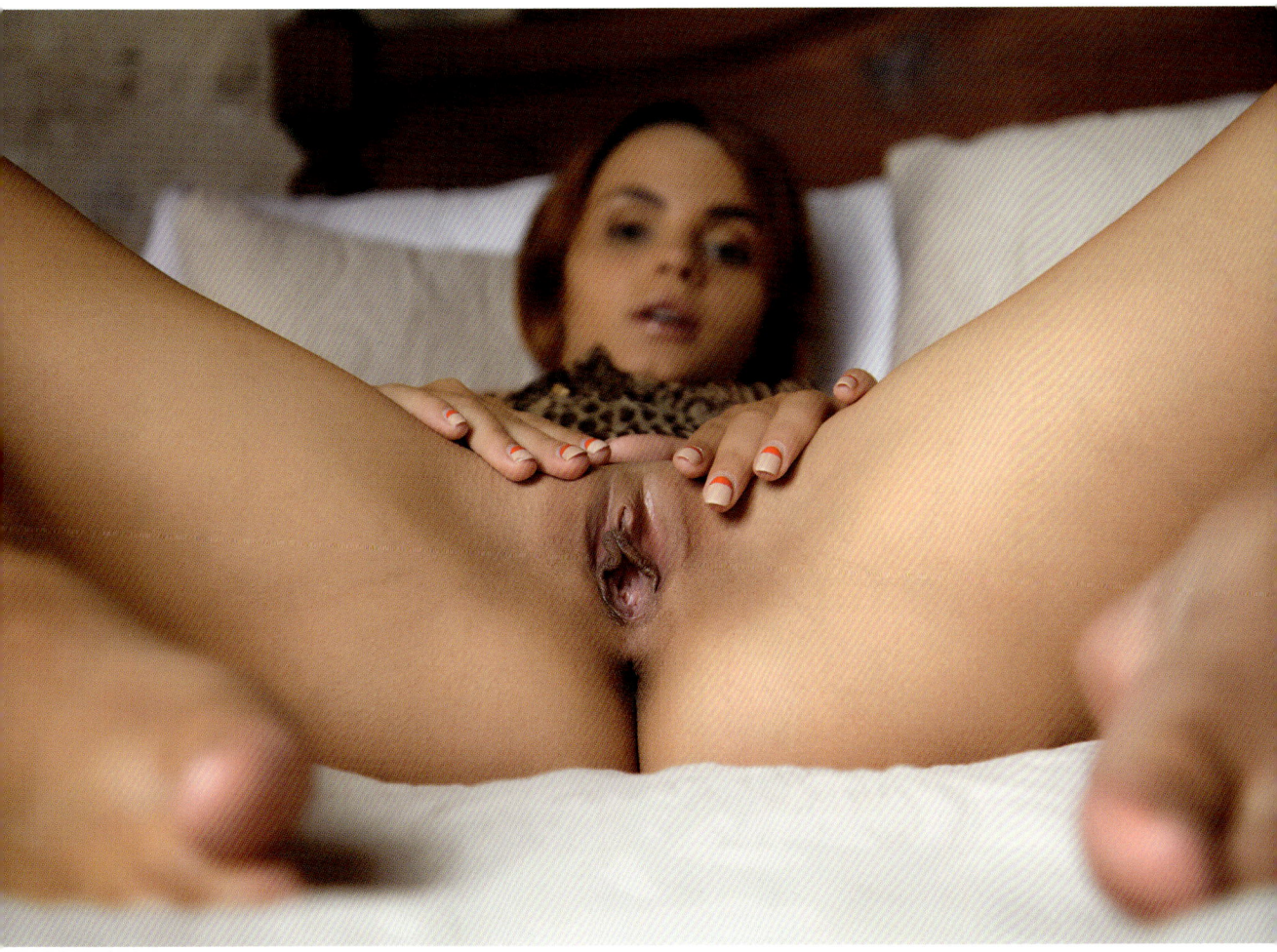

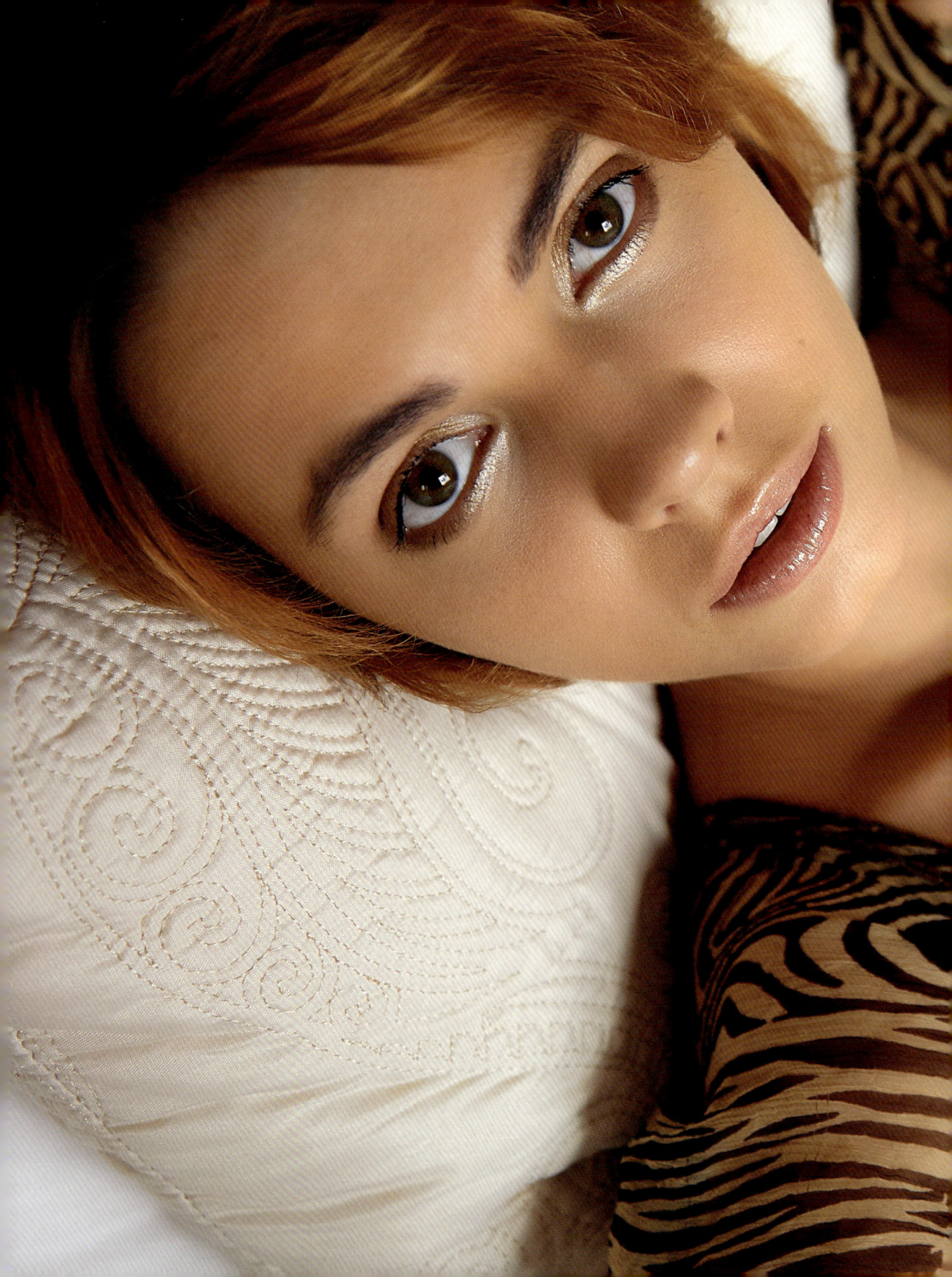

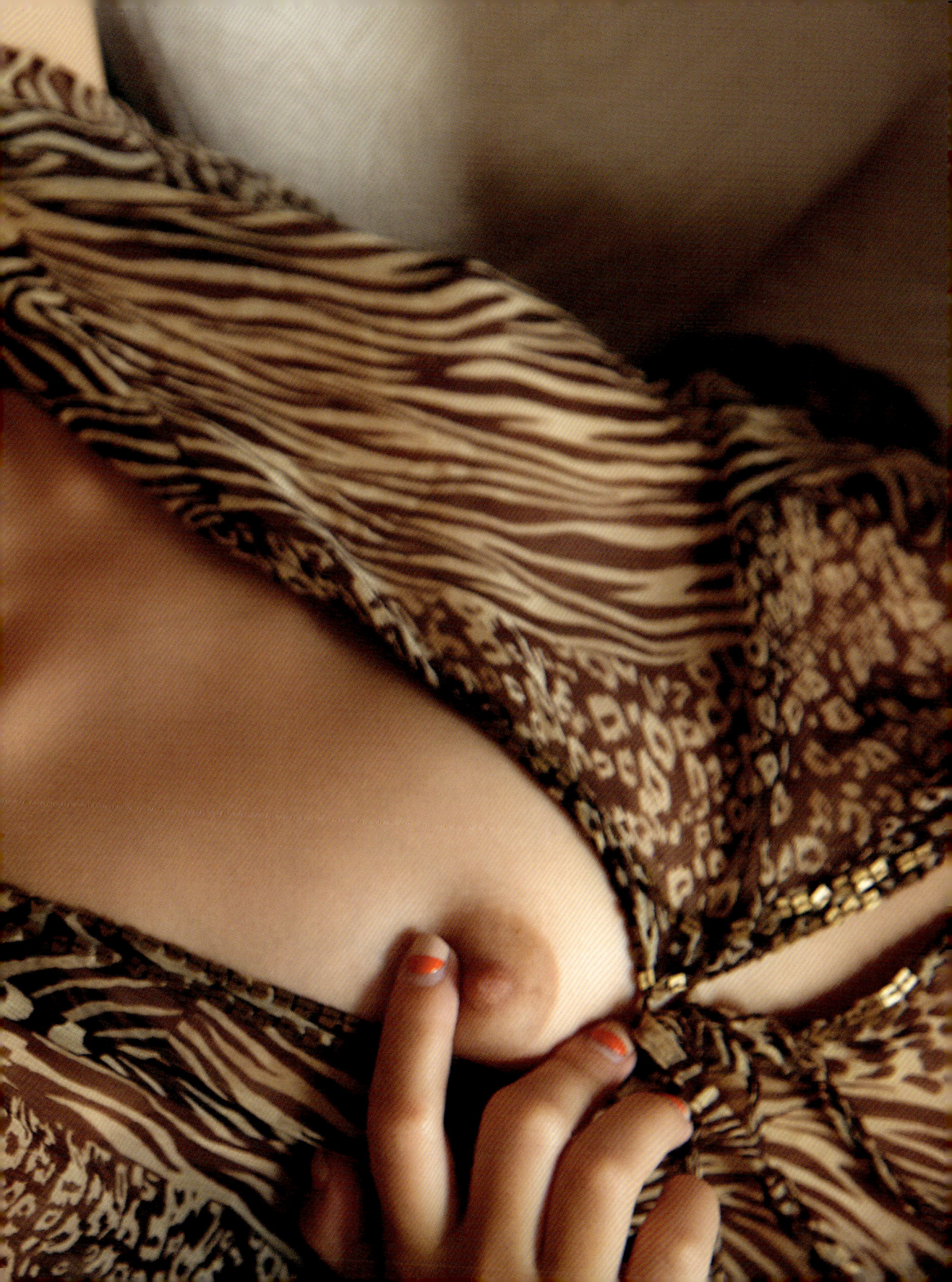

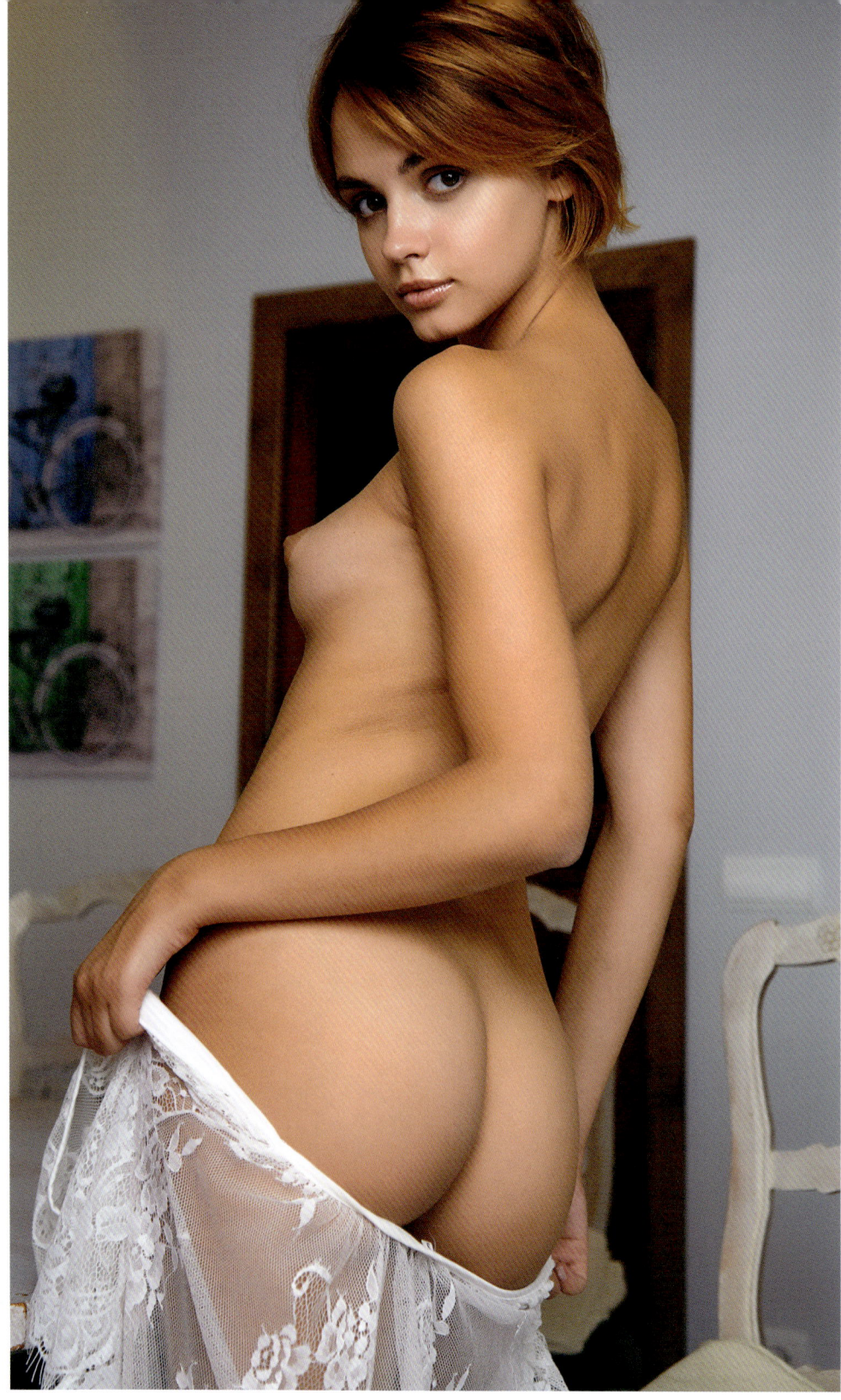

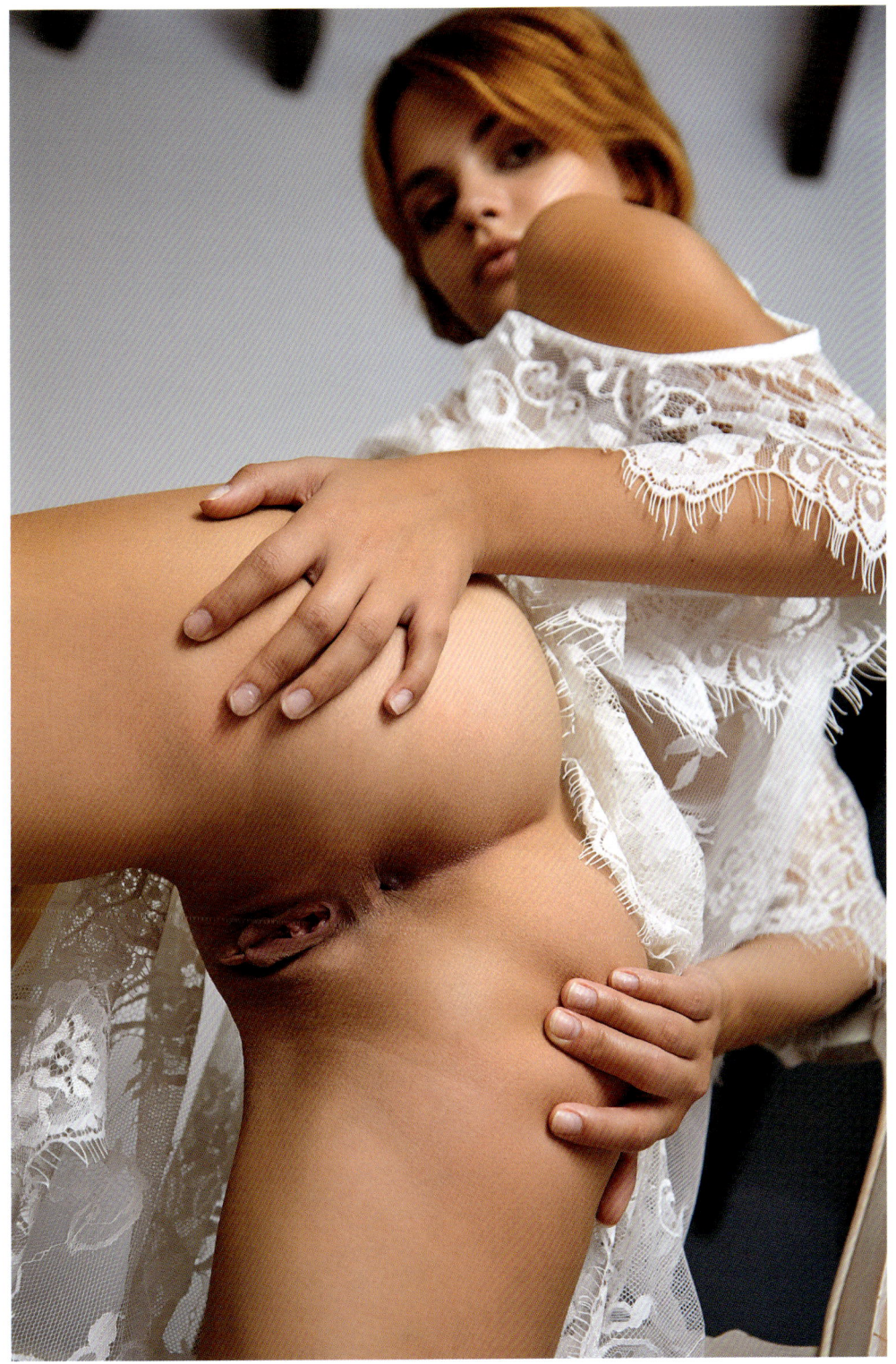

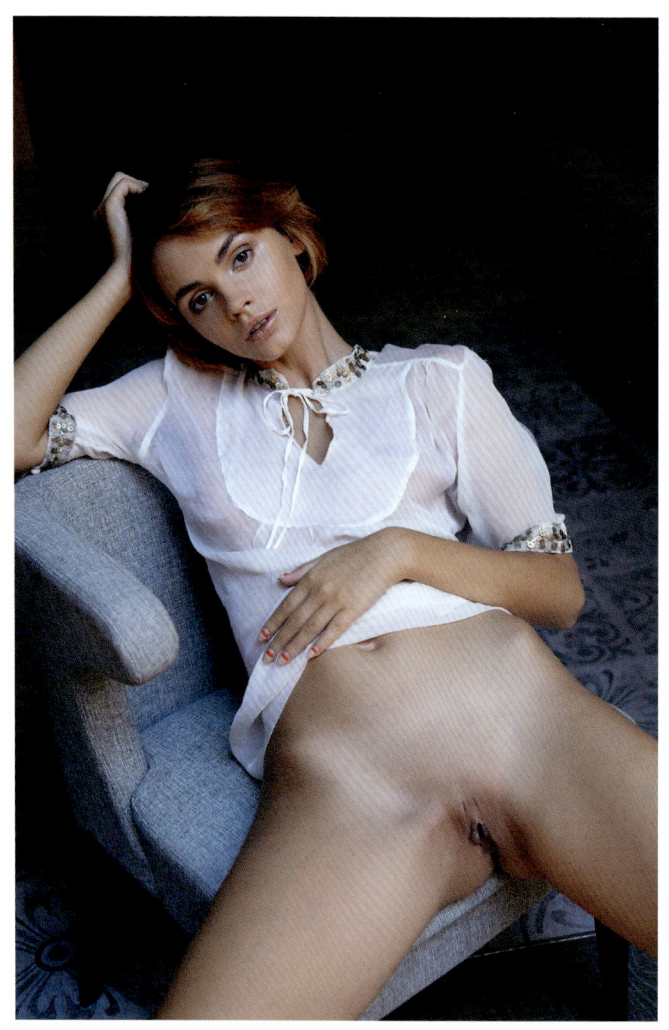

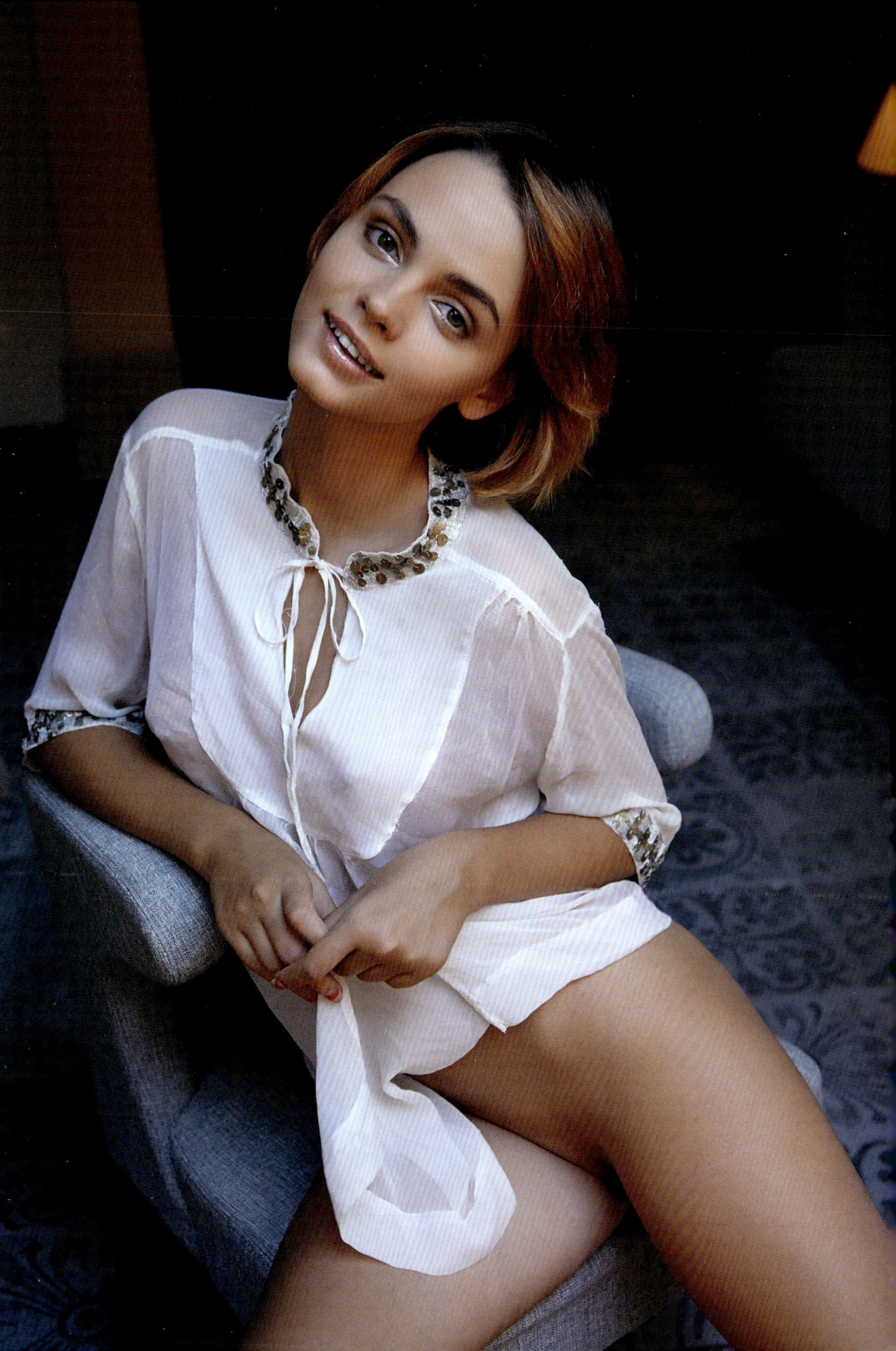

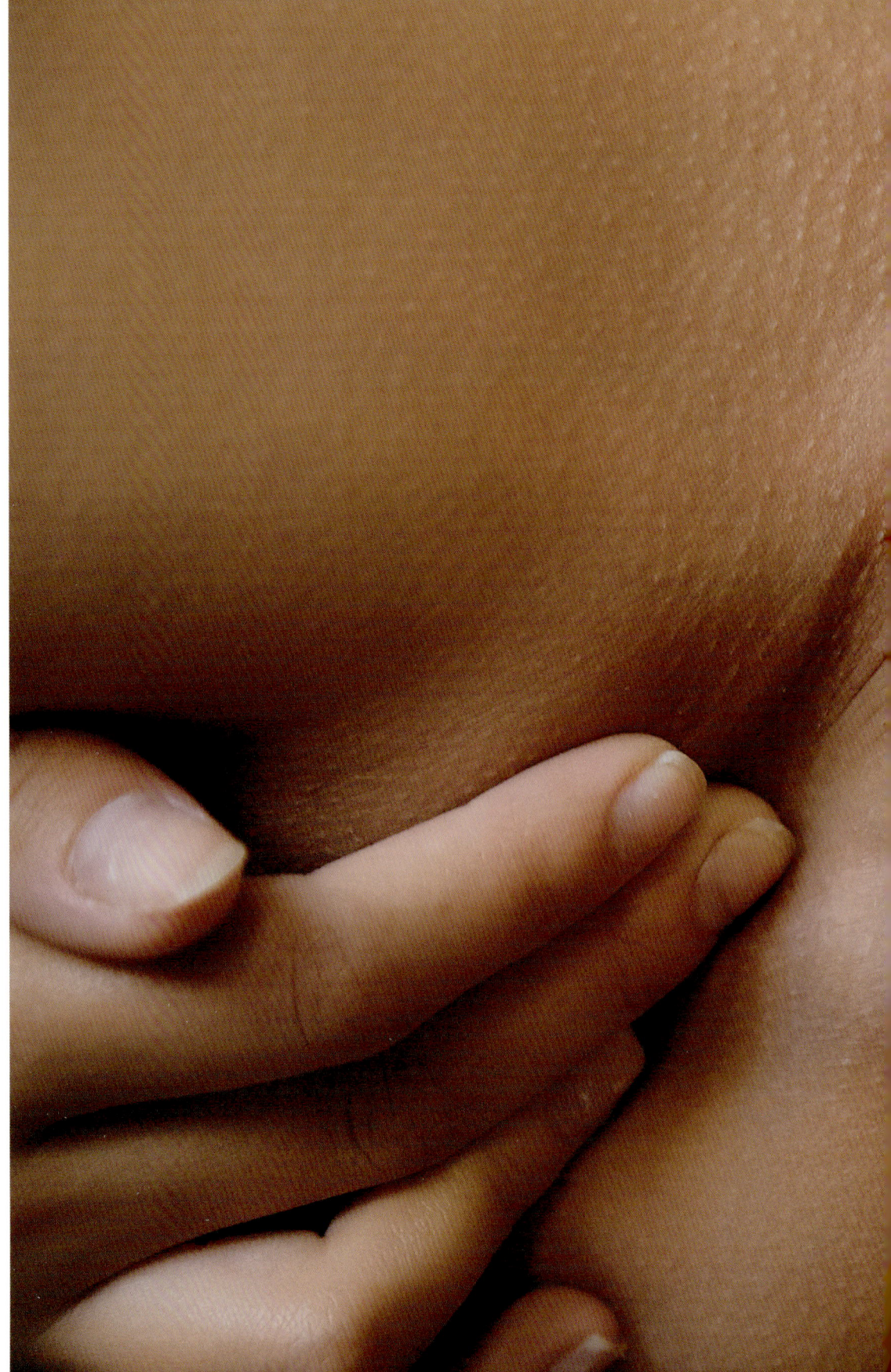

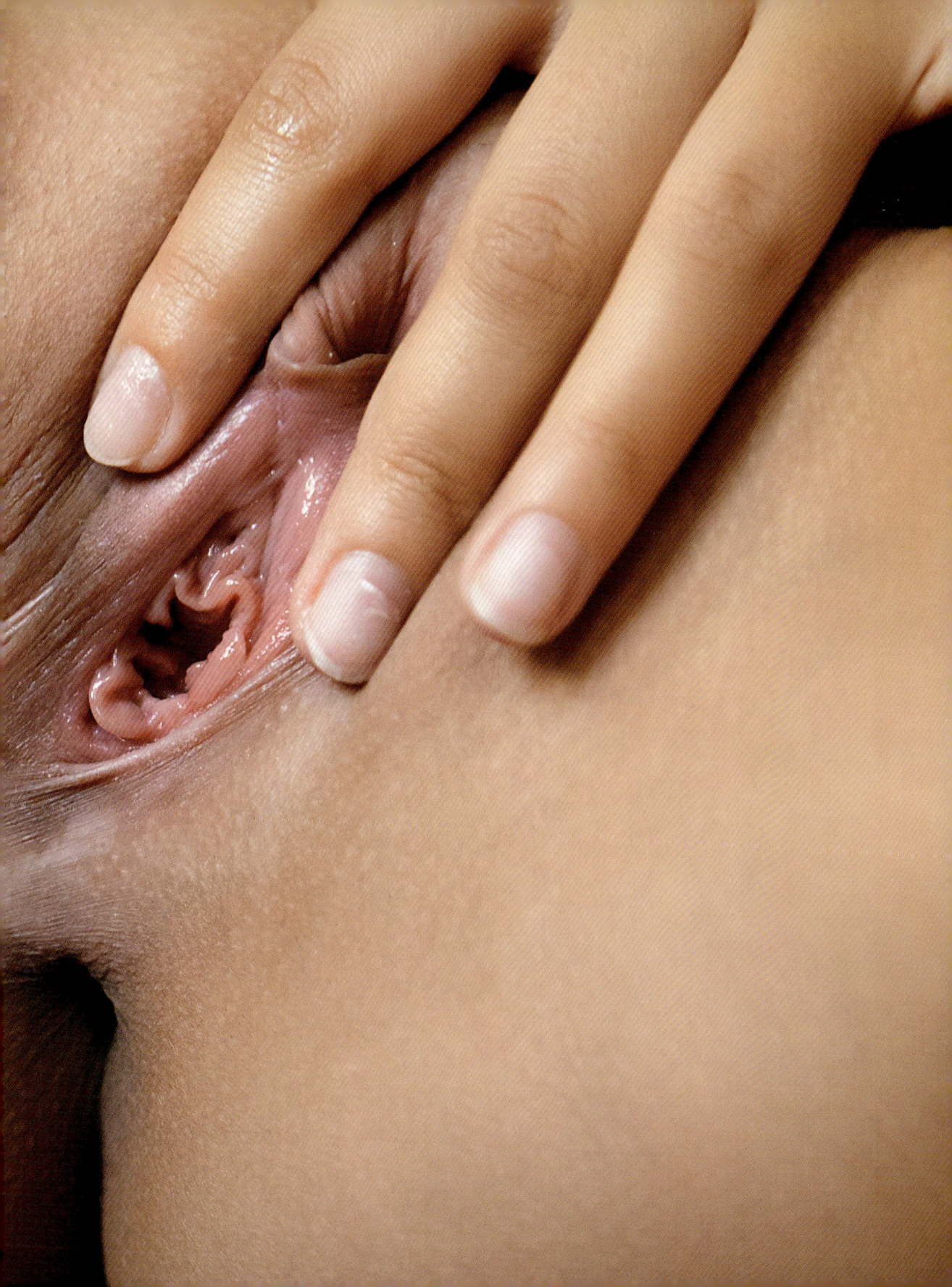

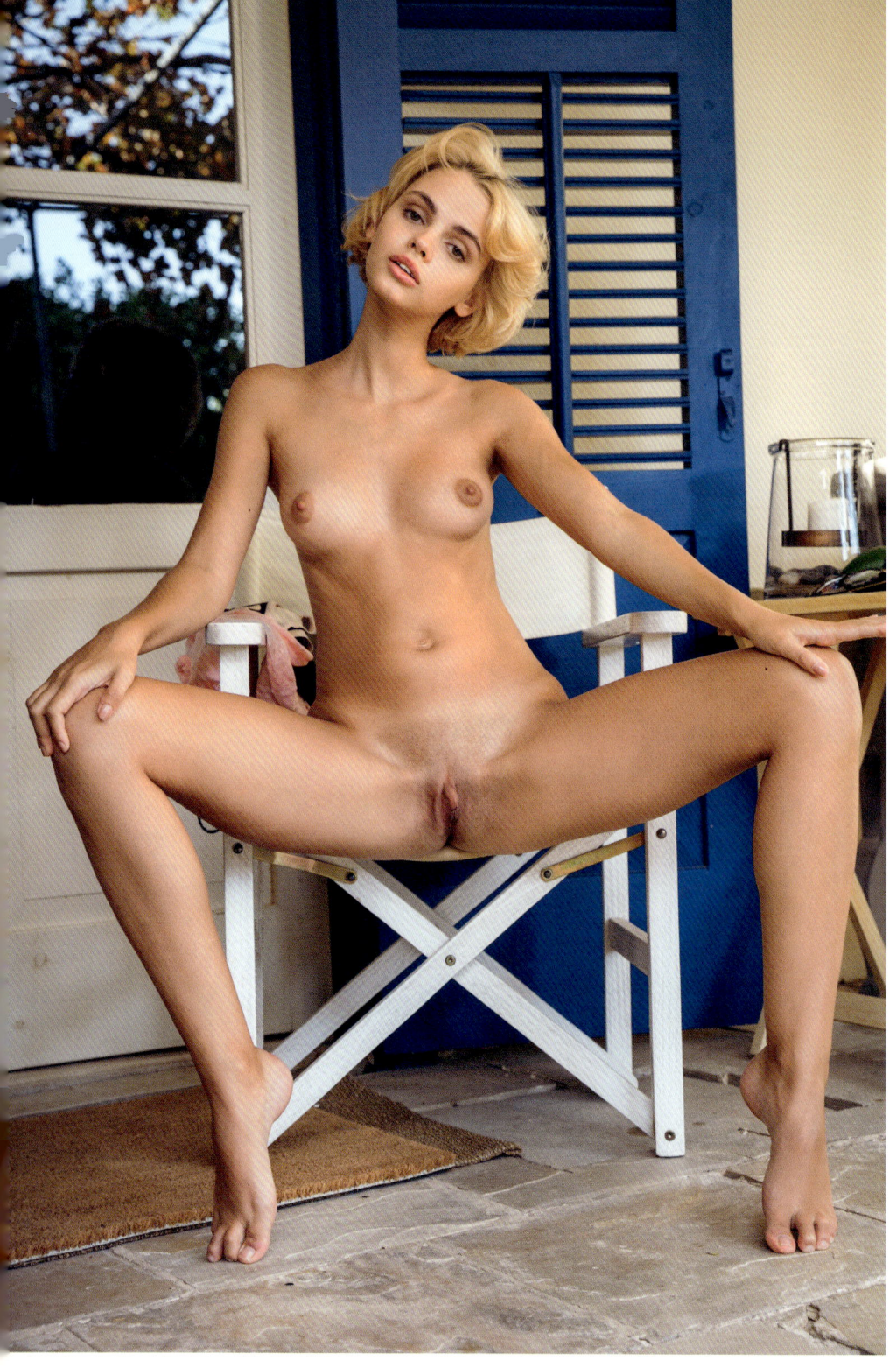

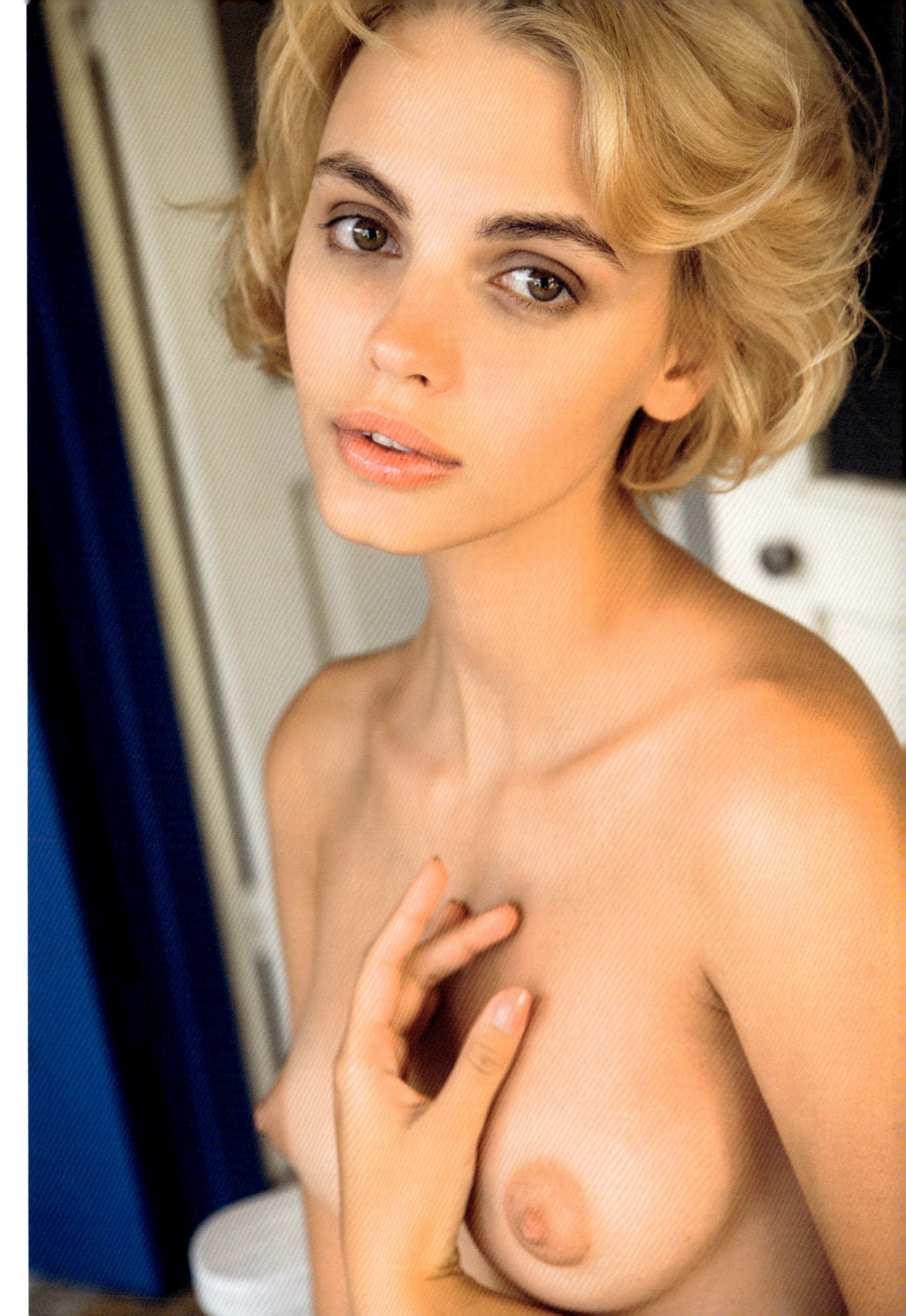

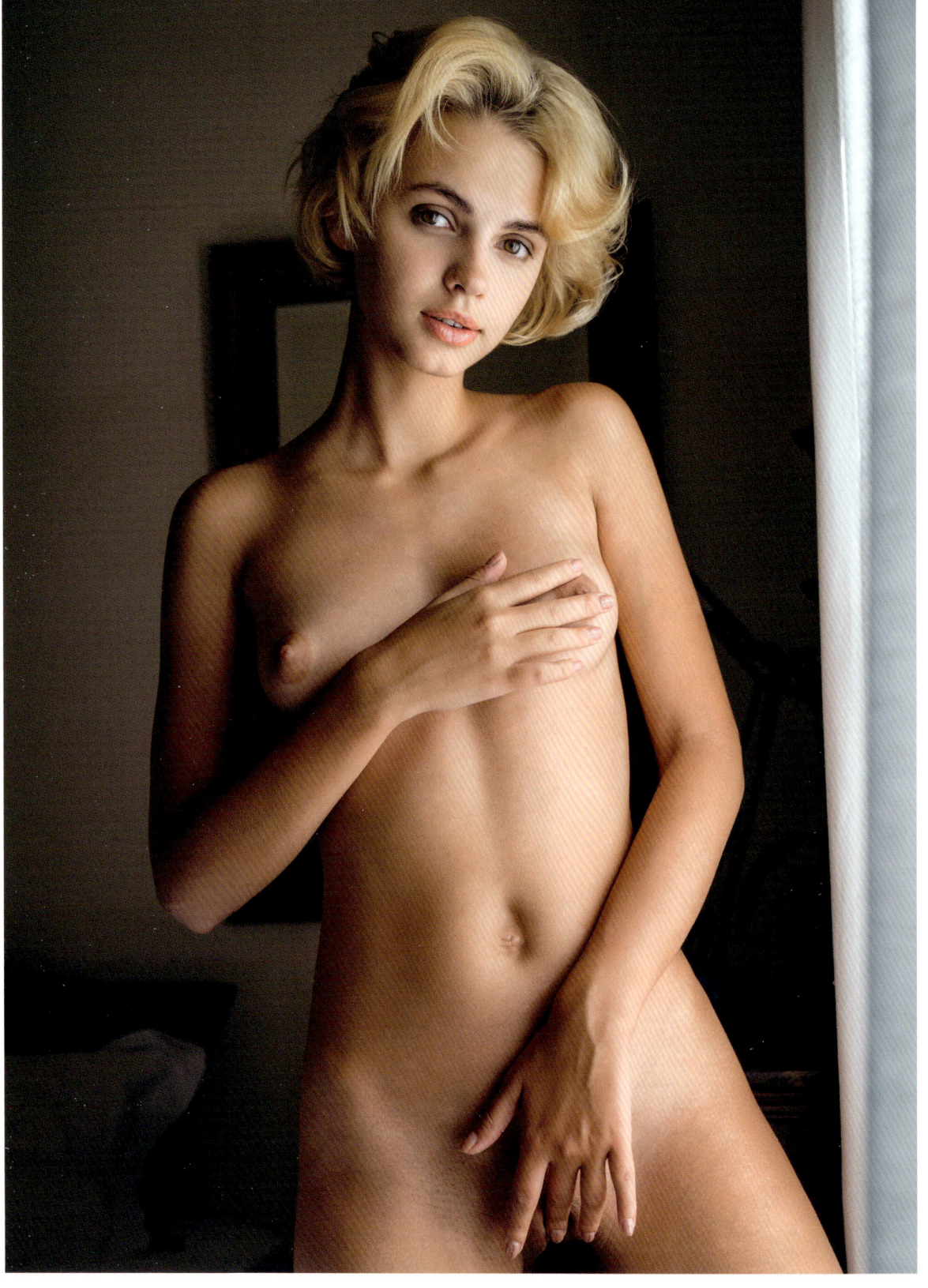

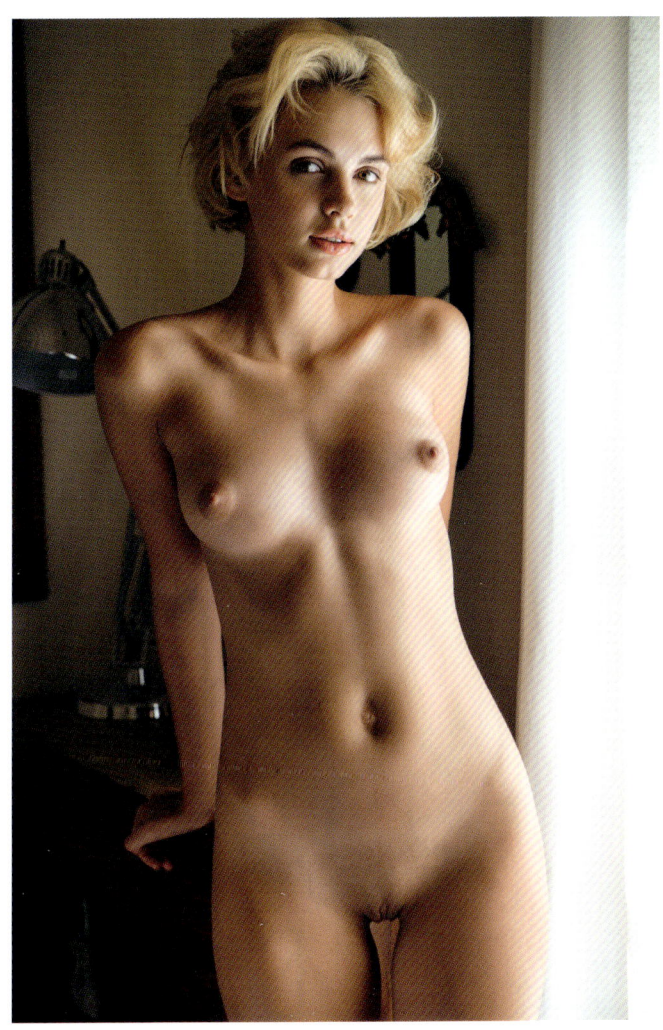

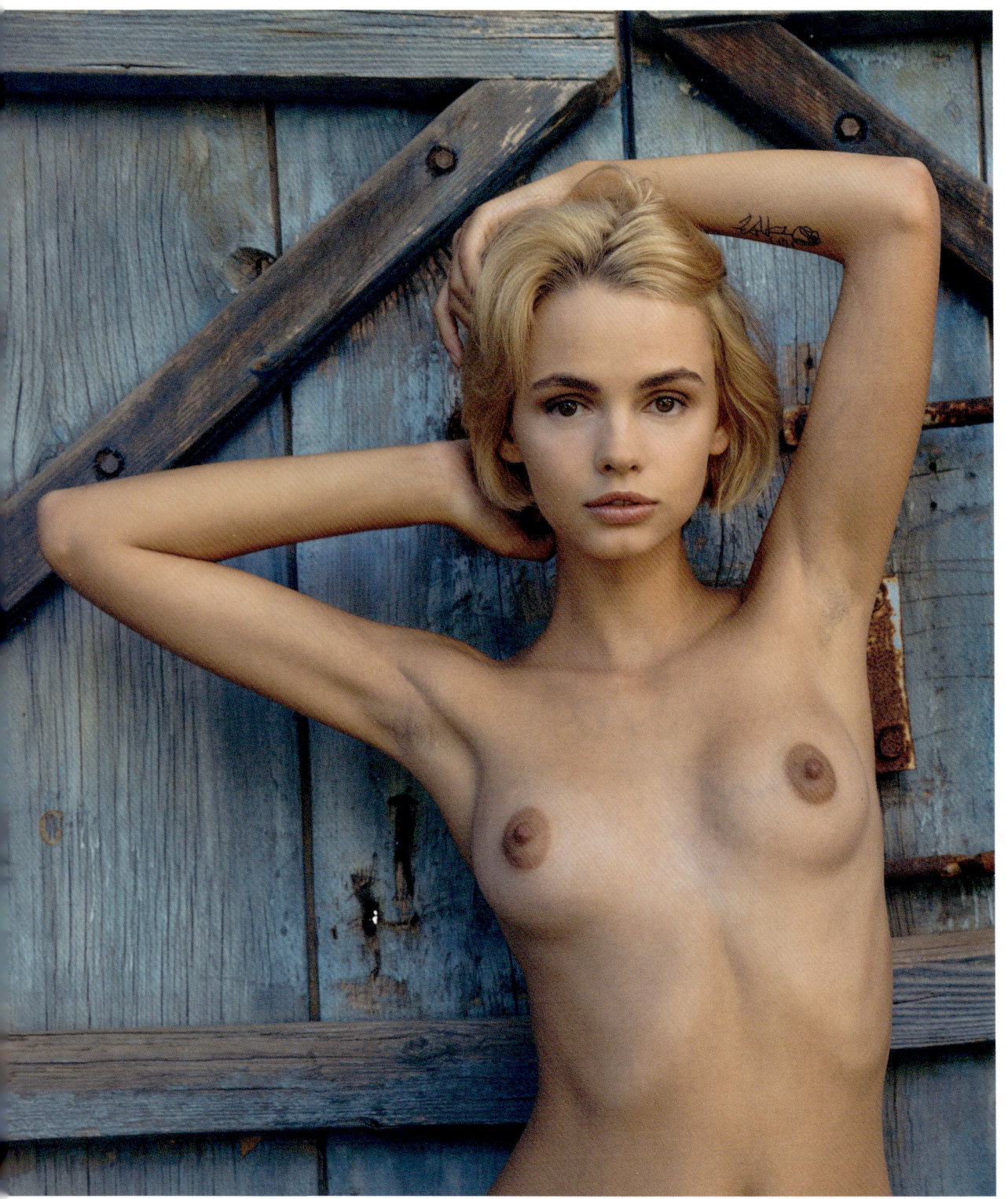

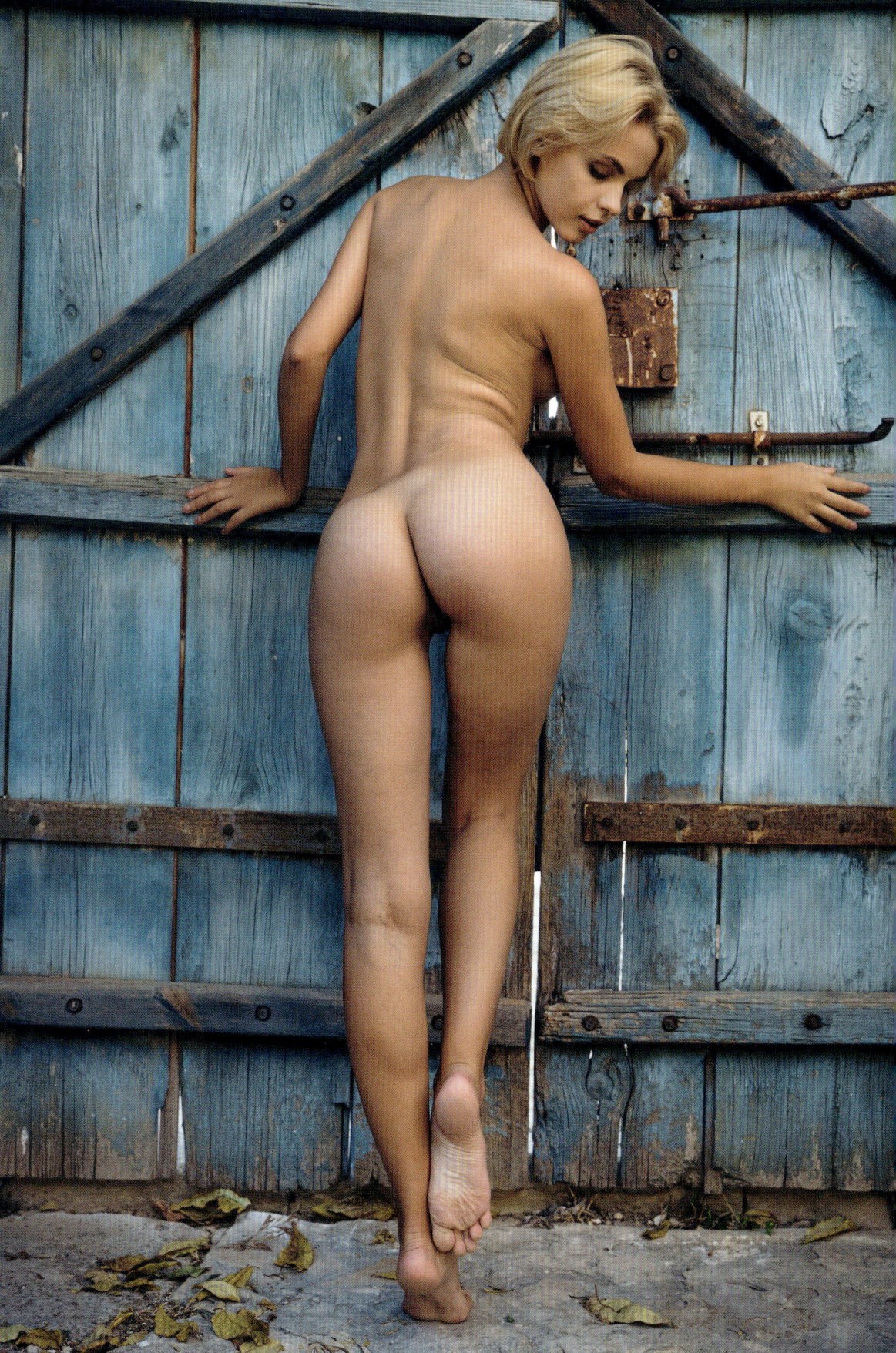

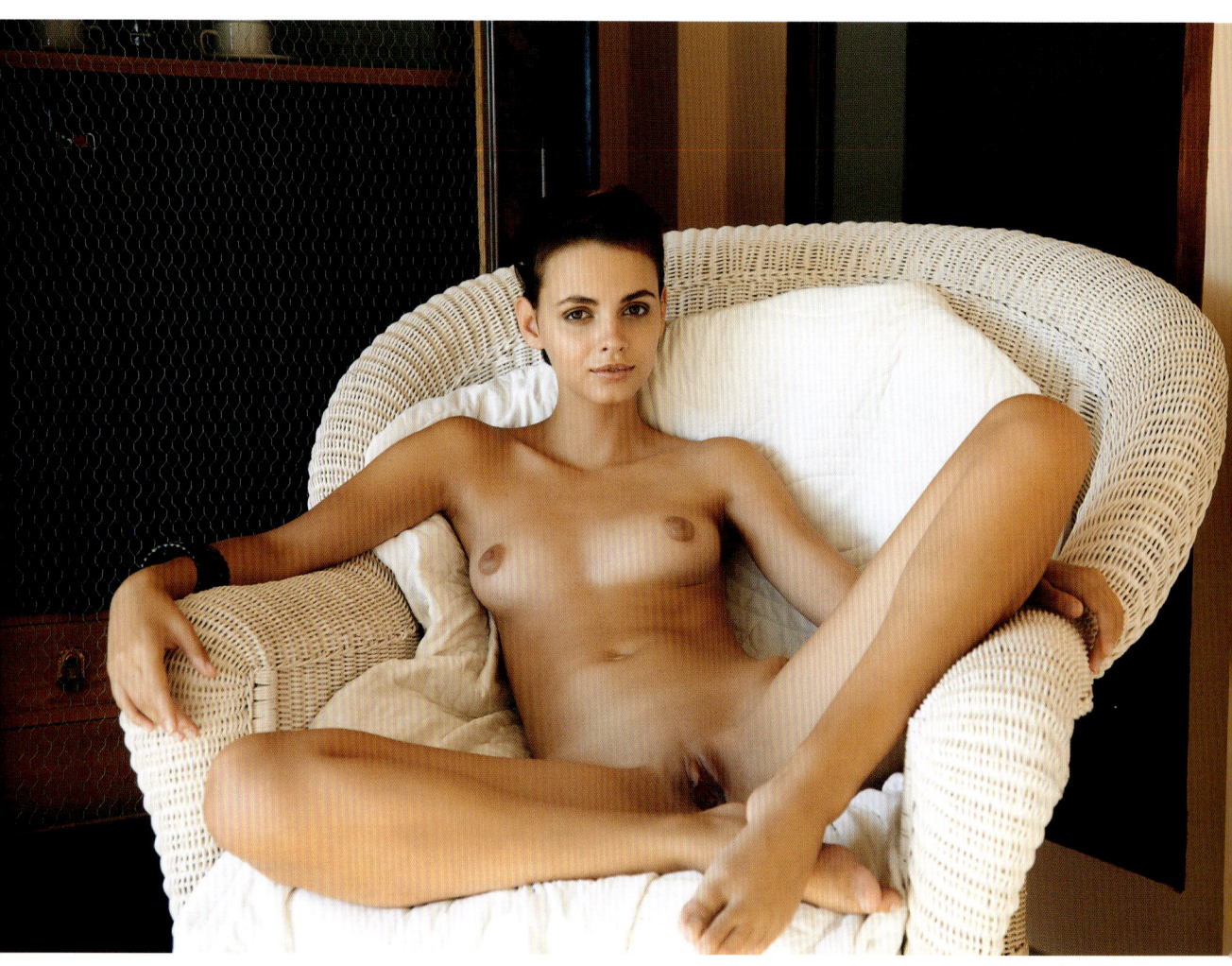

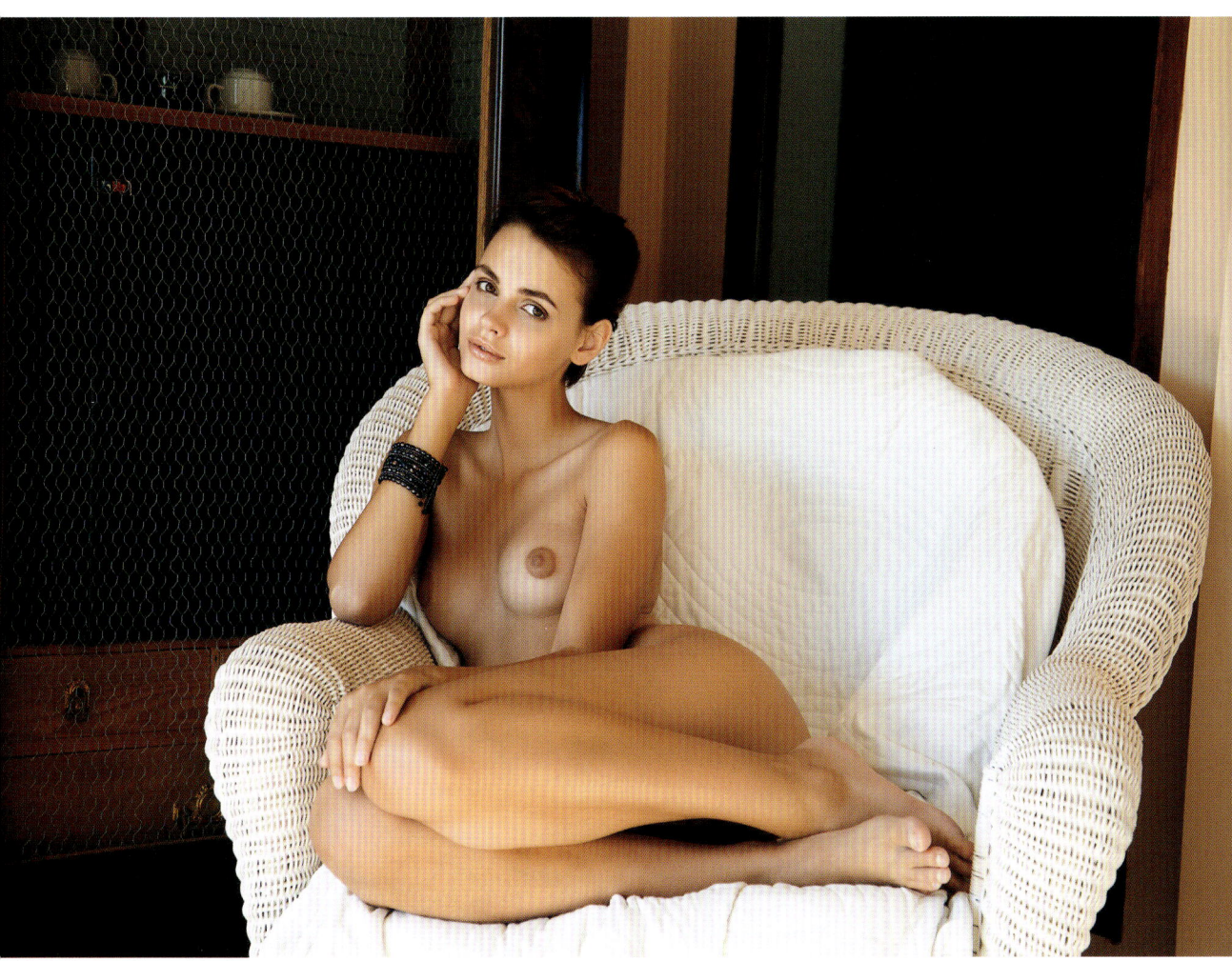

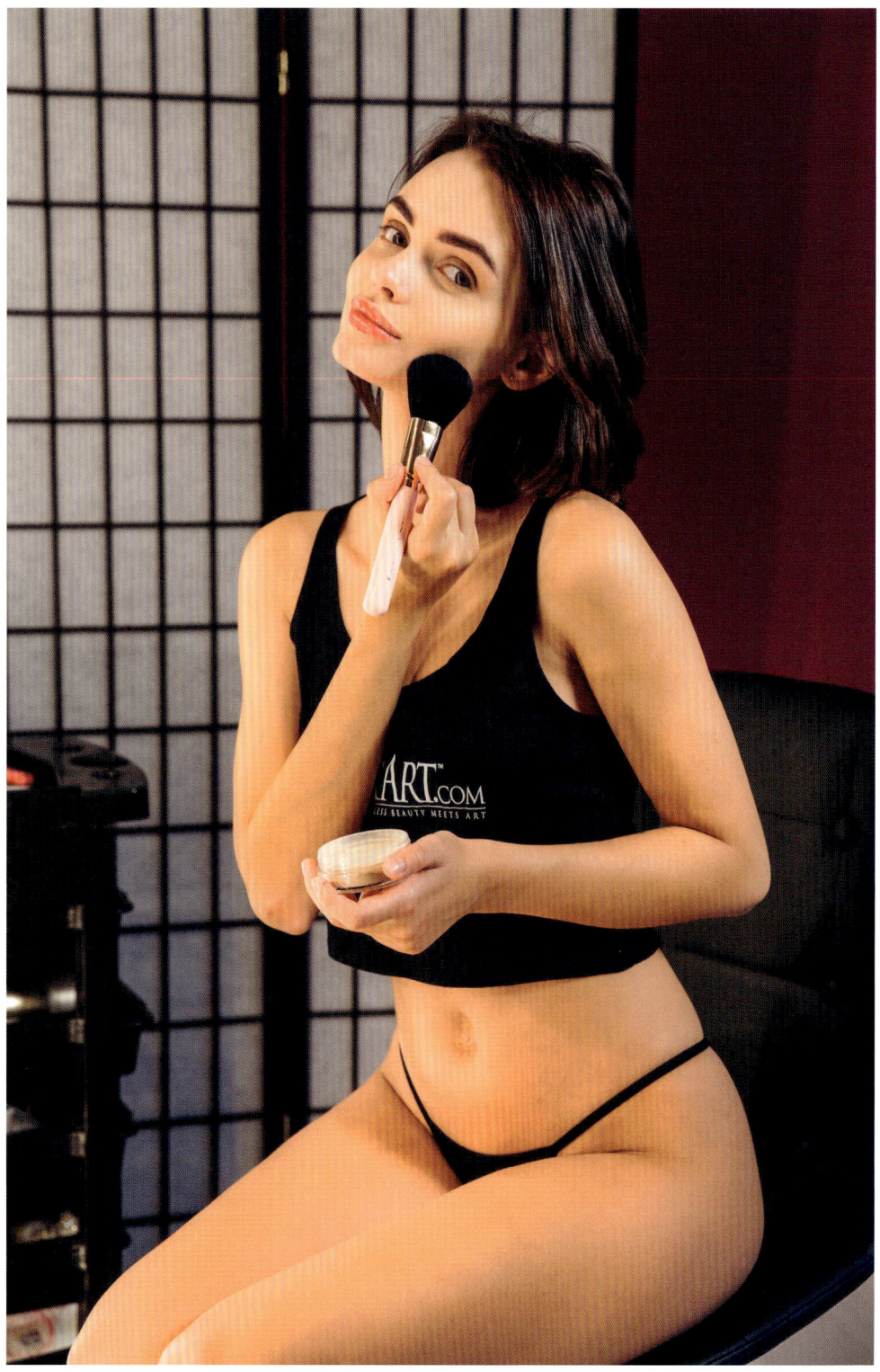

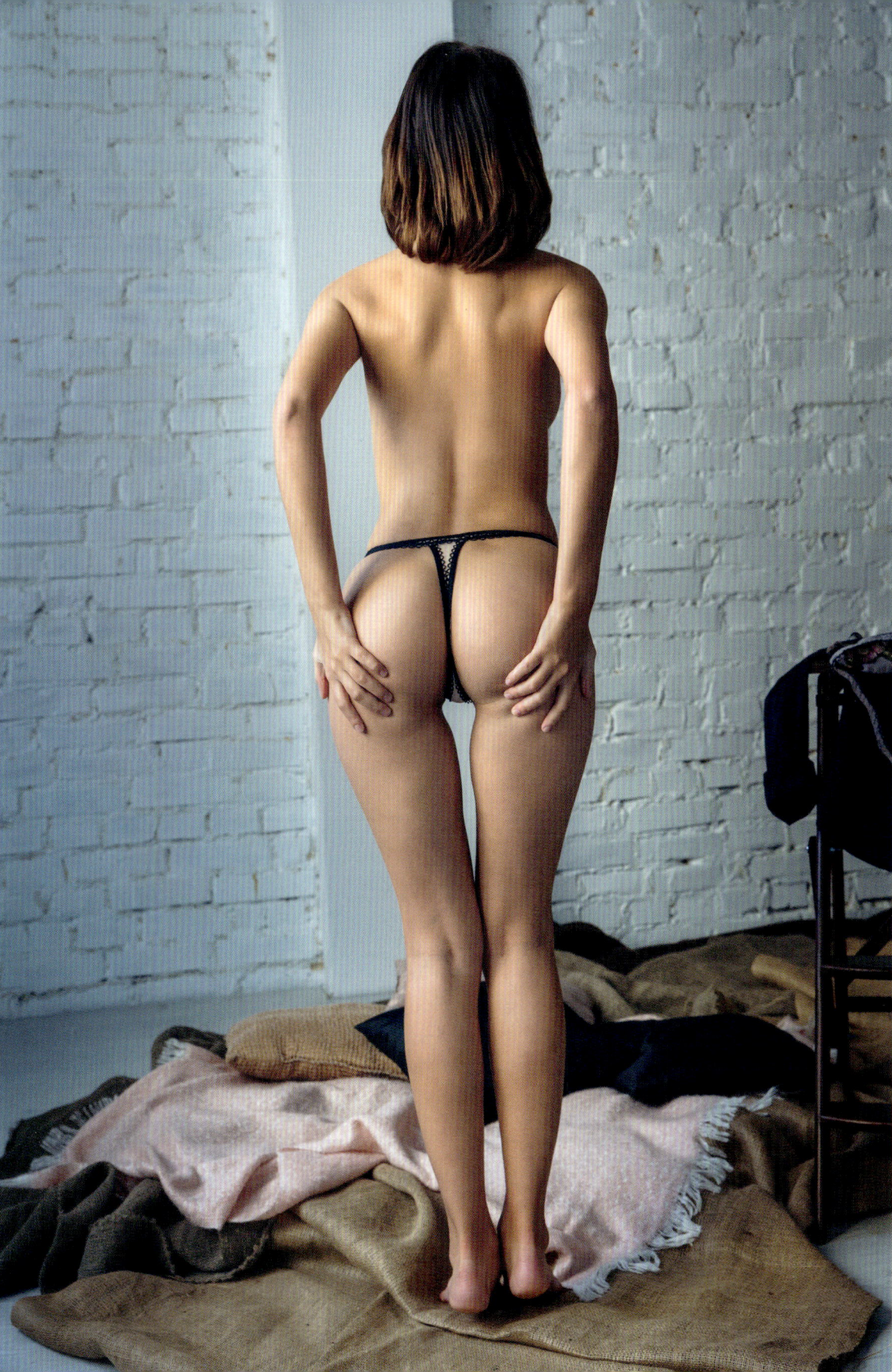

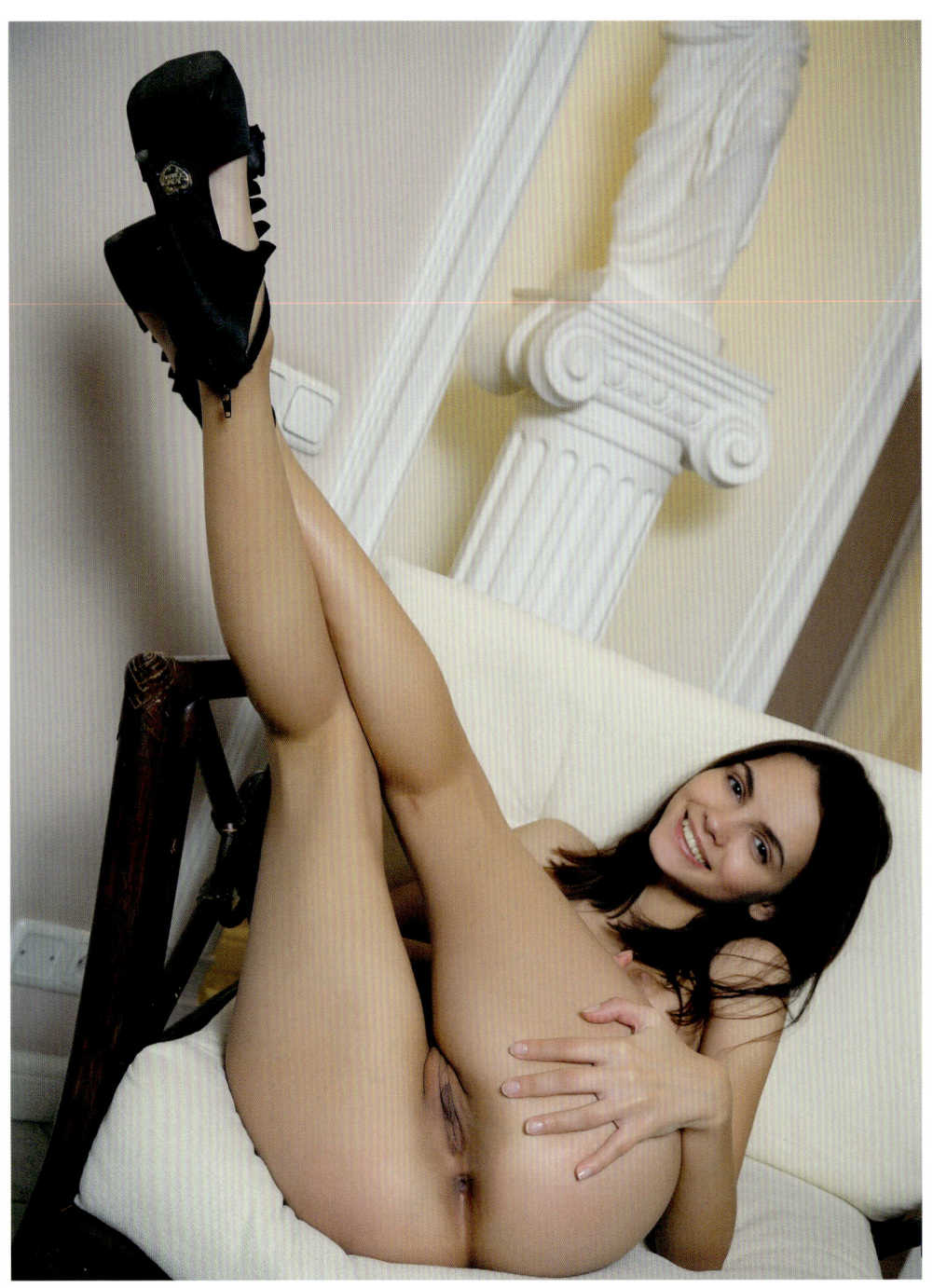

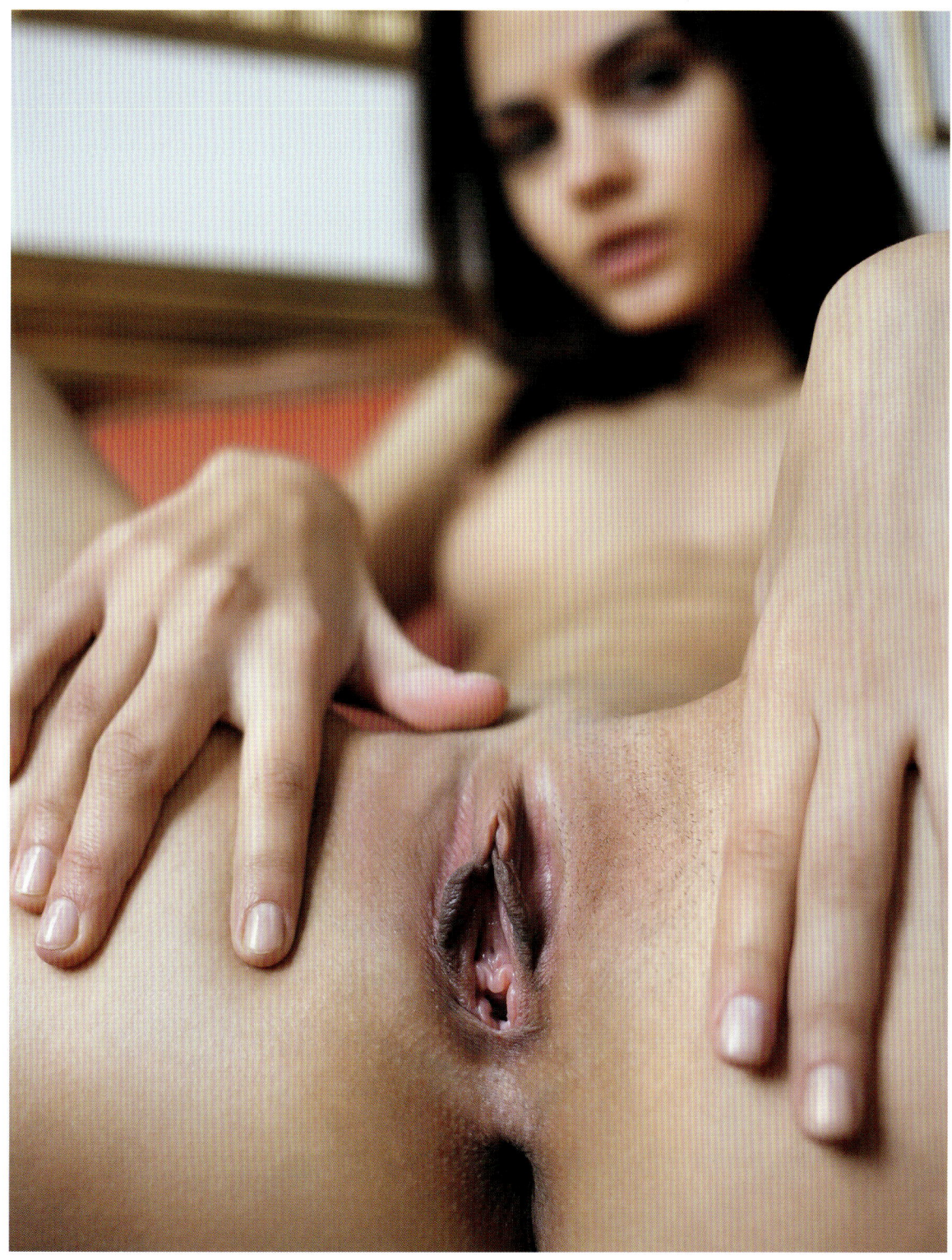

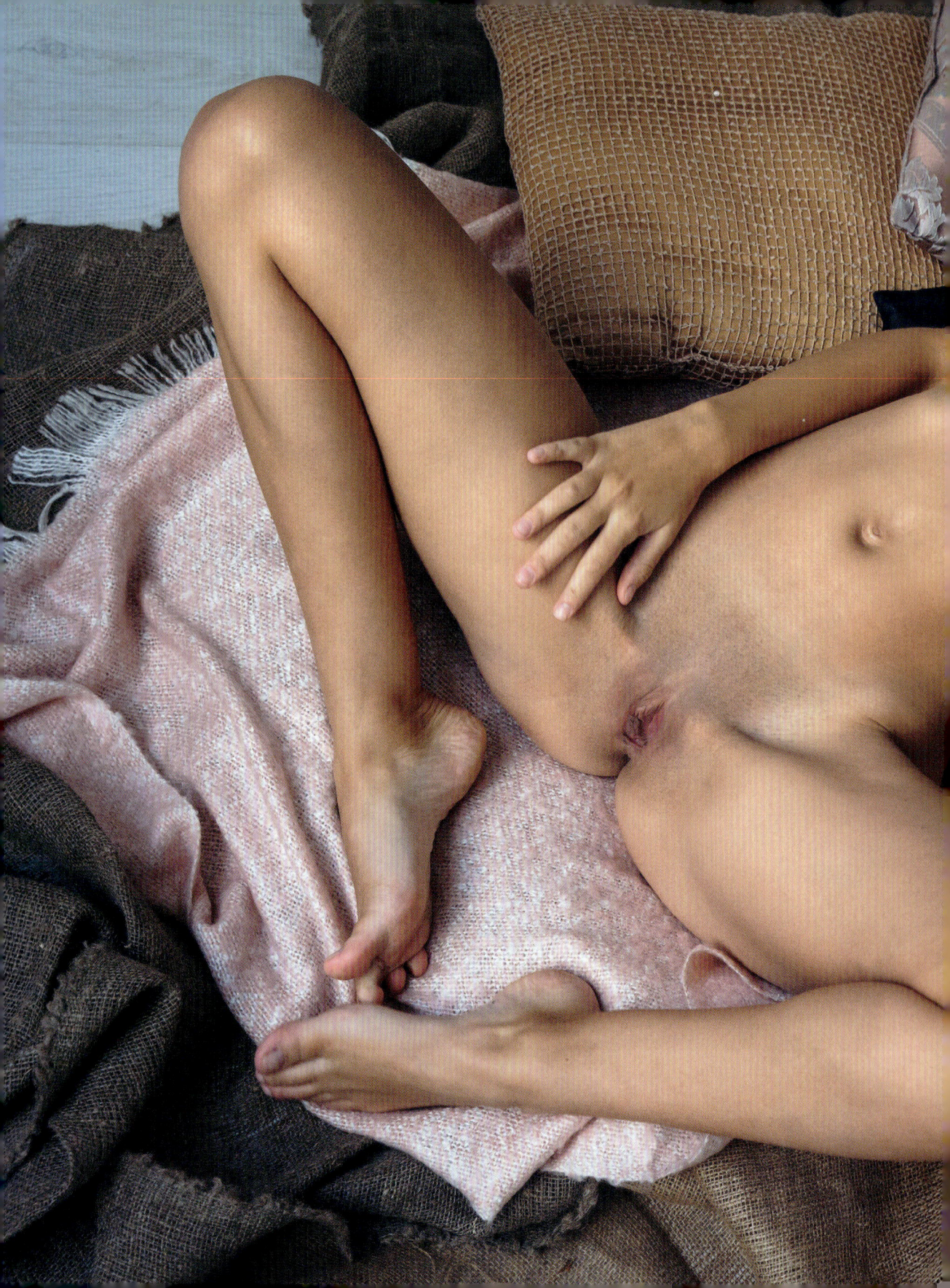

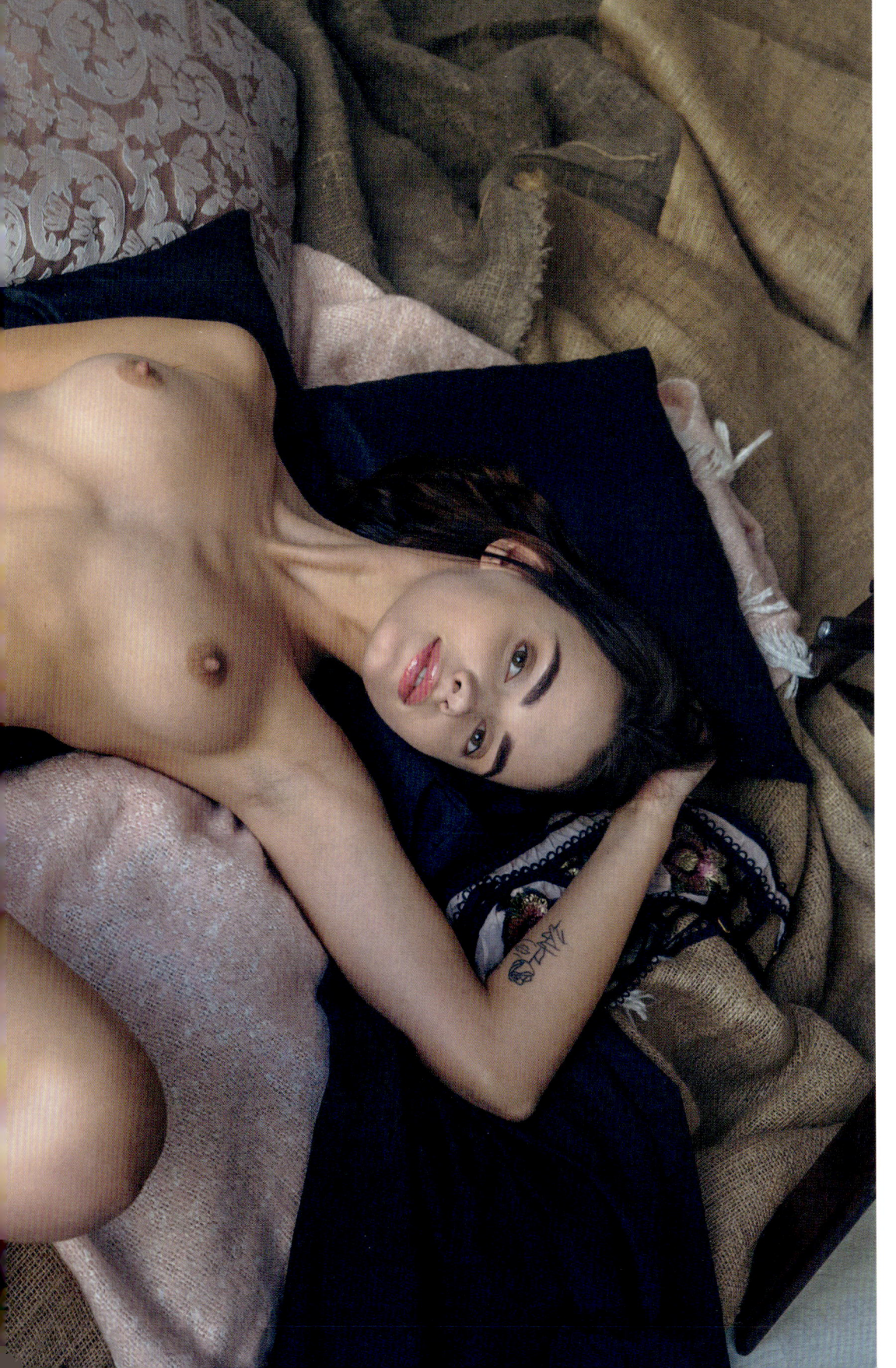

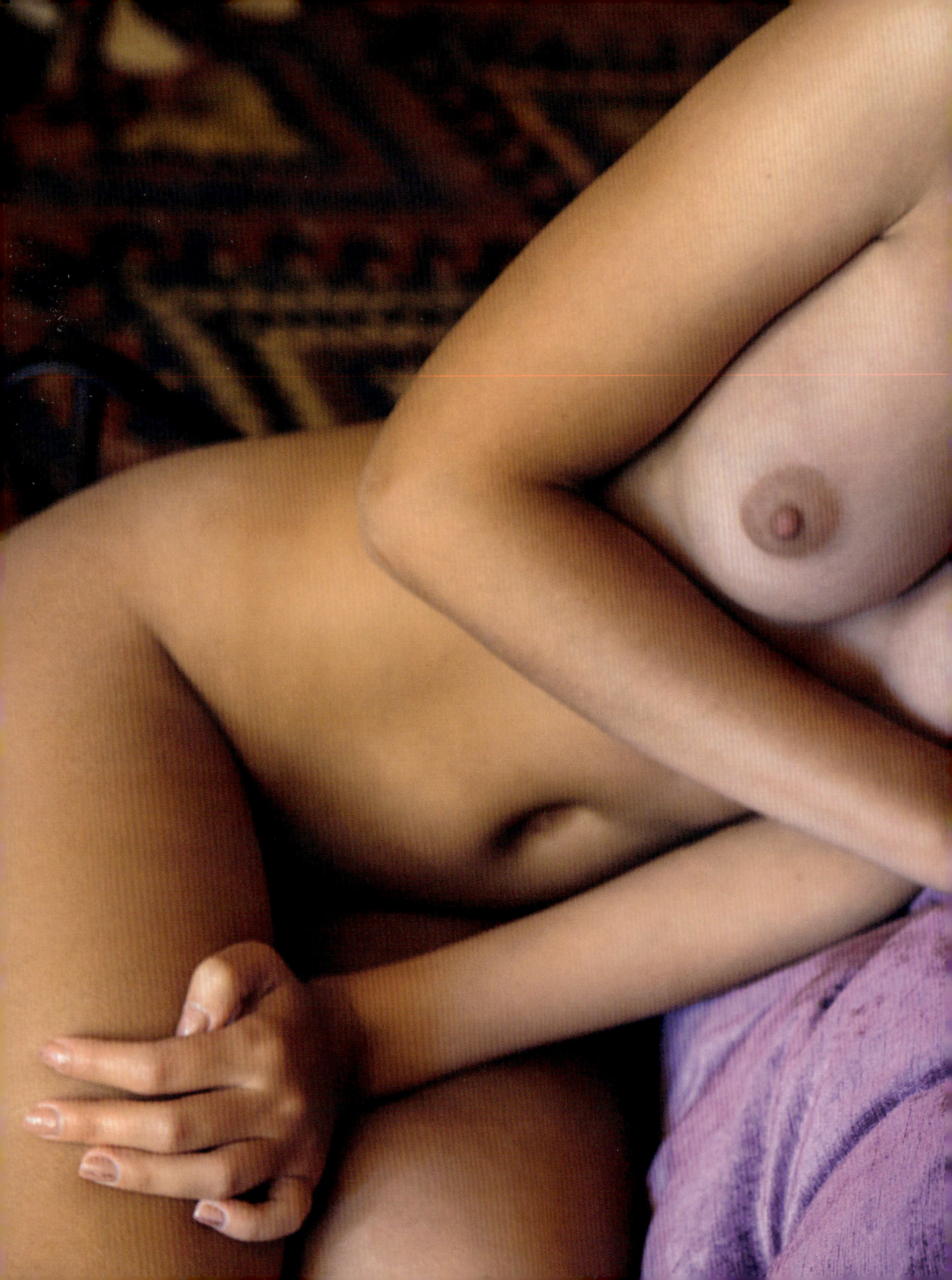

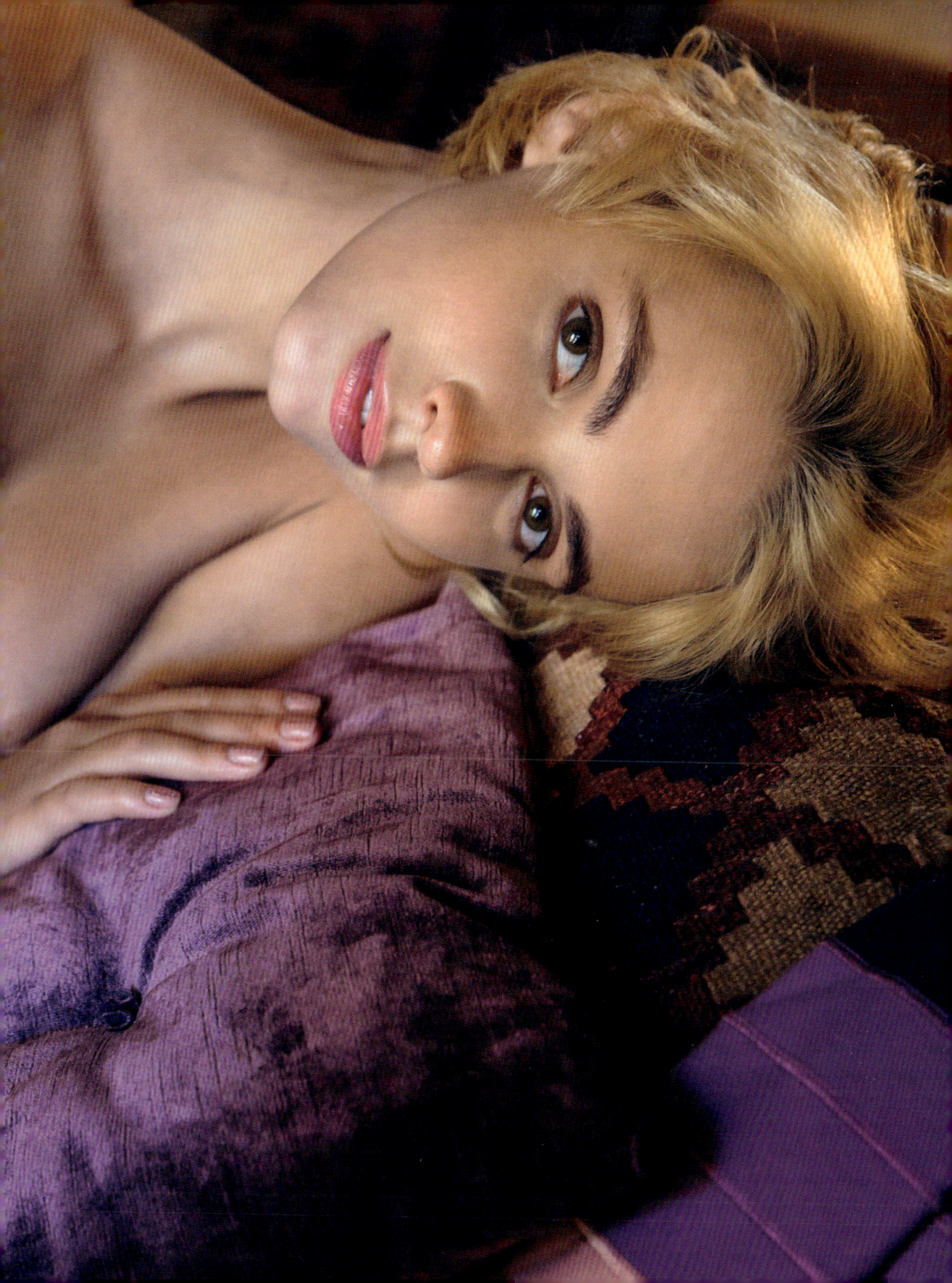

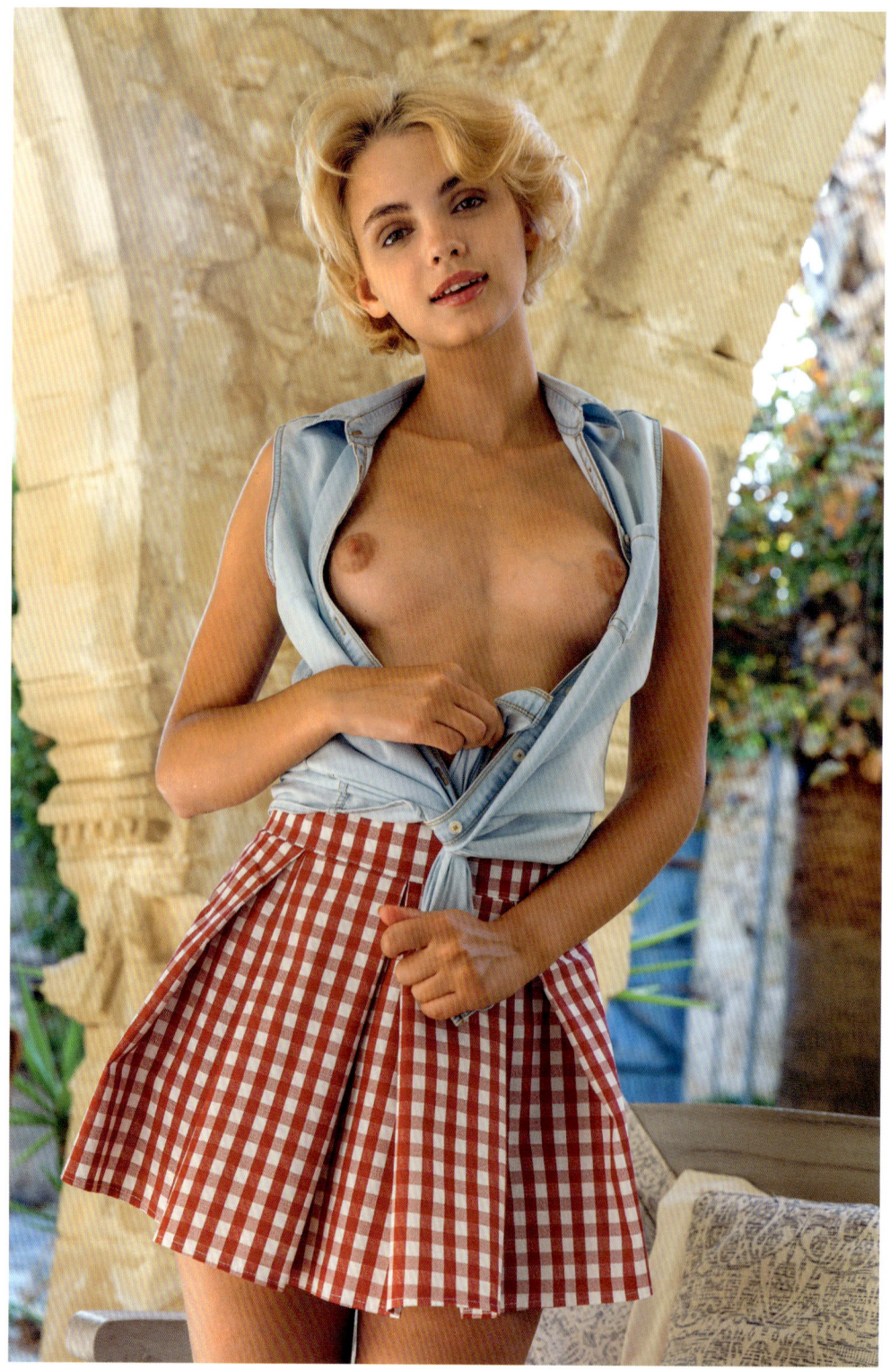

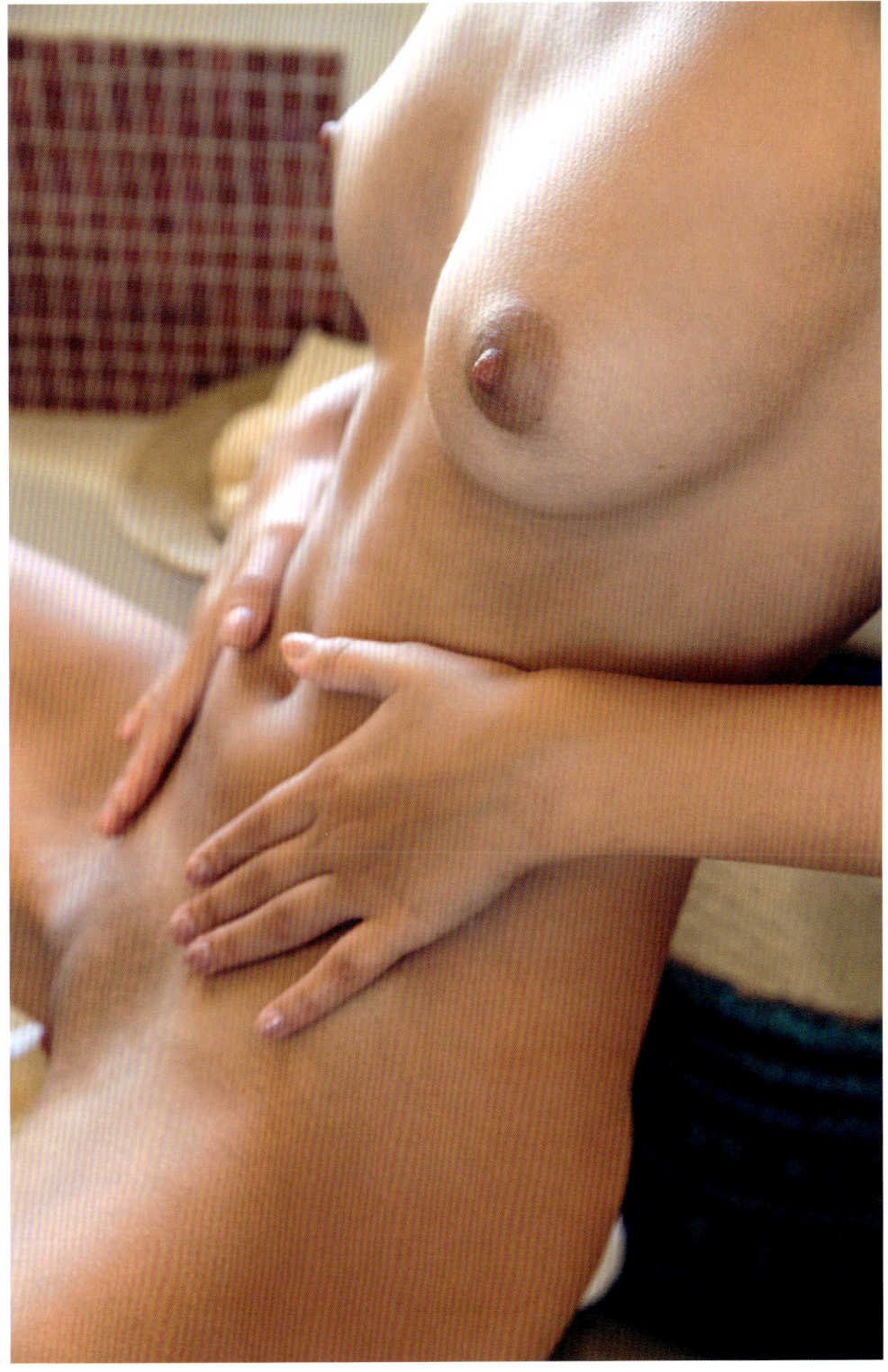

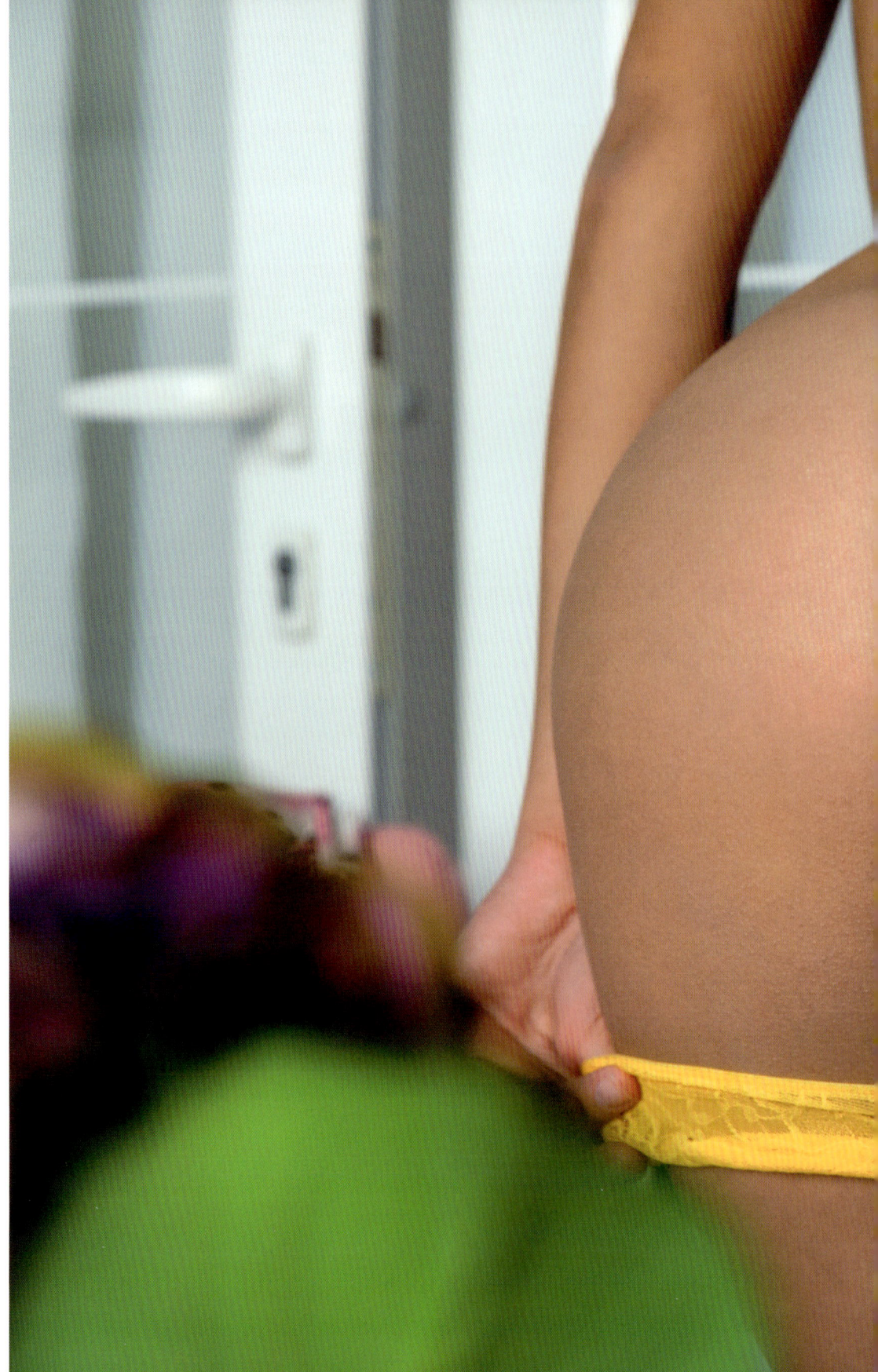

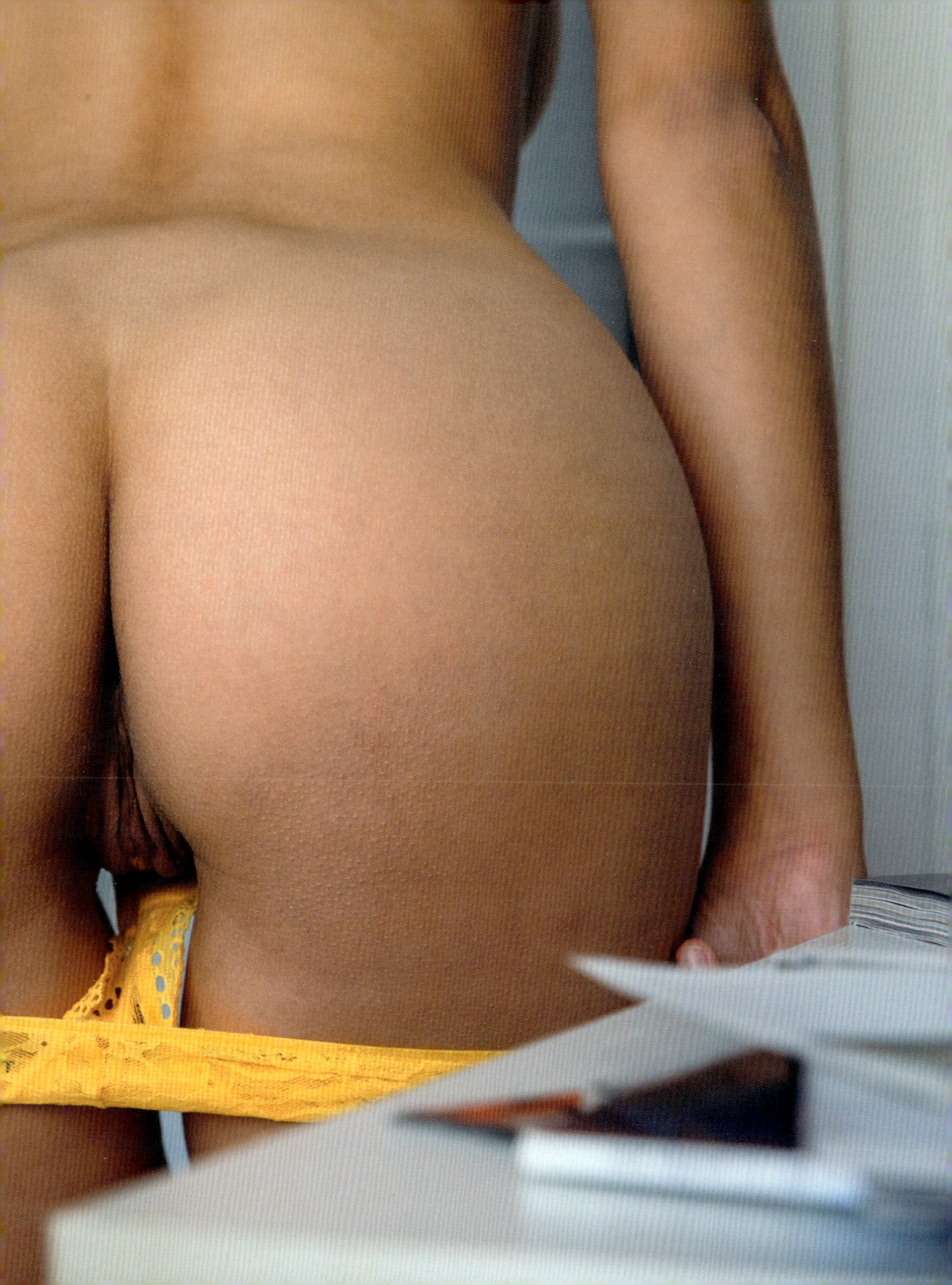

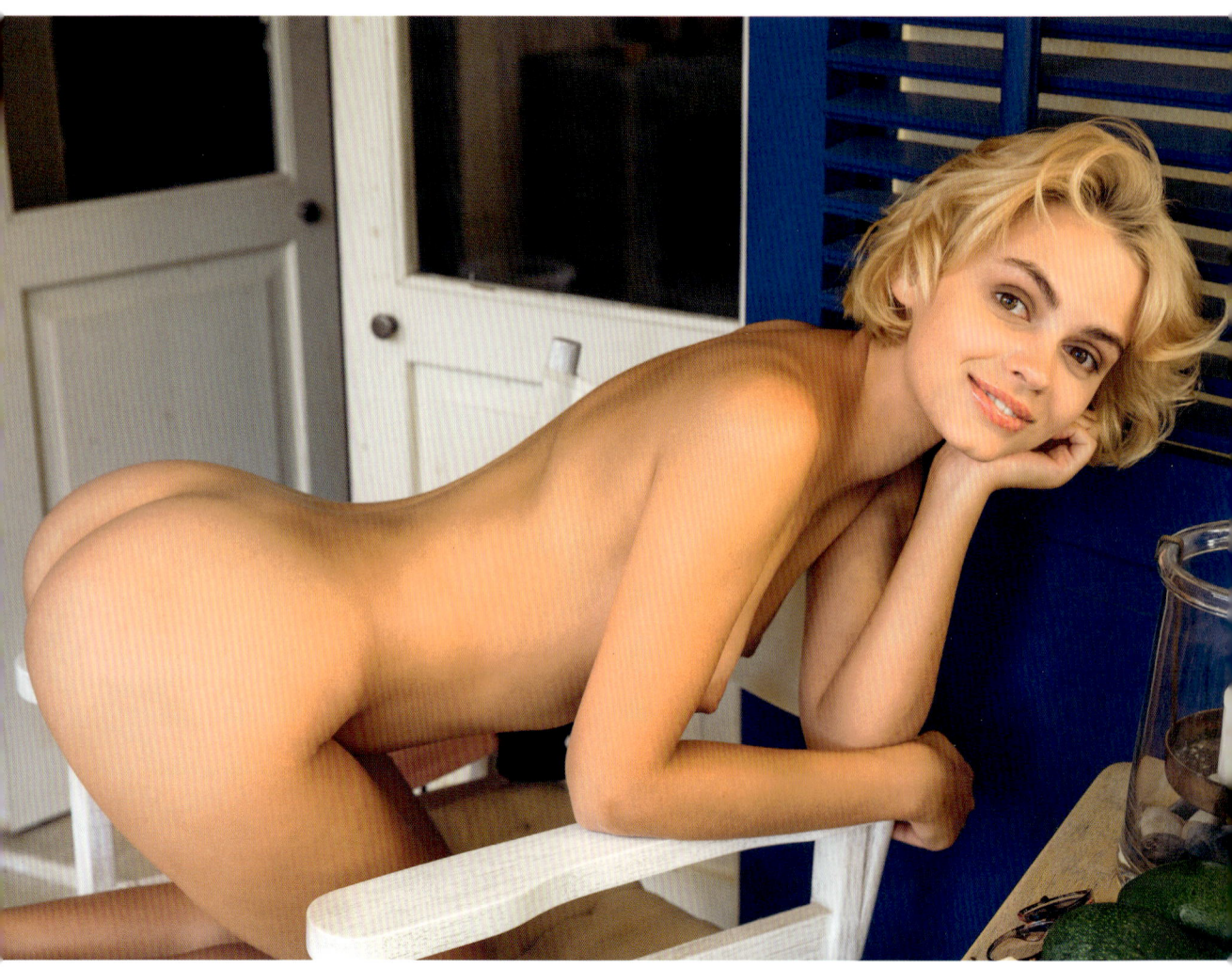

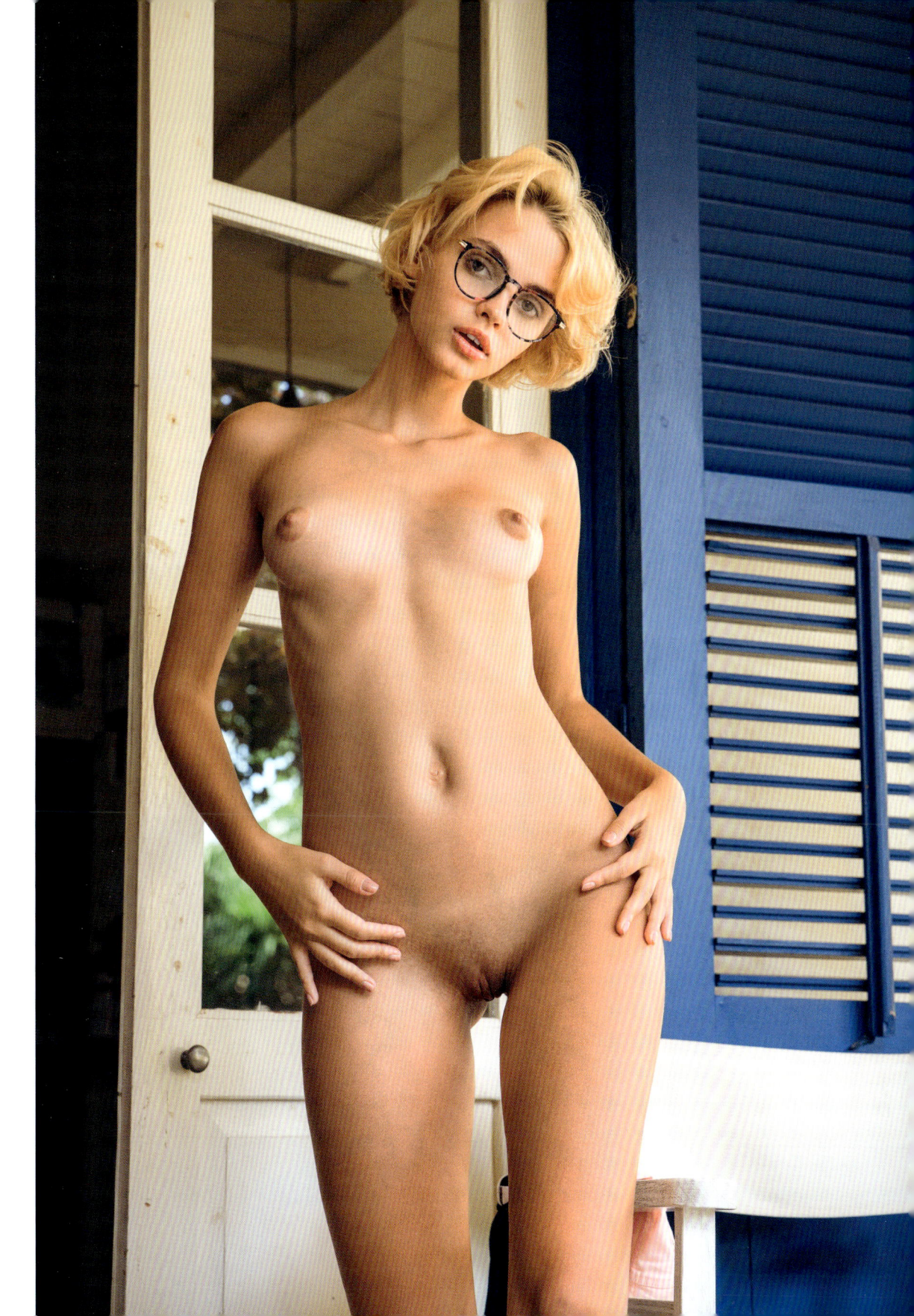

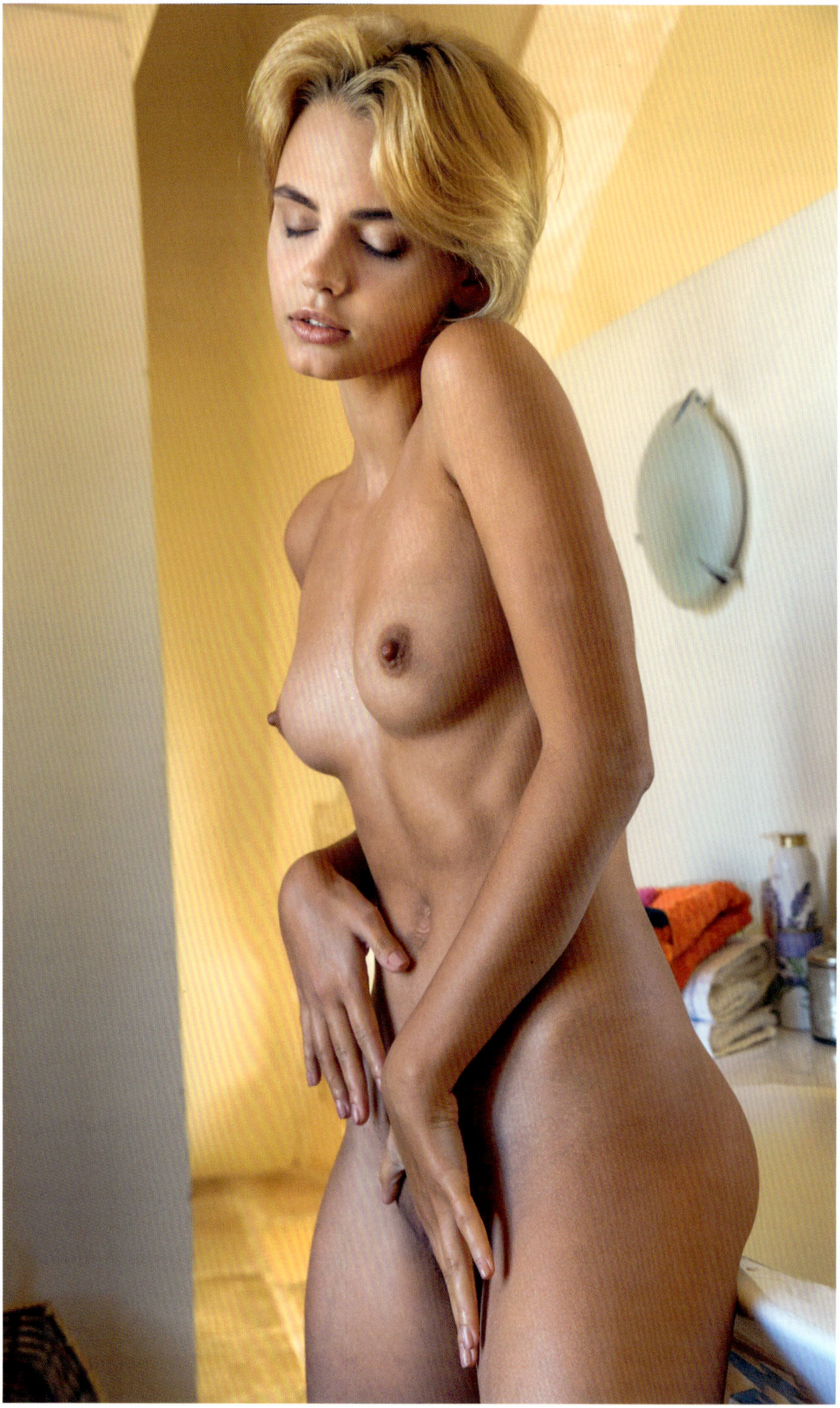

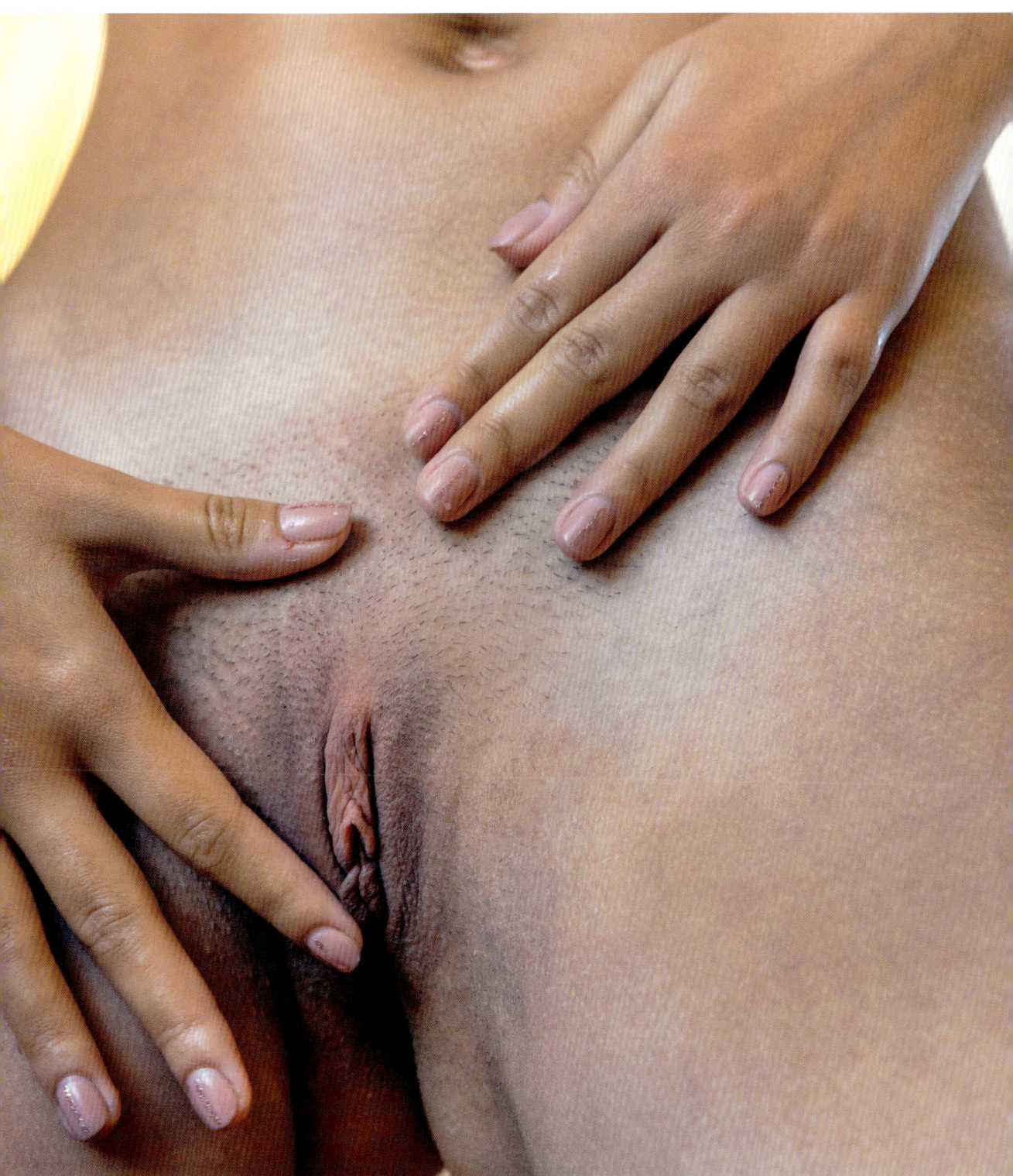

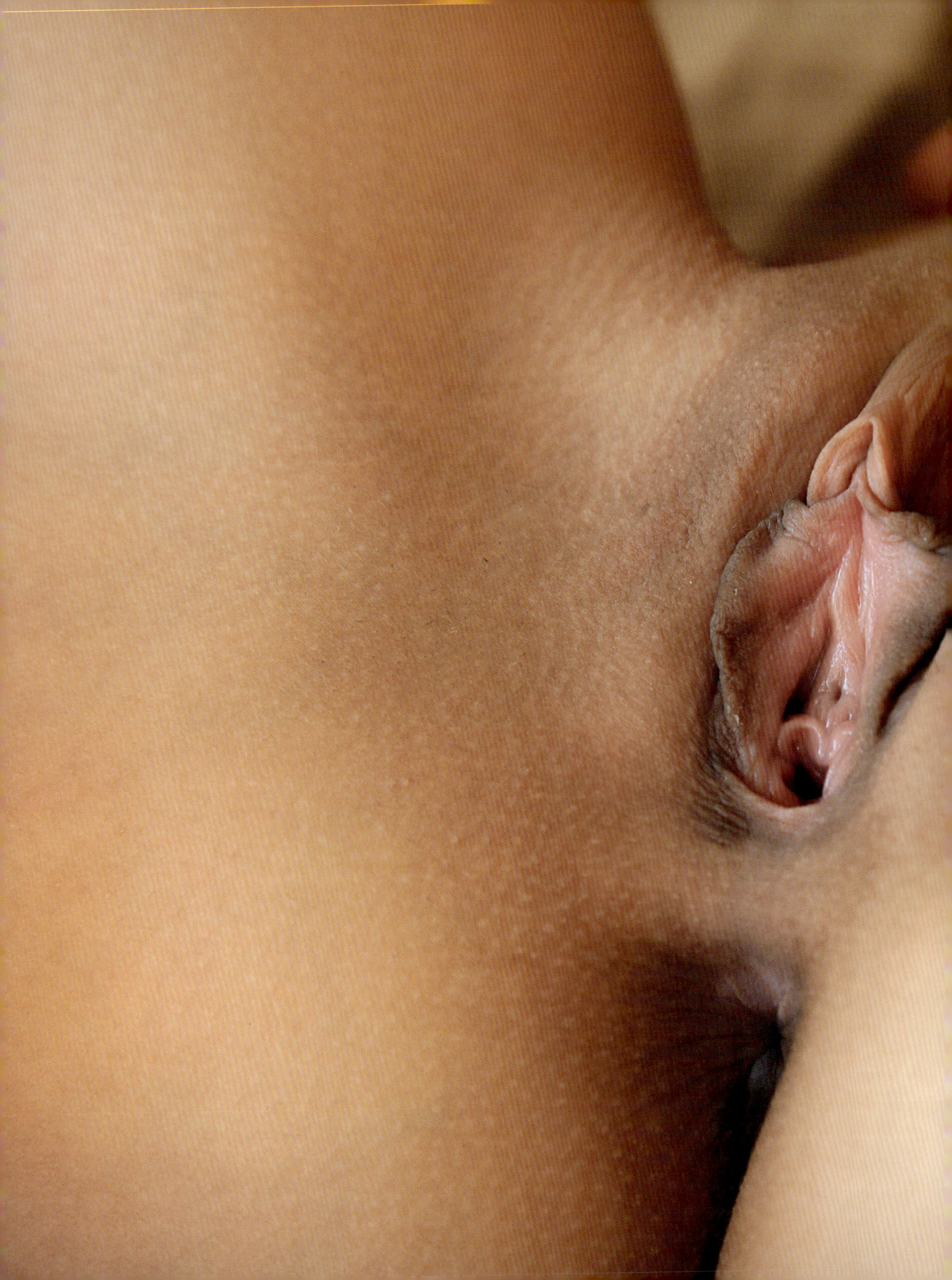

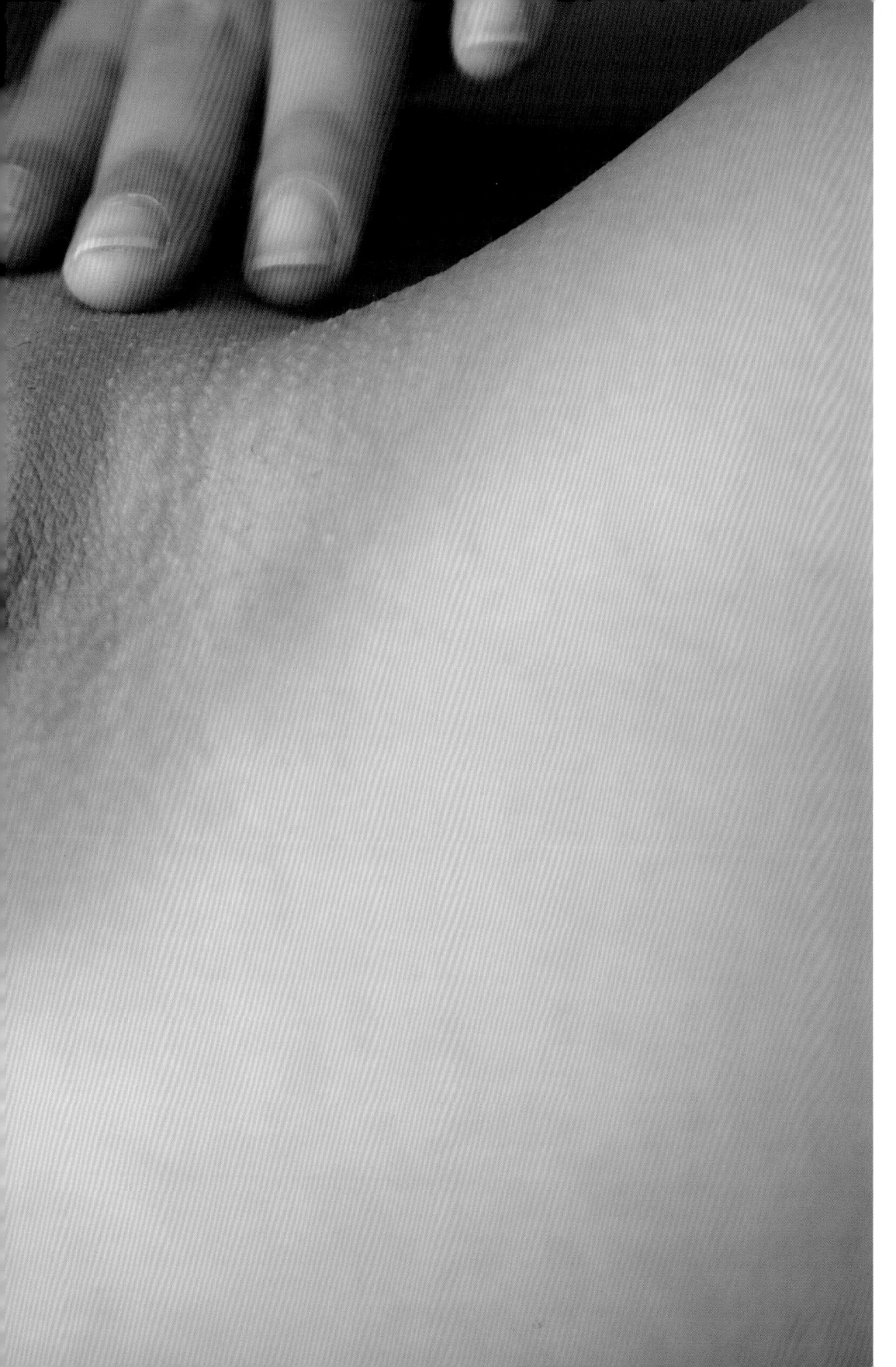

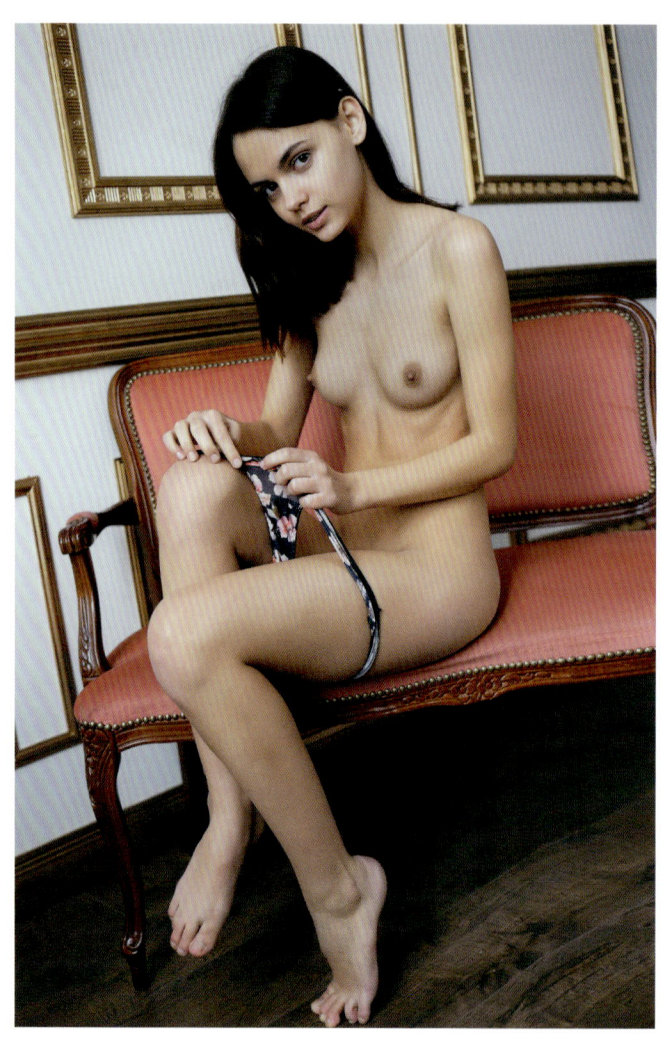

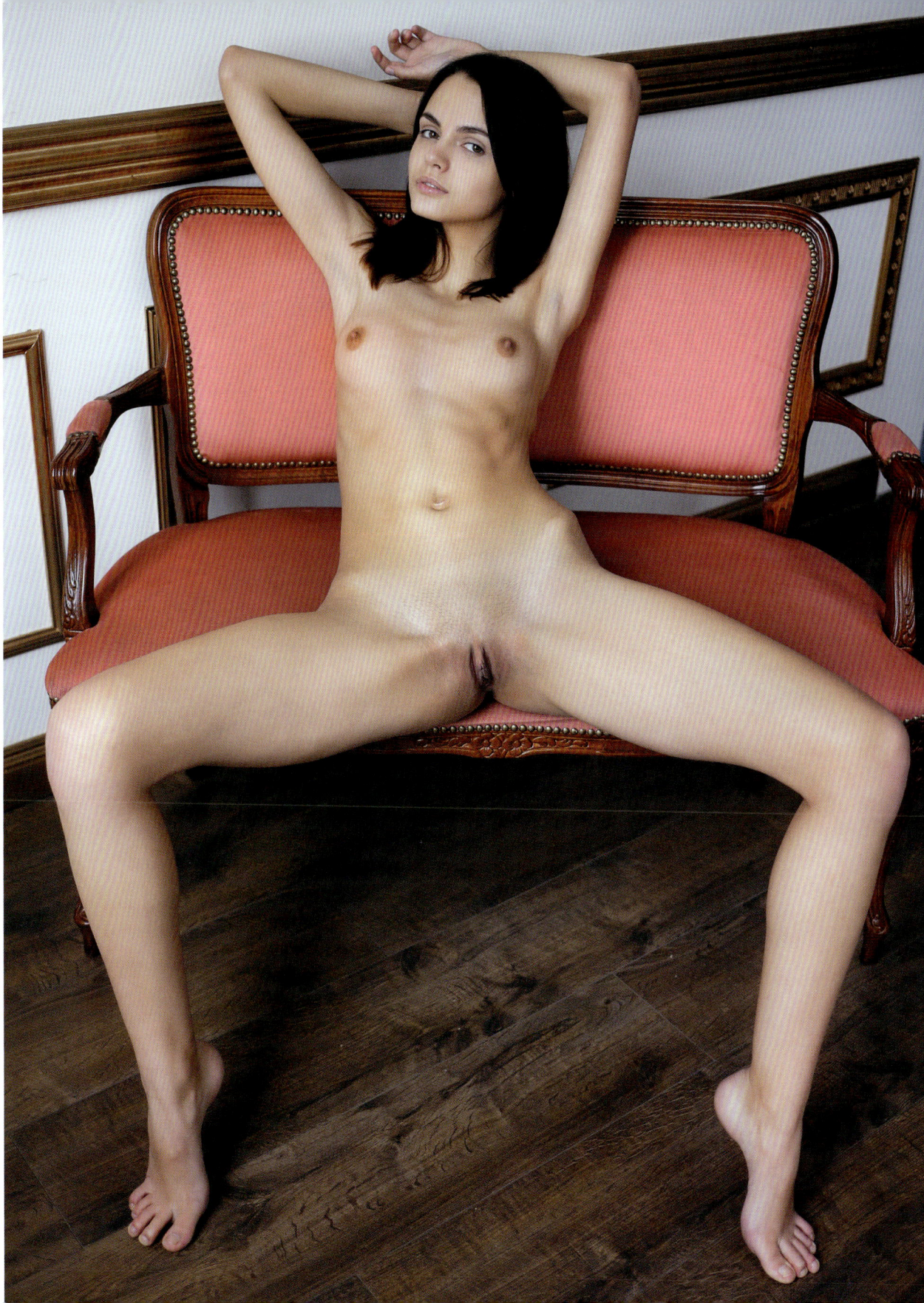

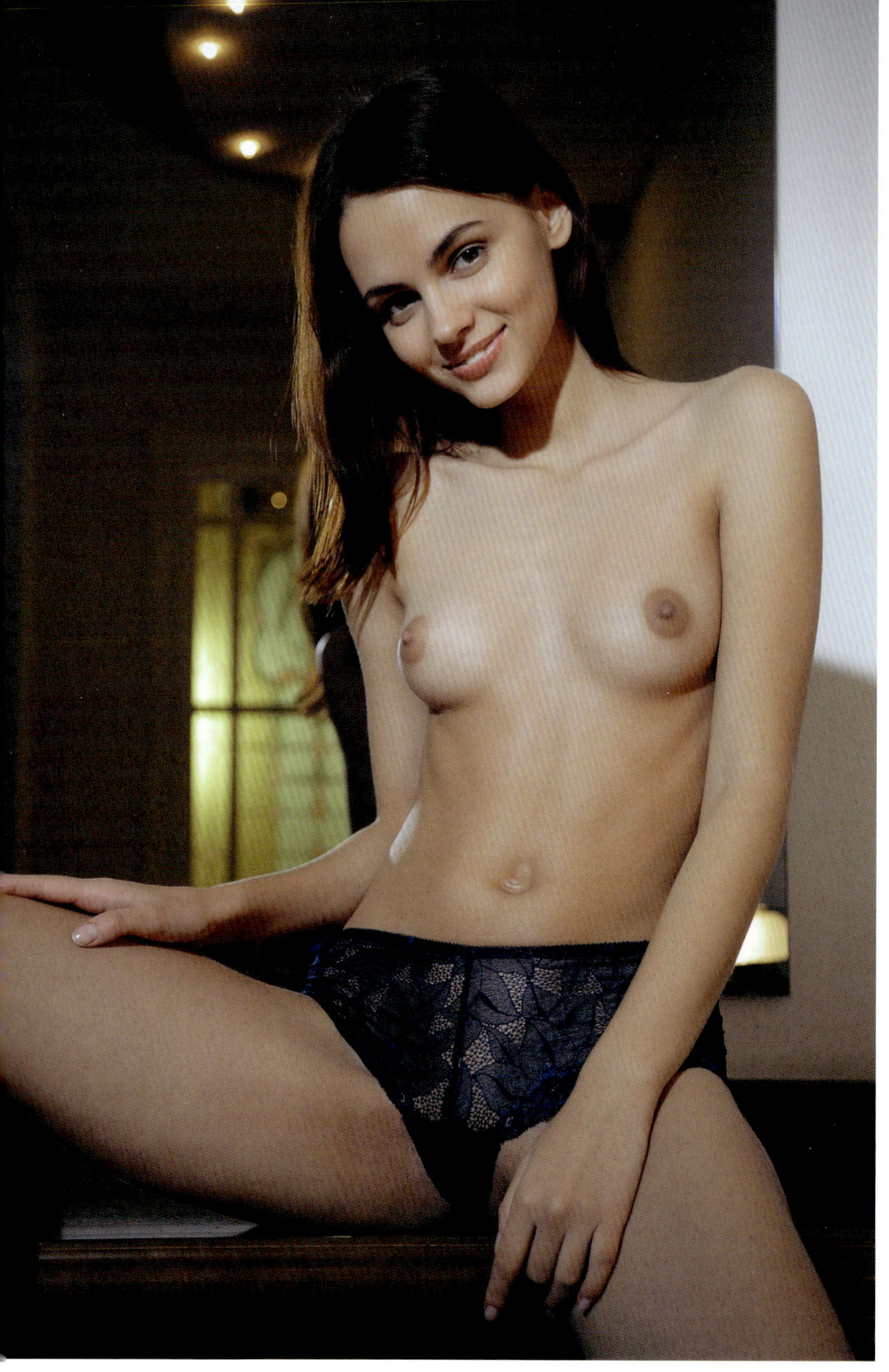

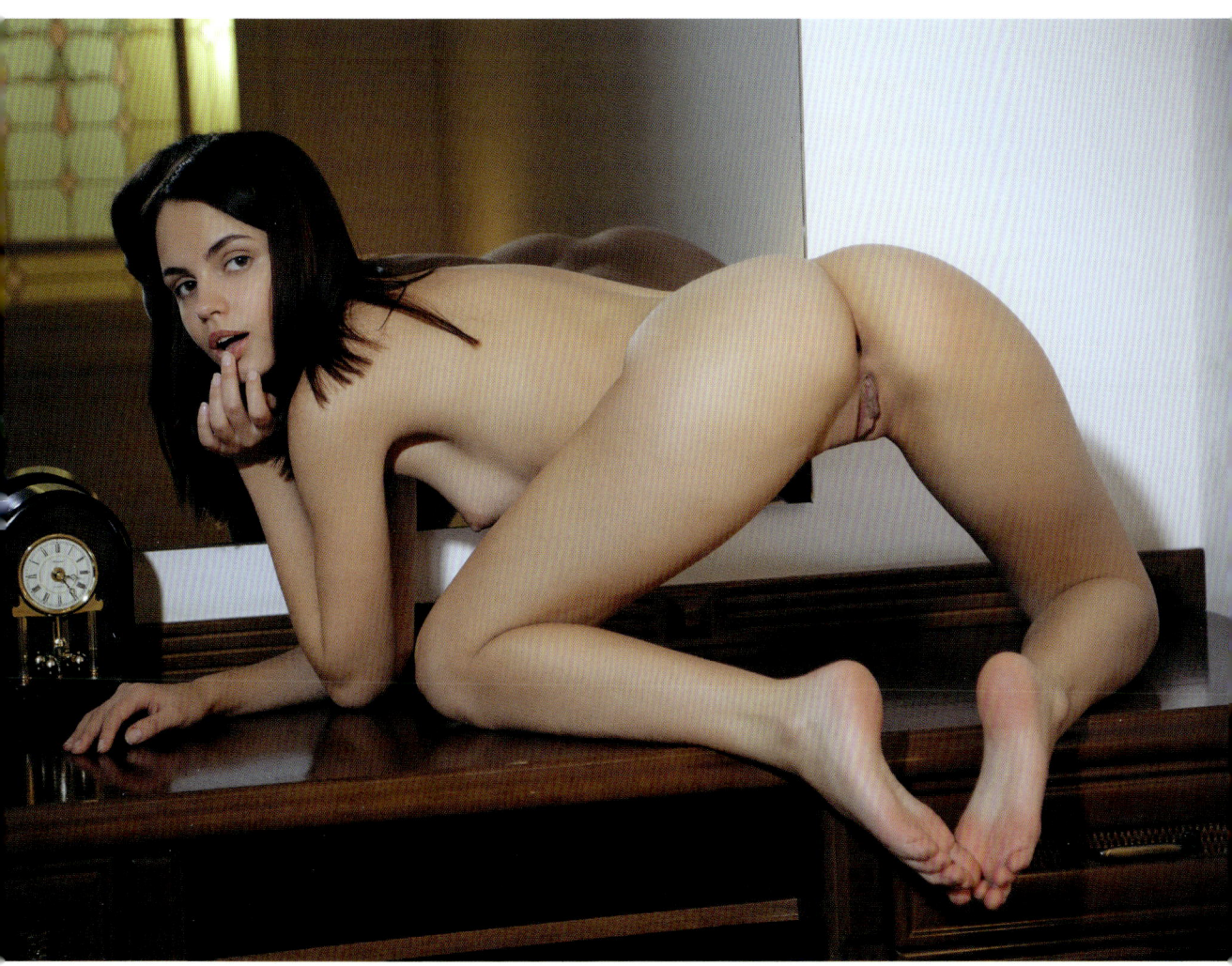

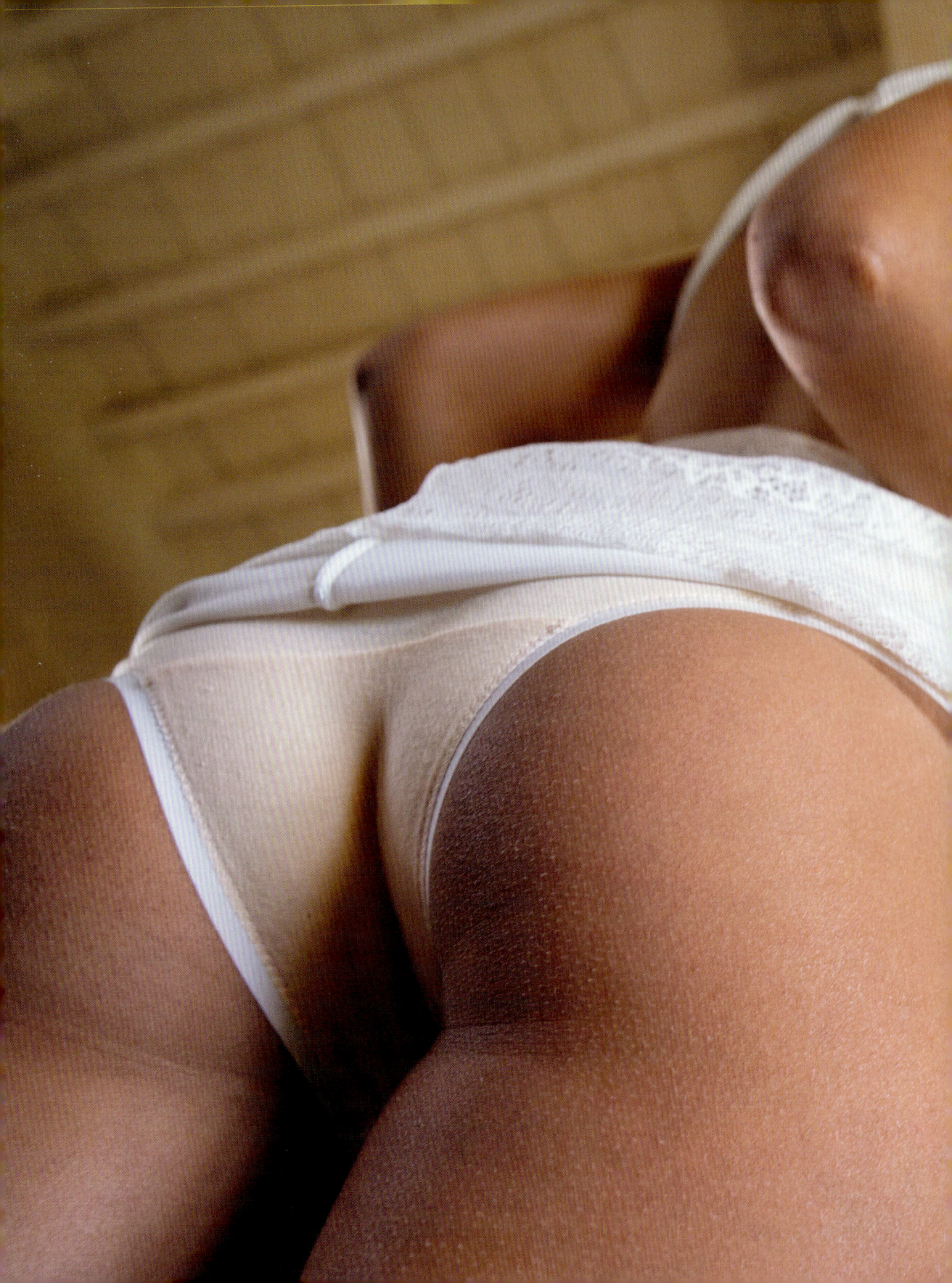

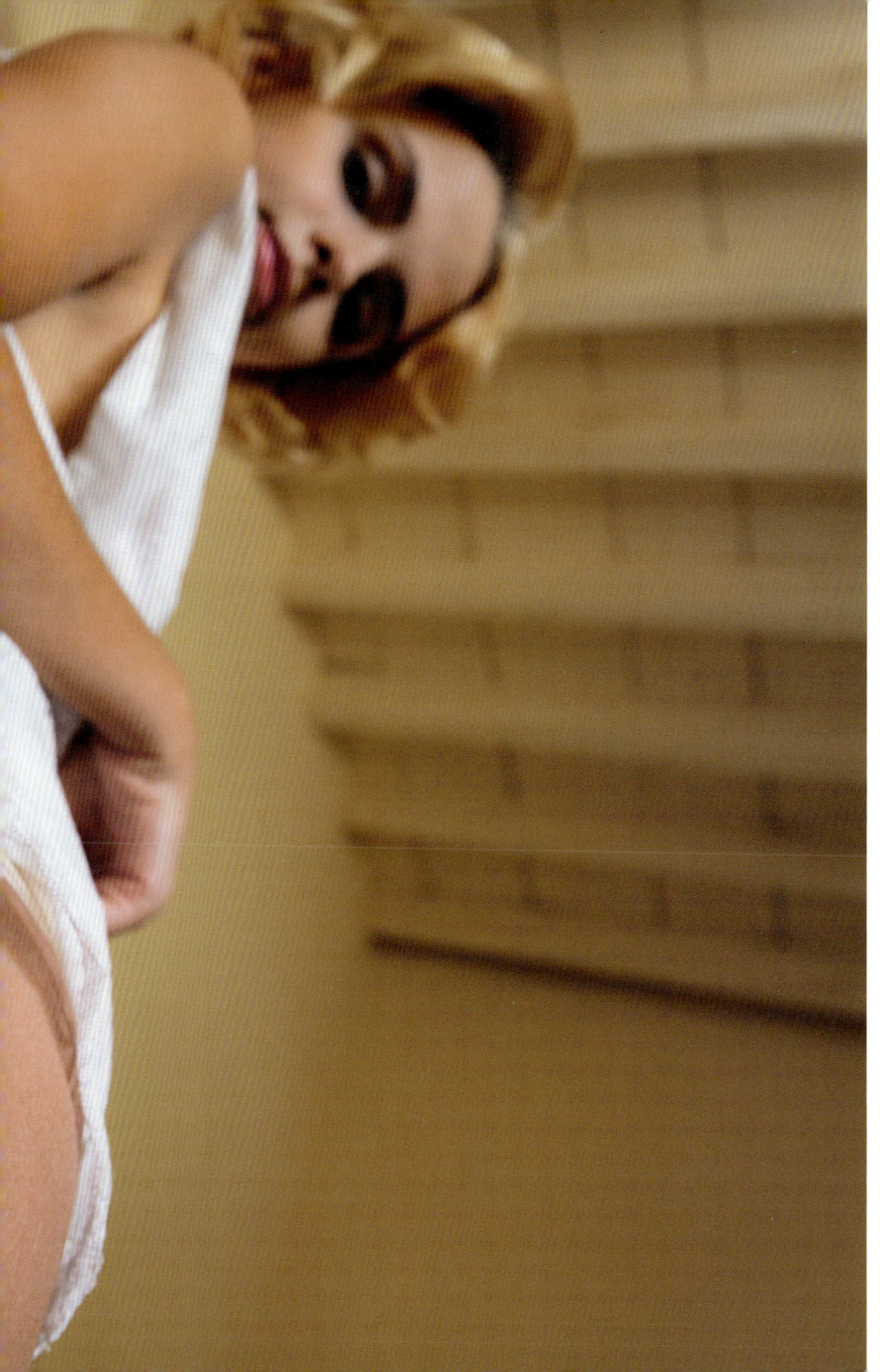

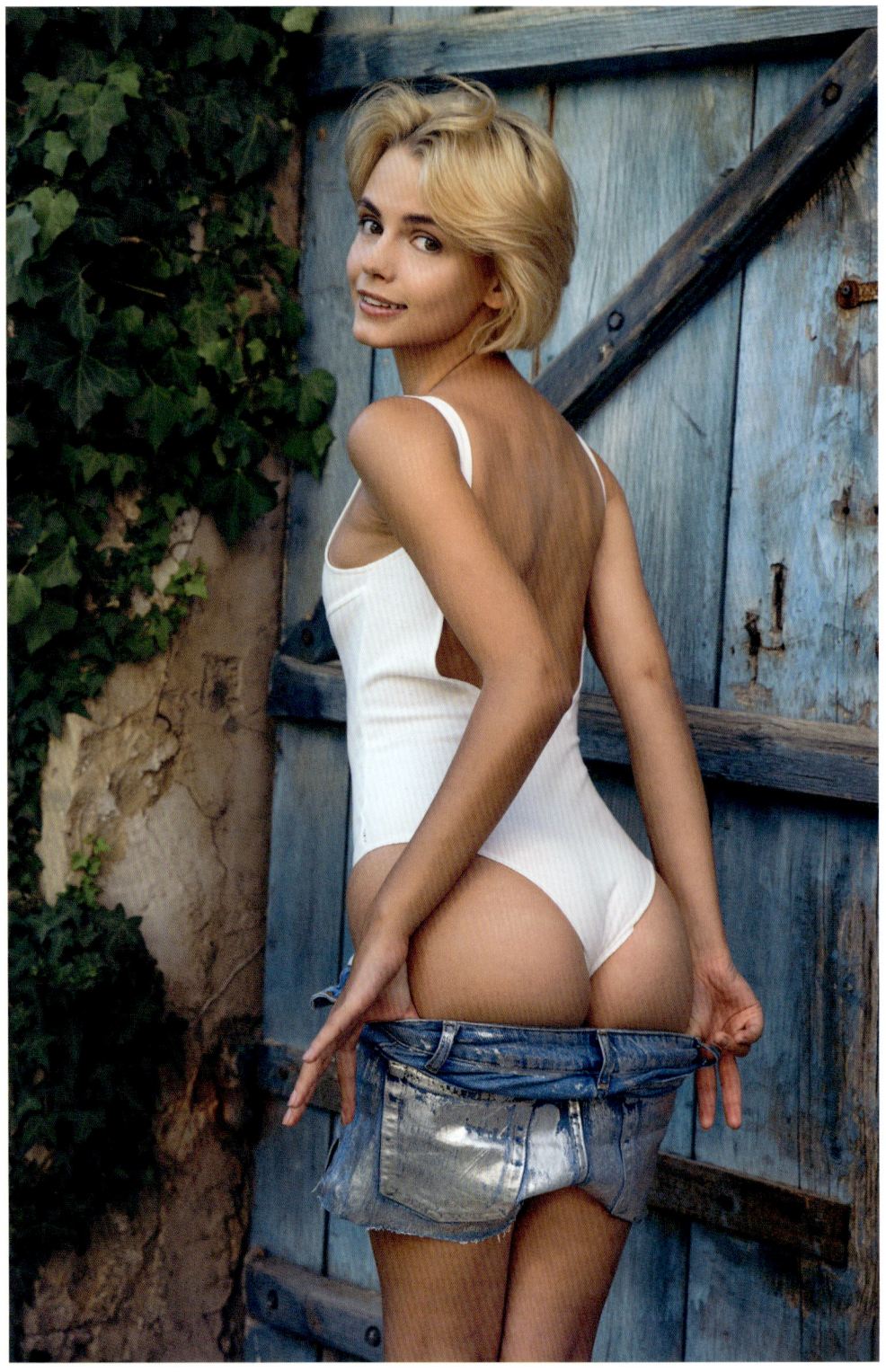

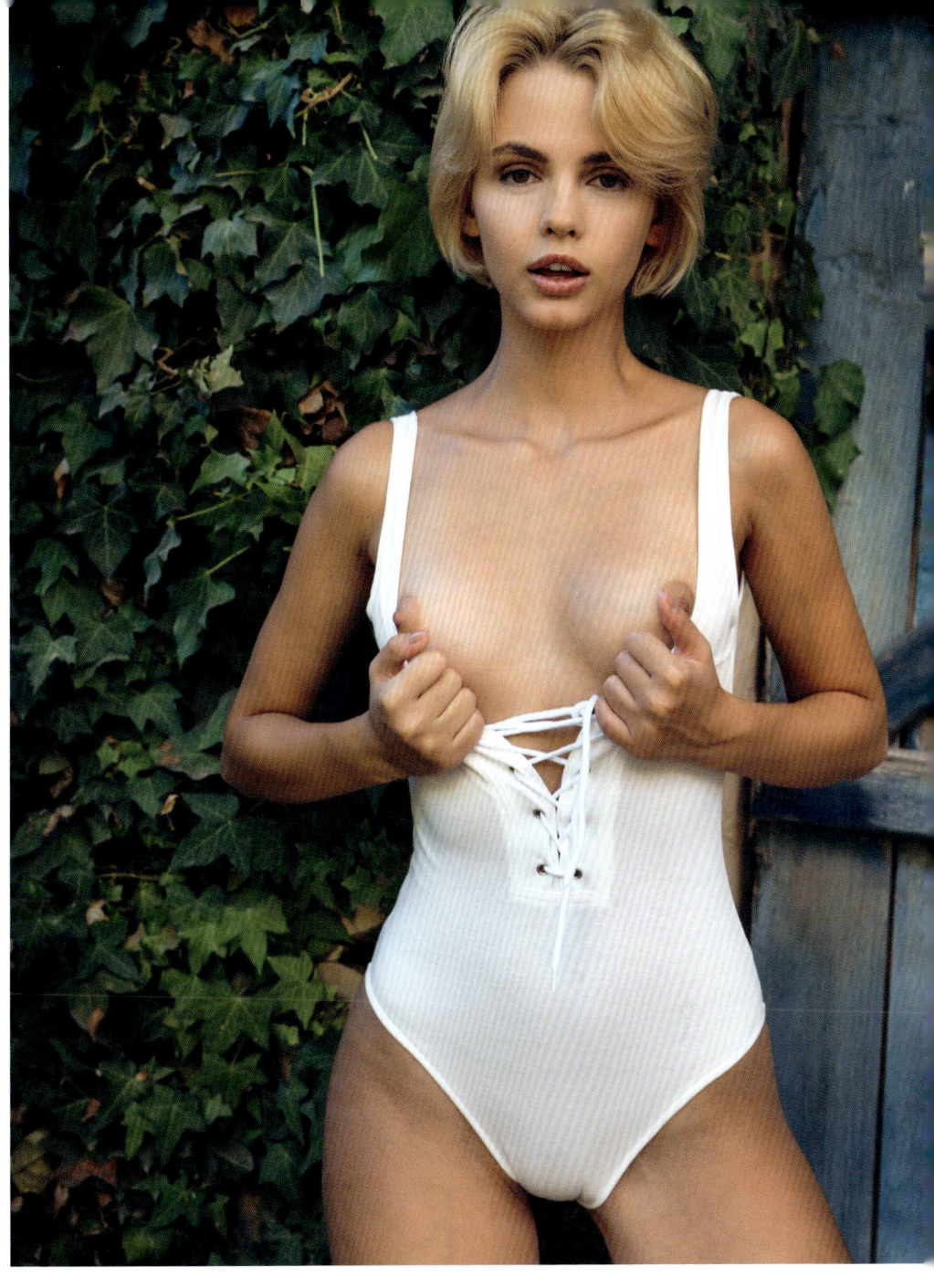

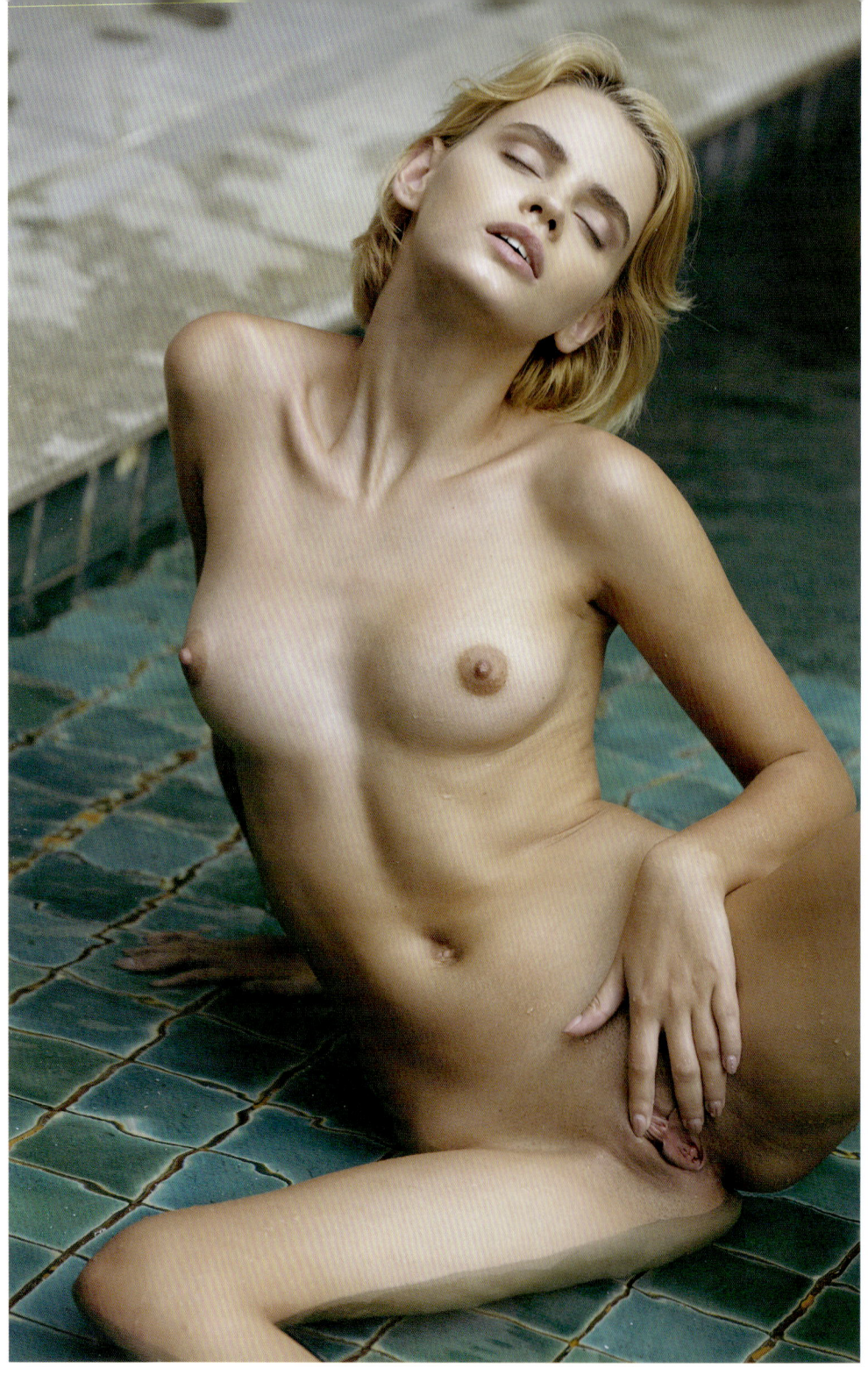

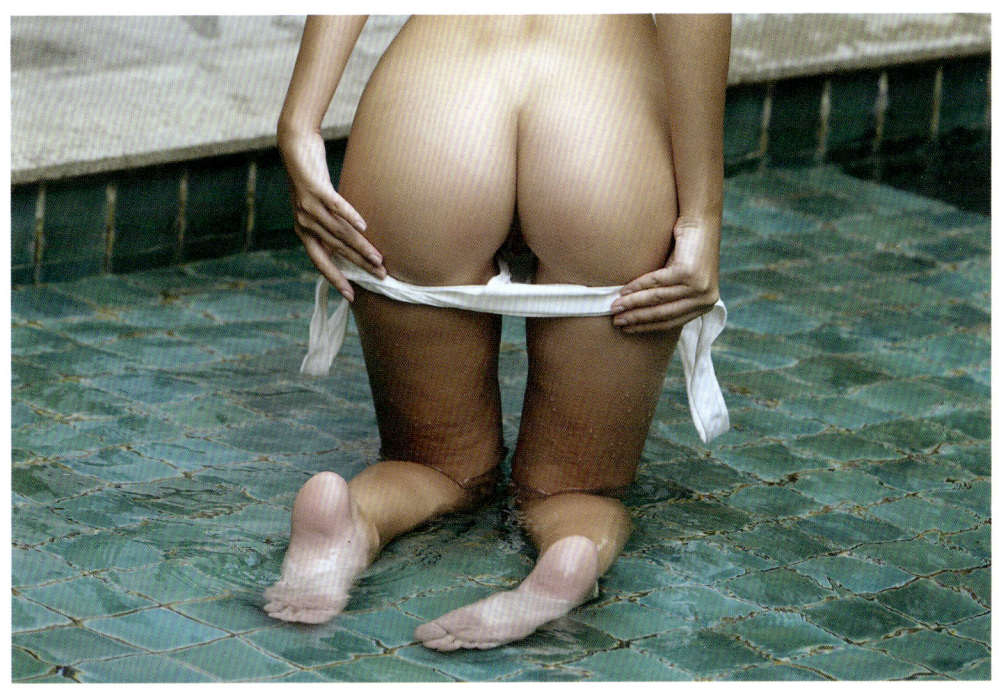

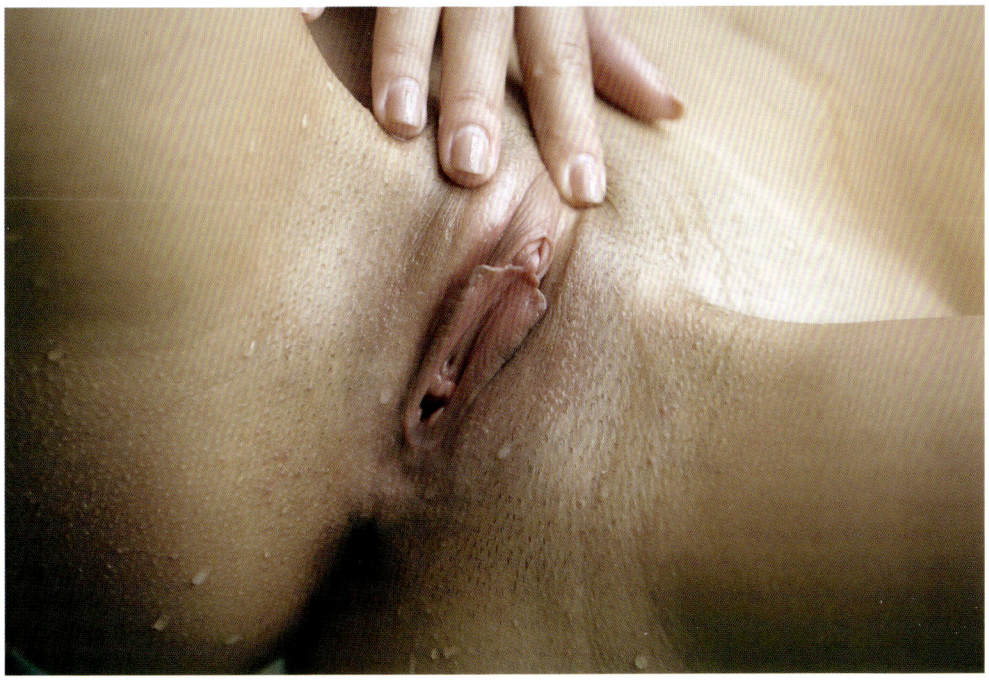

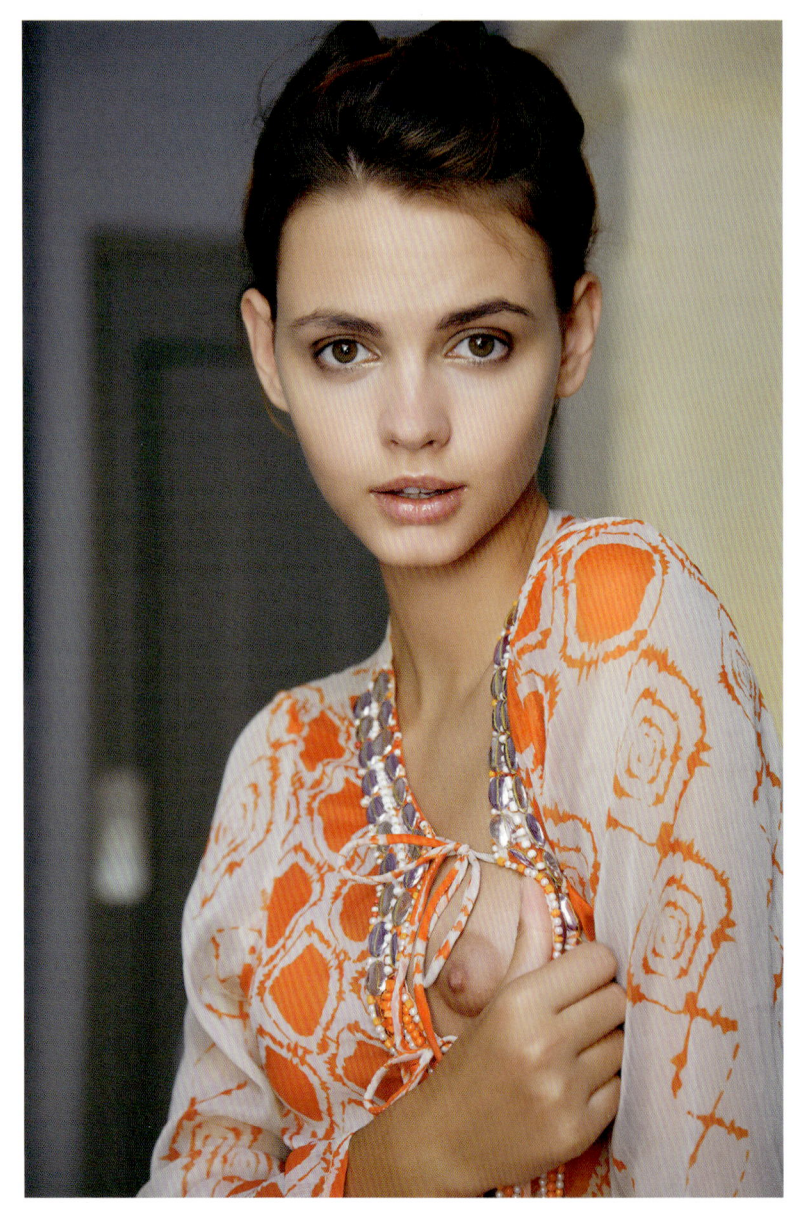

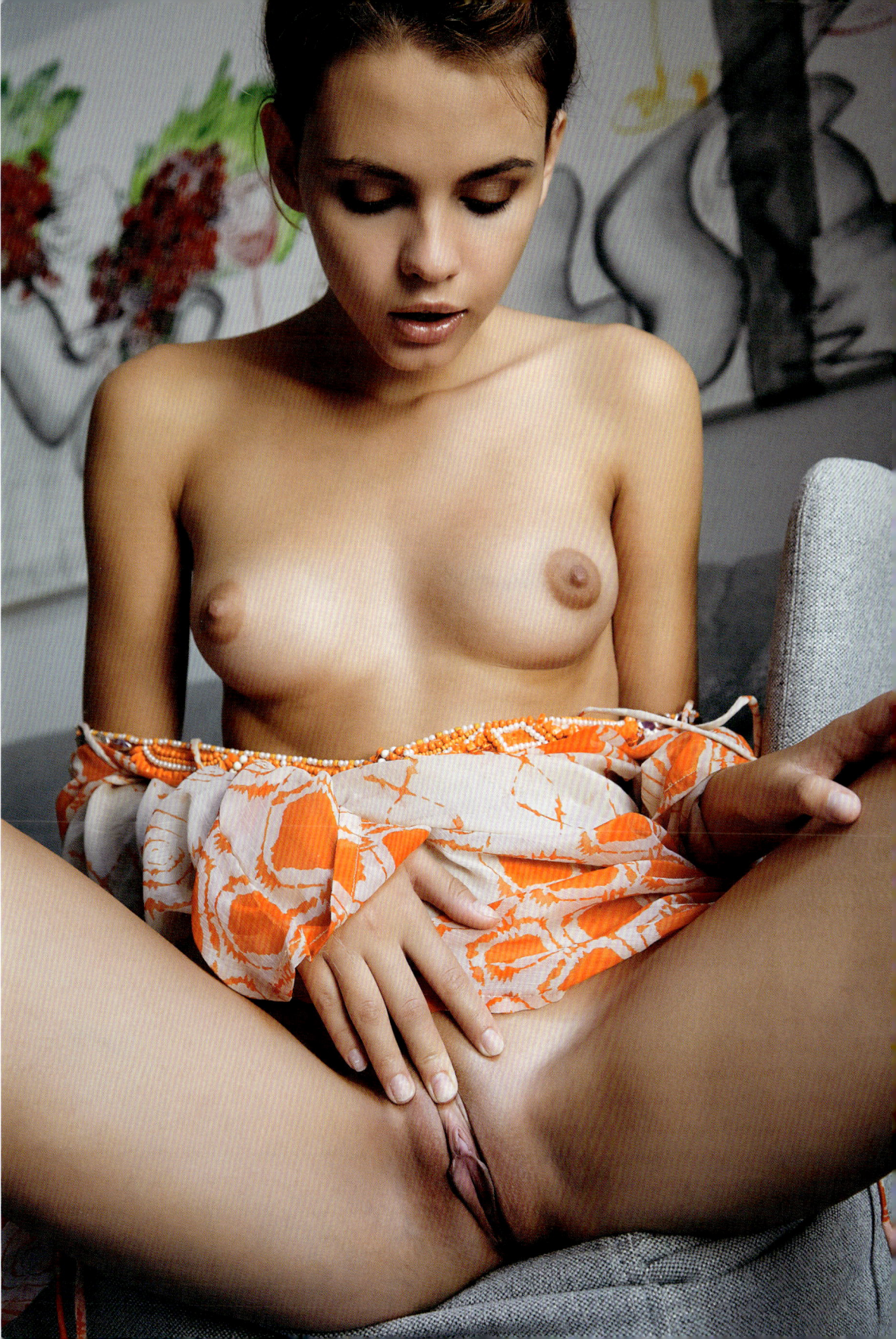

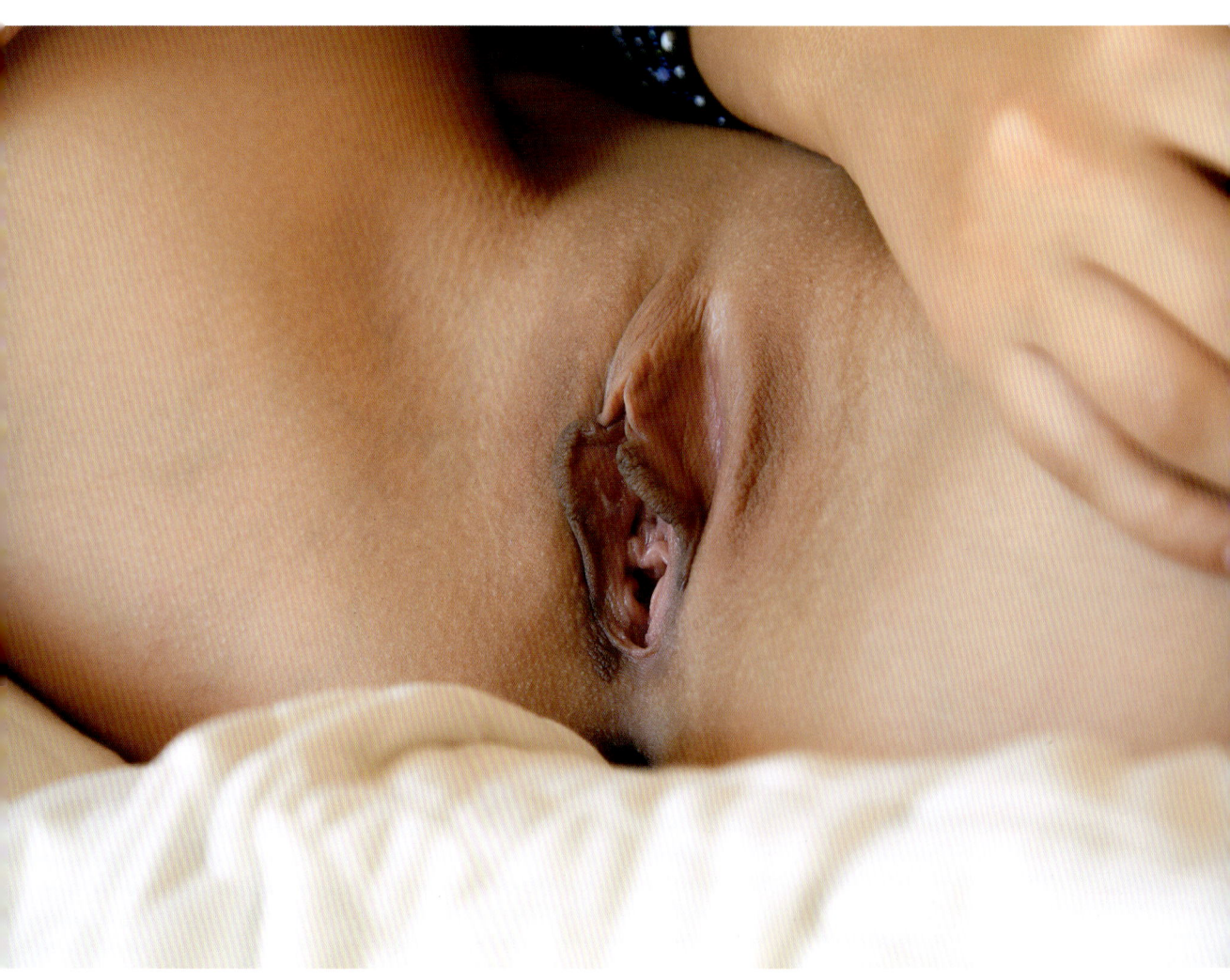

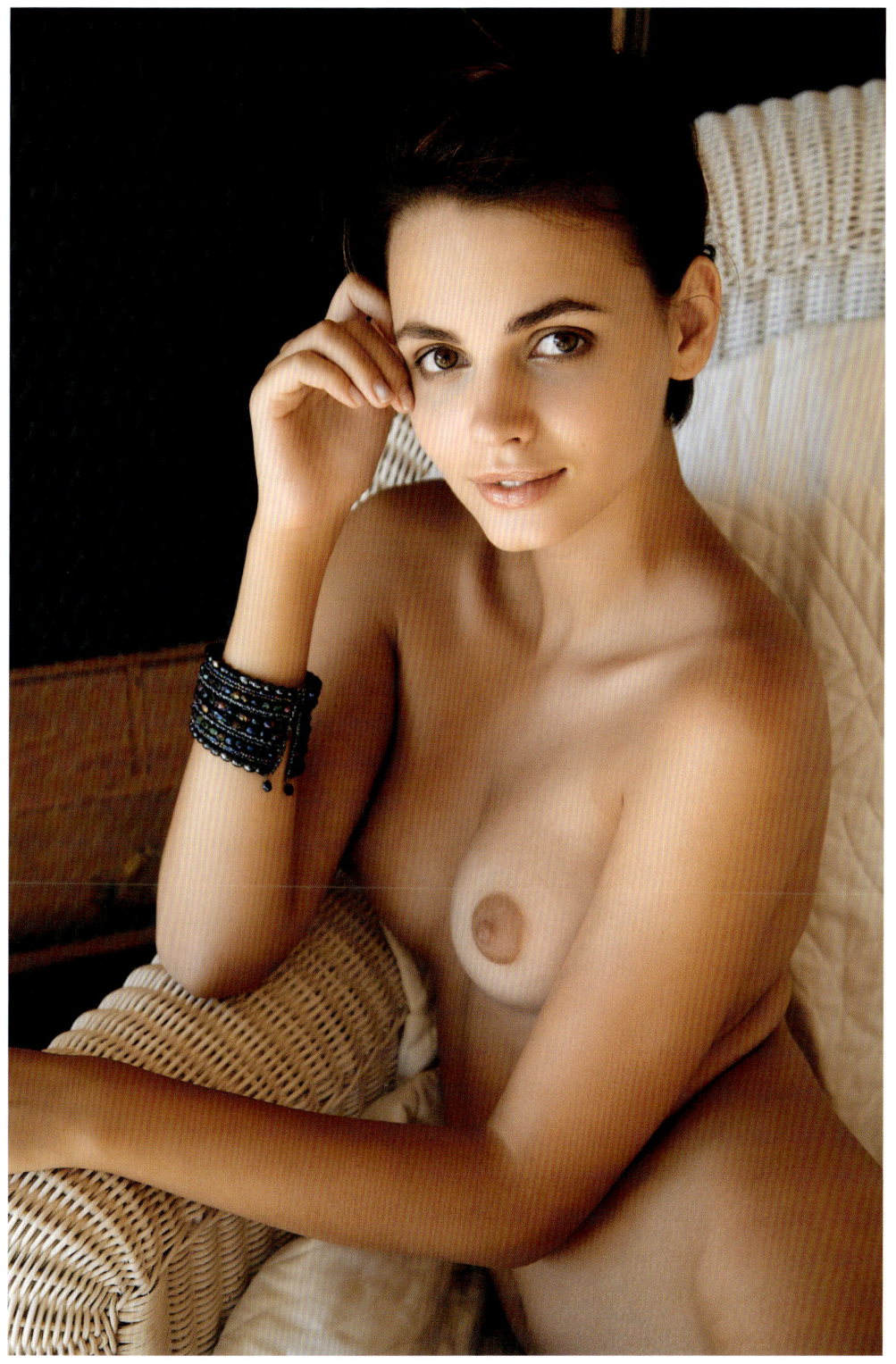

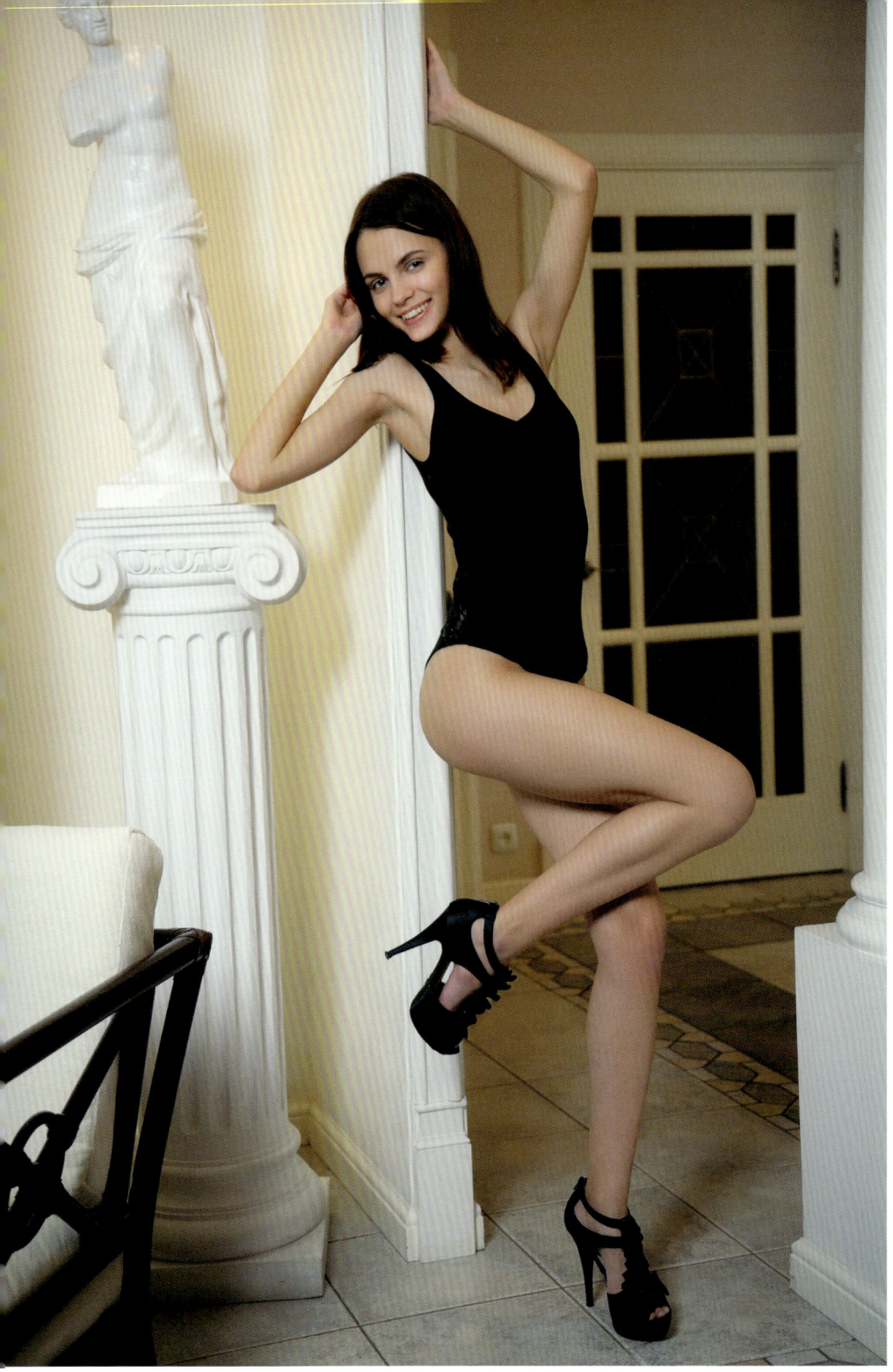

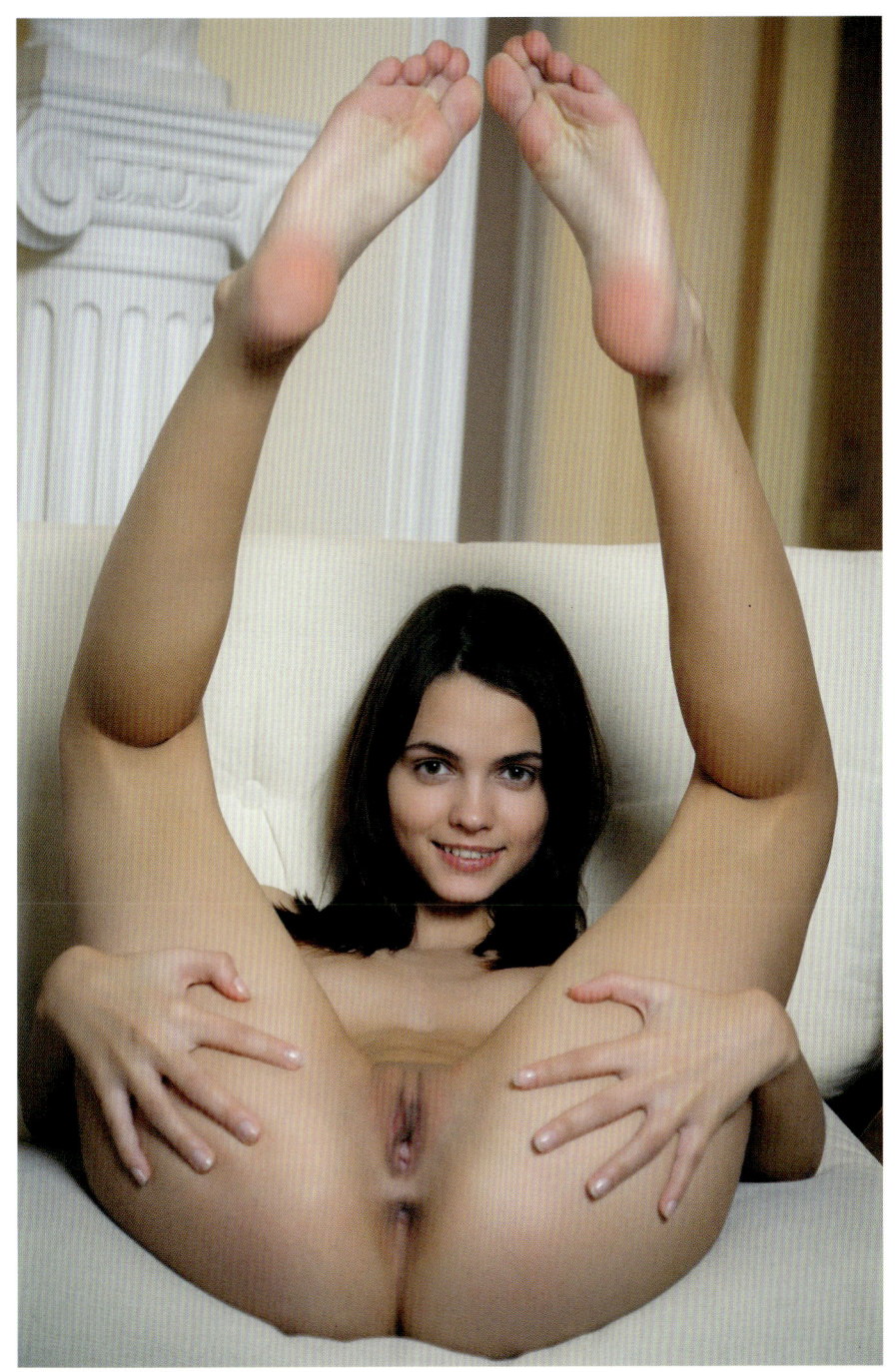

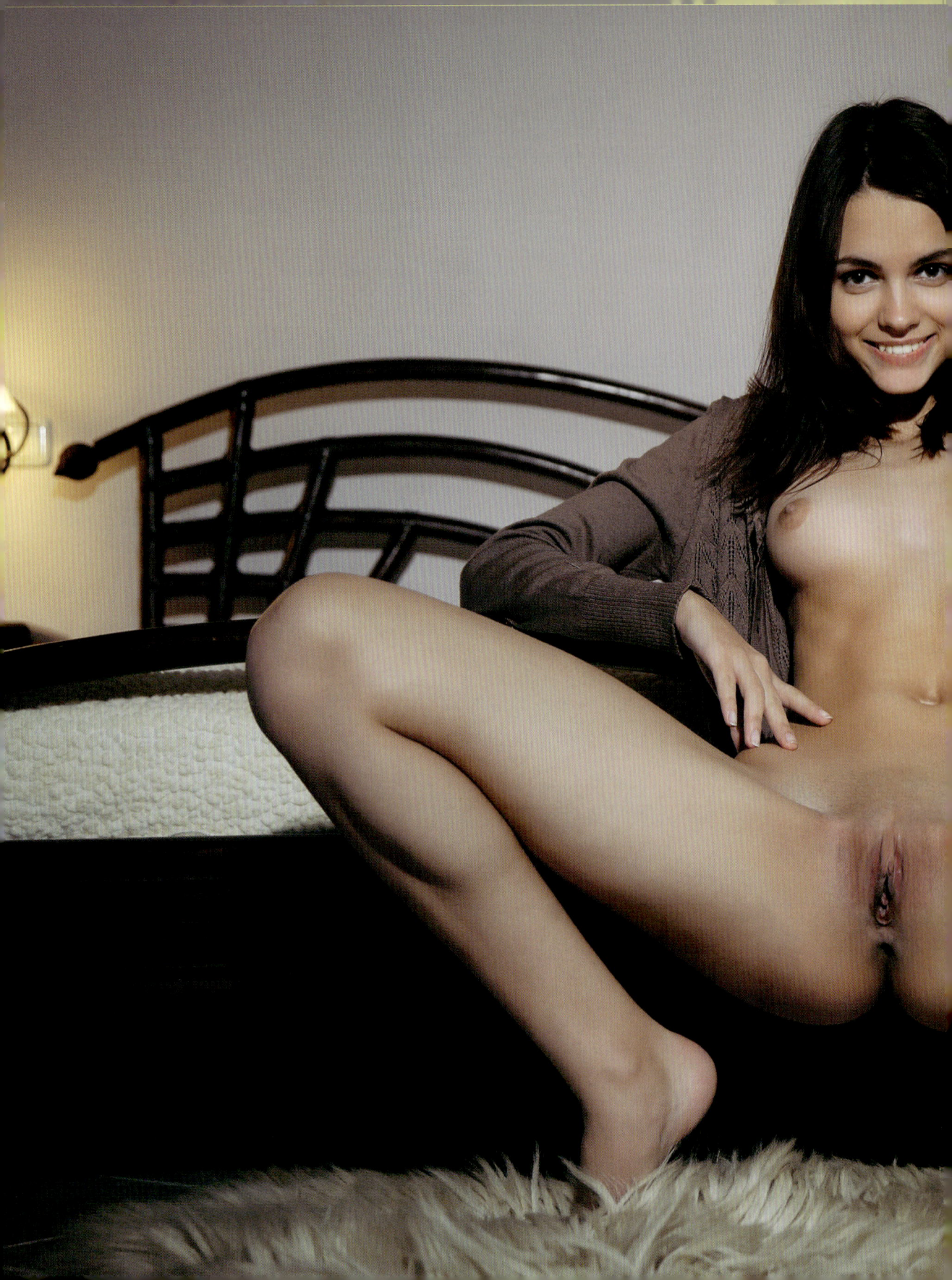

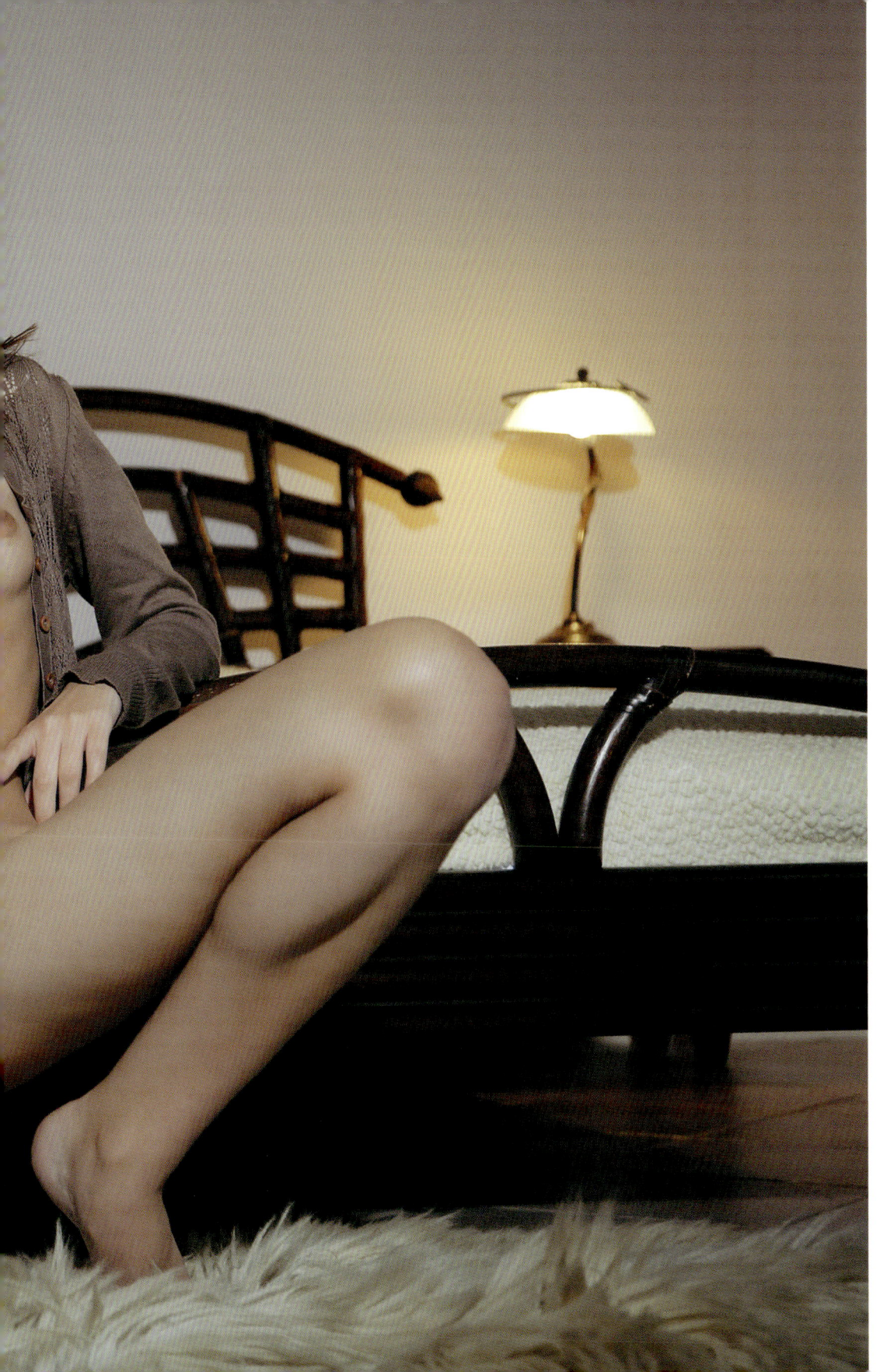

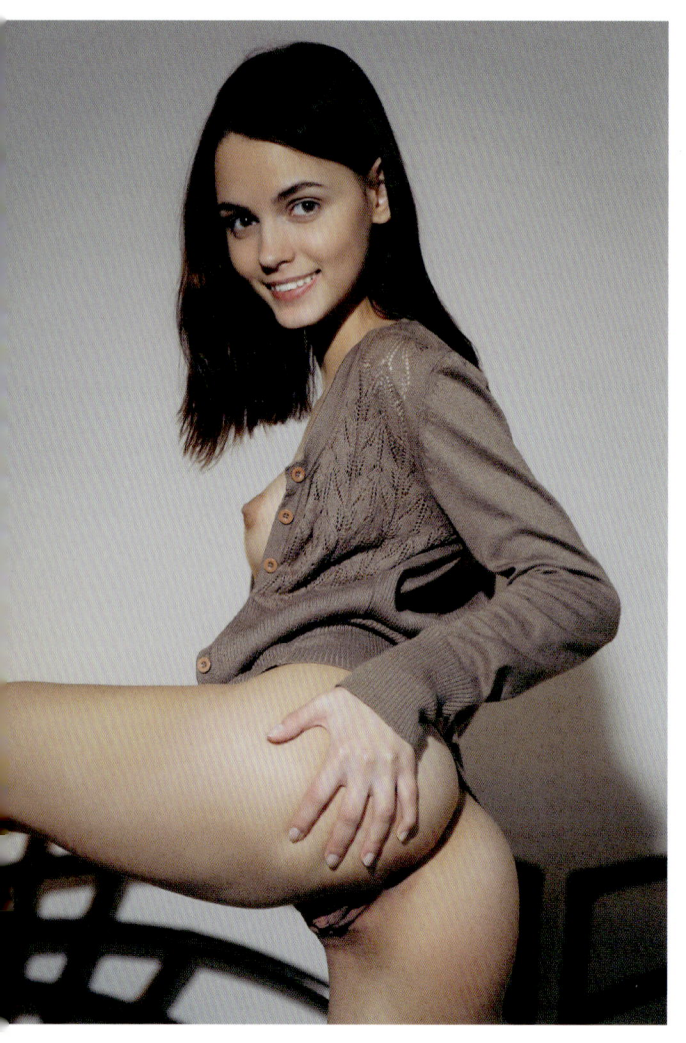
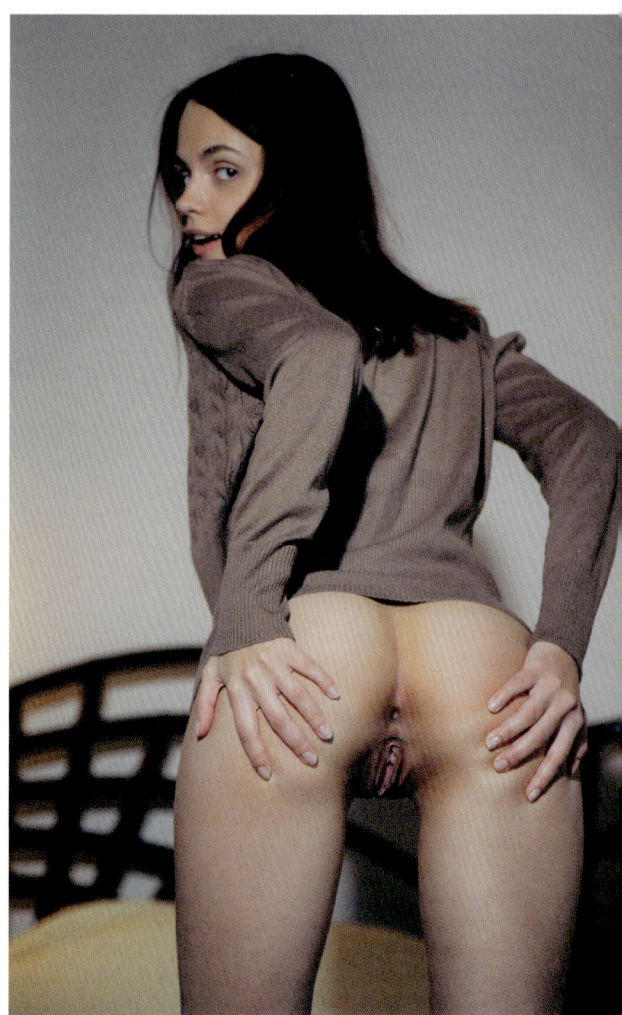

104

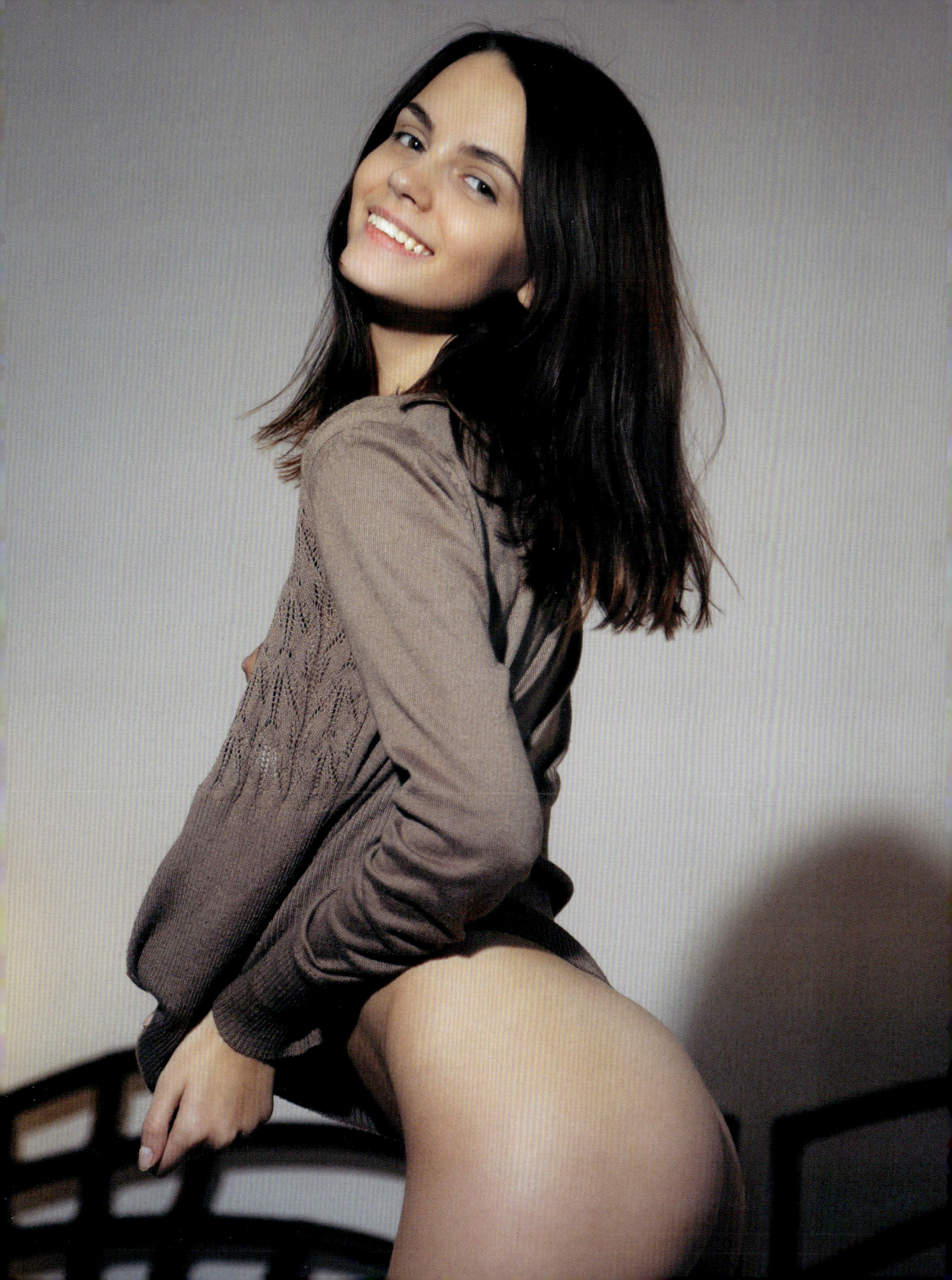

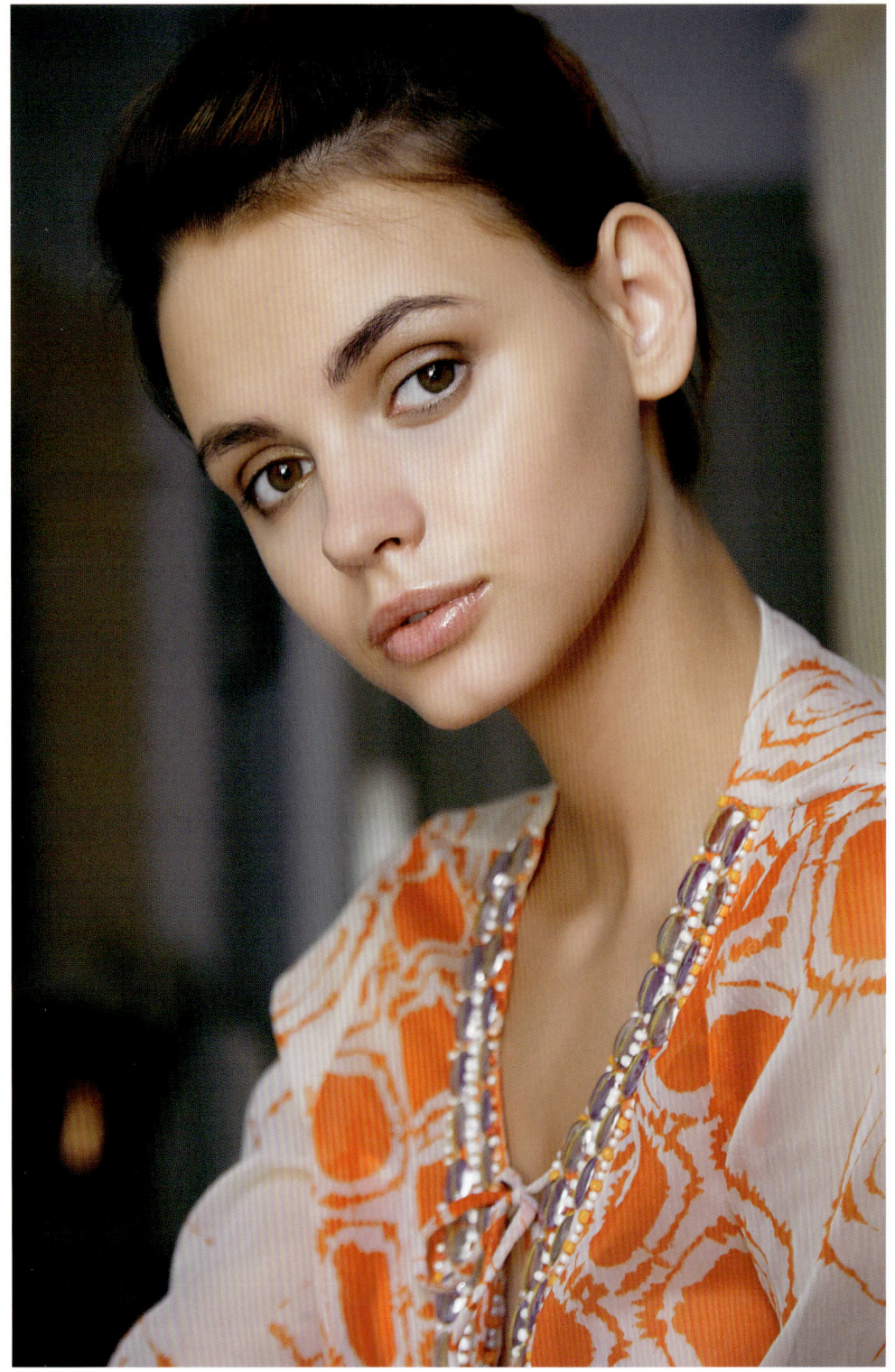

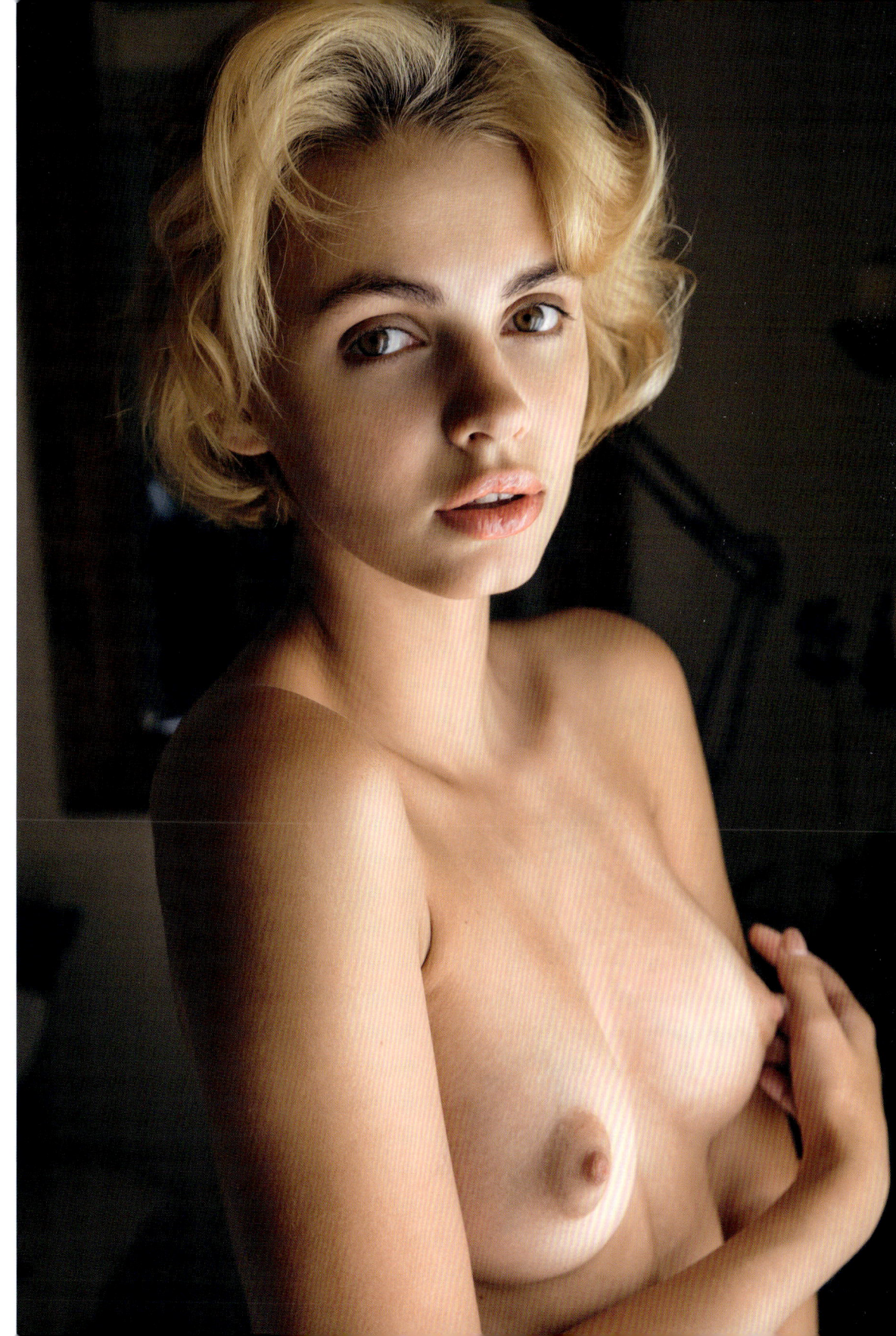

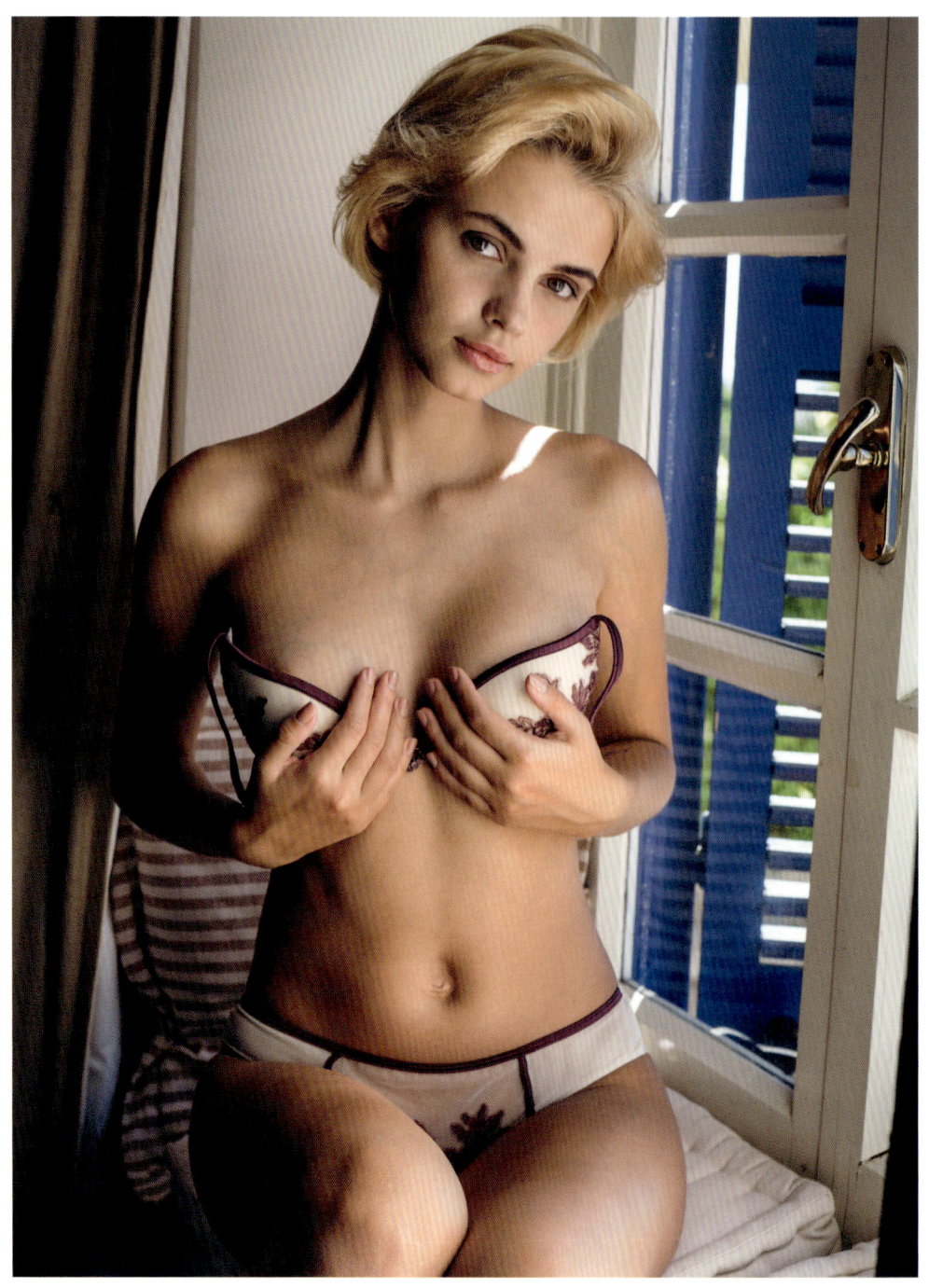

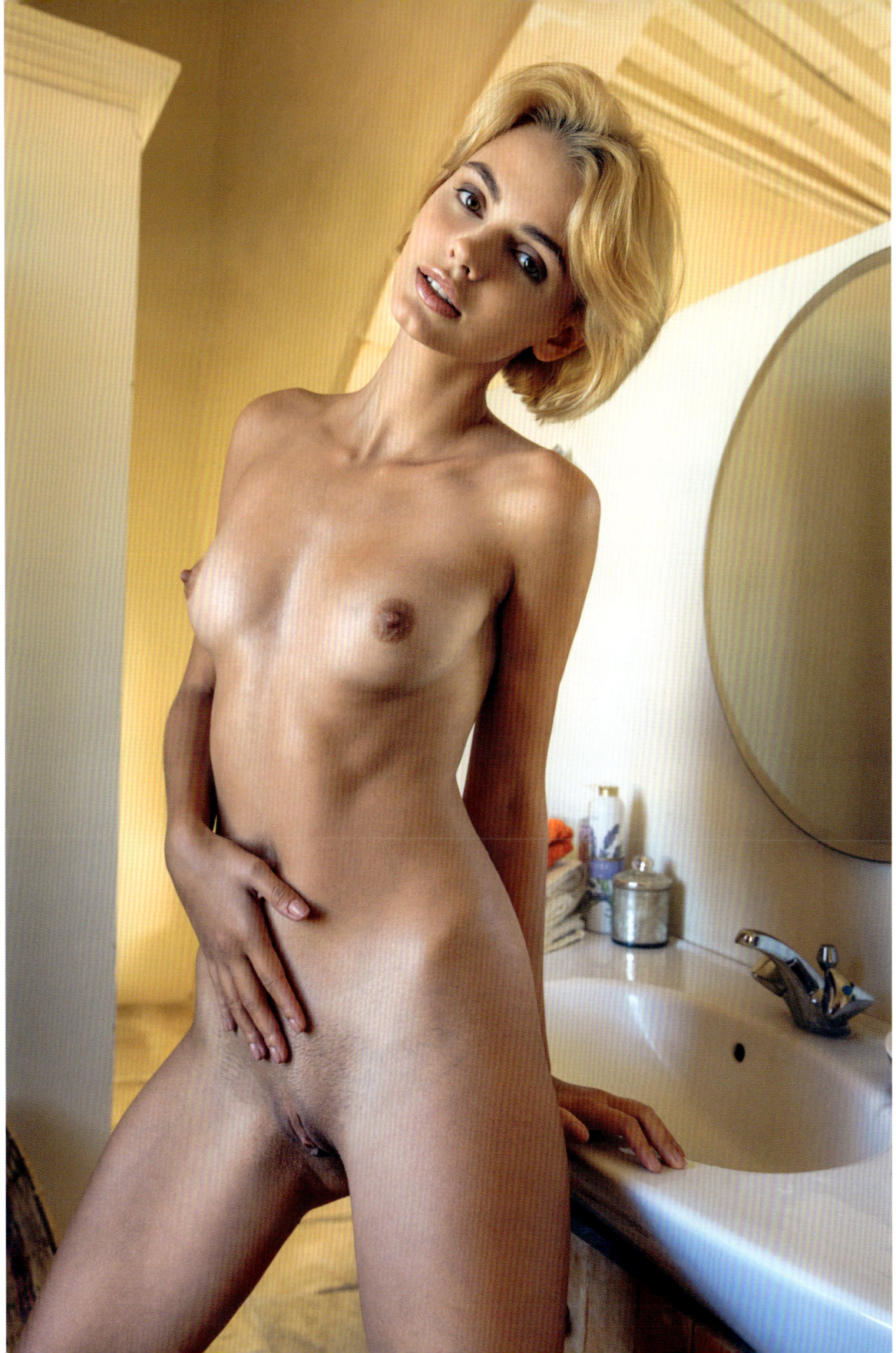

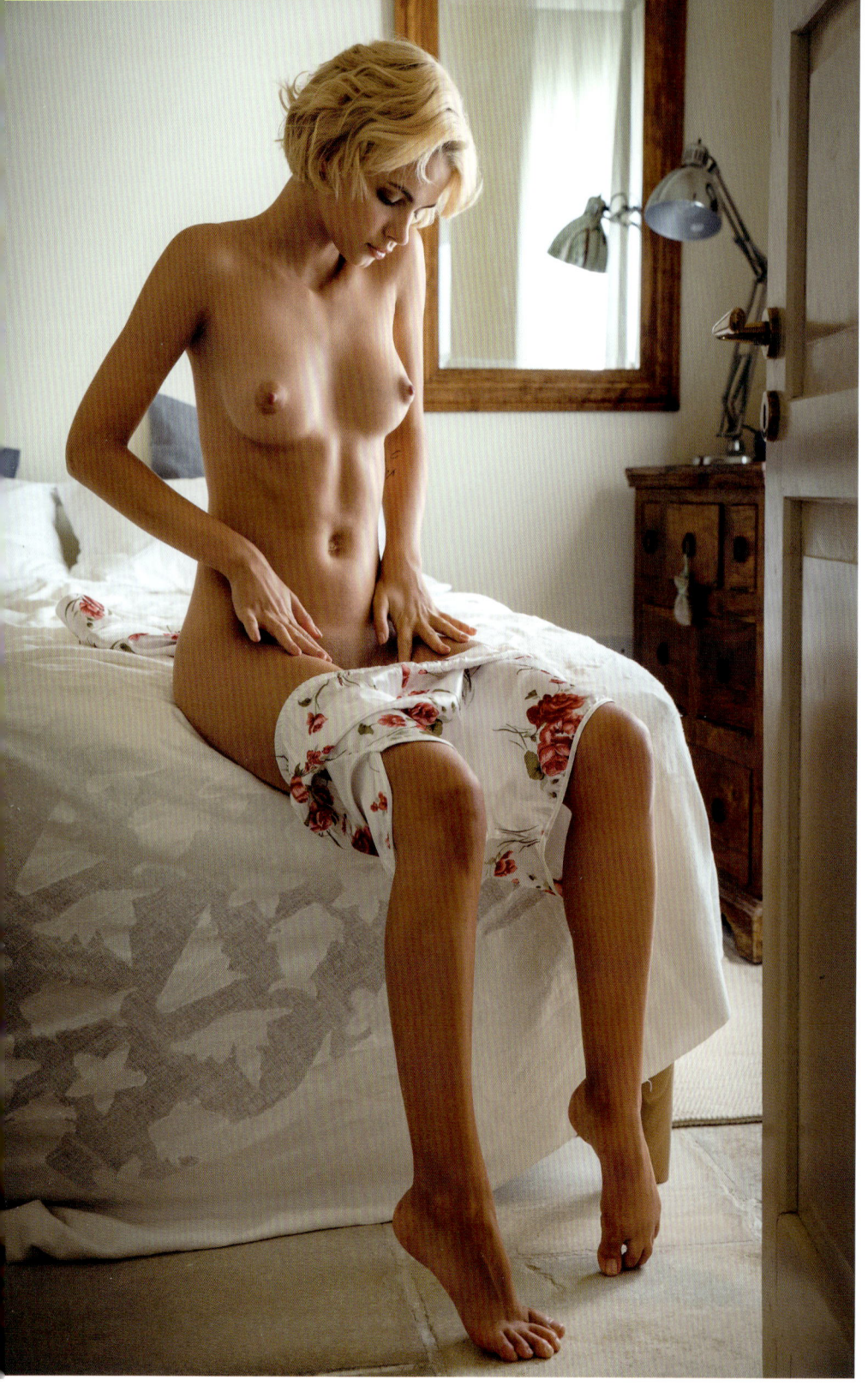

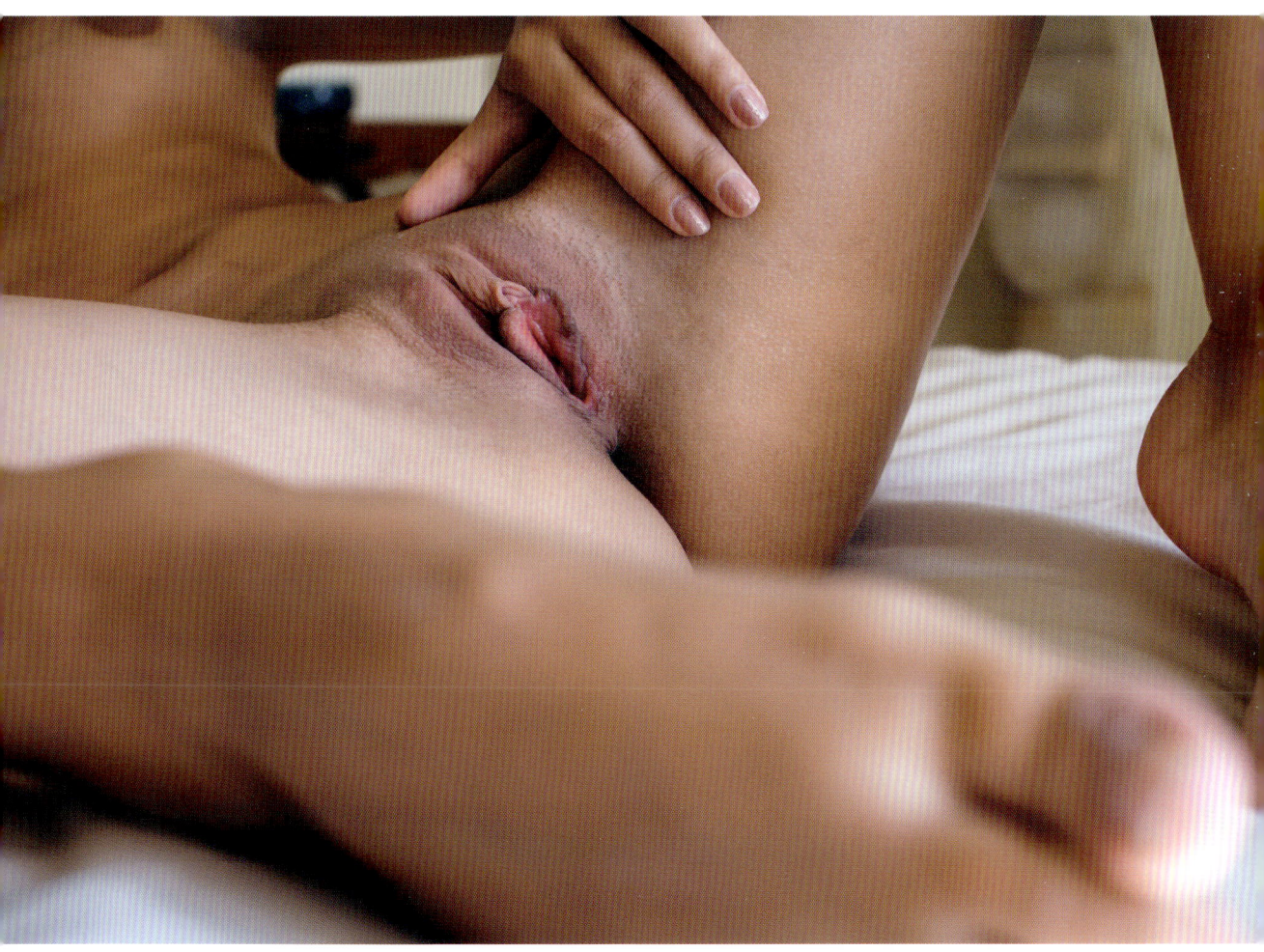

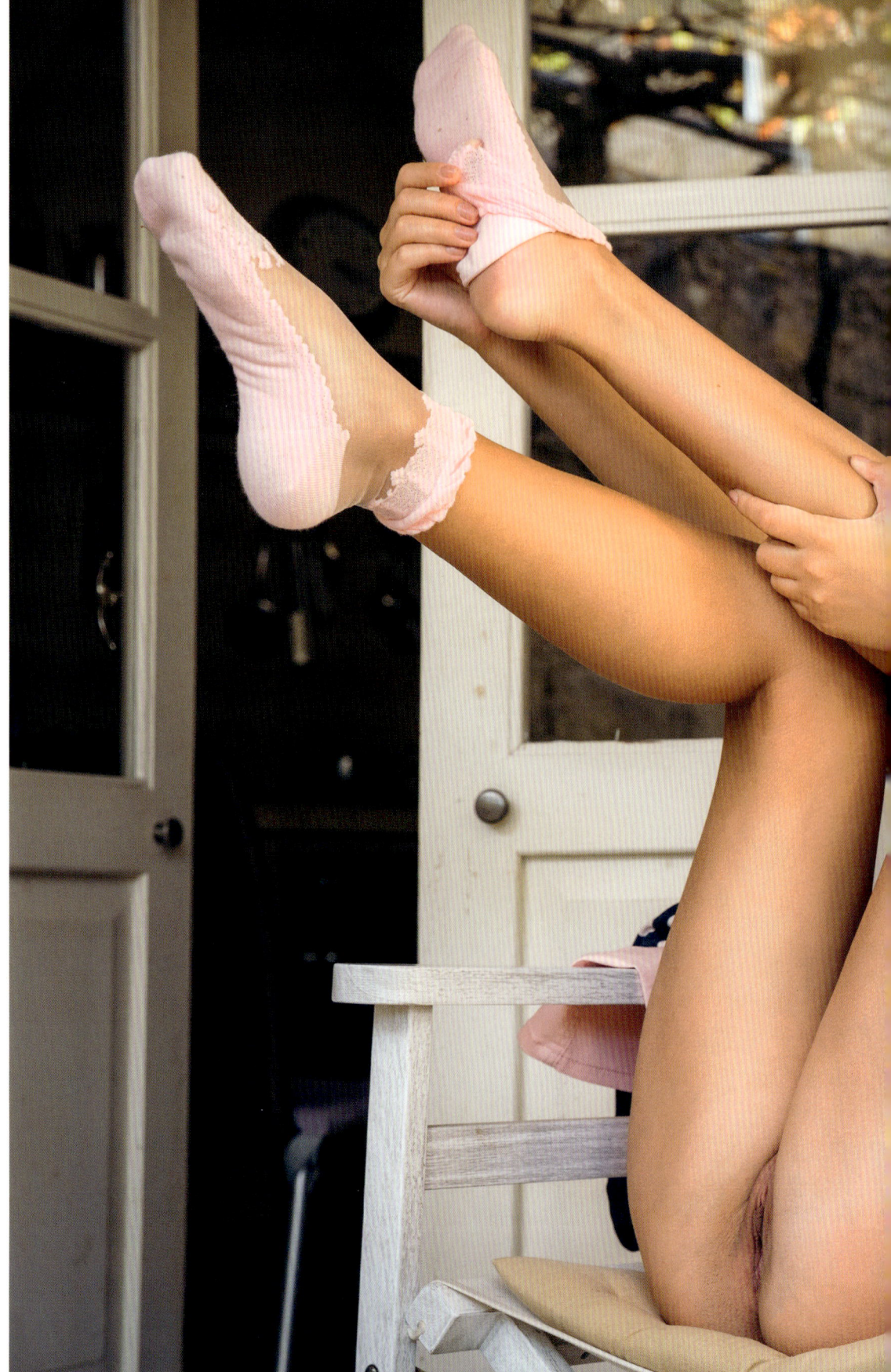

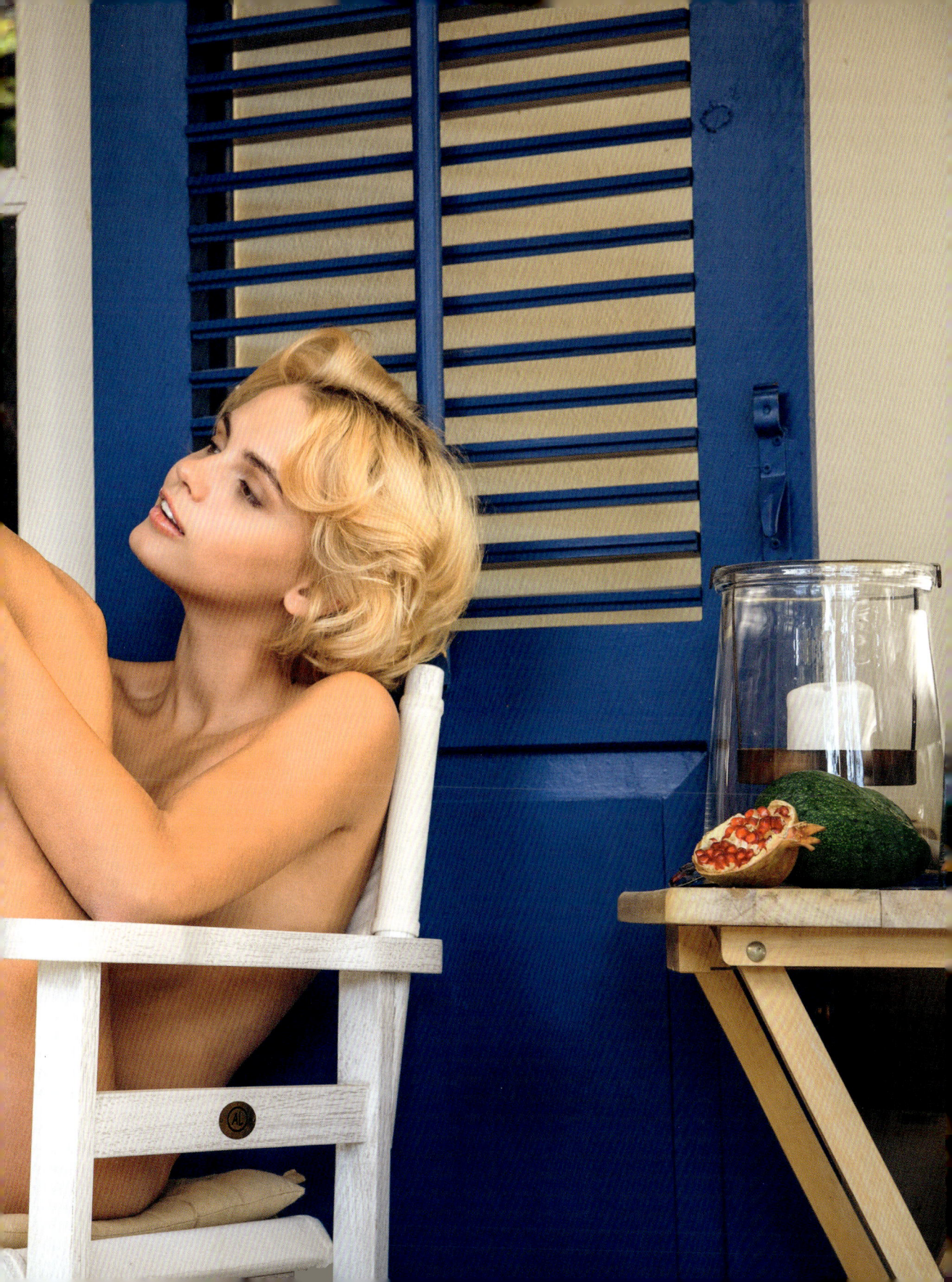

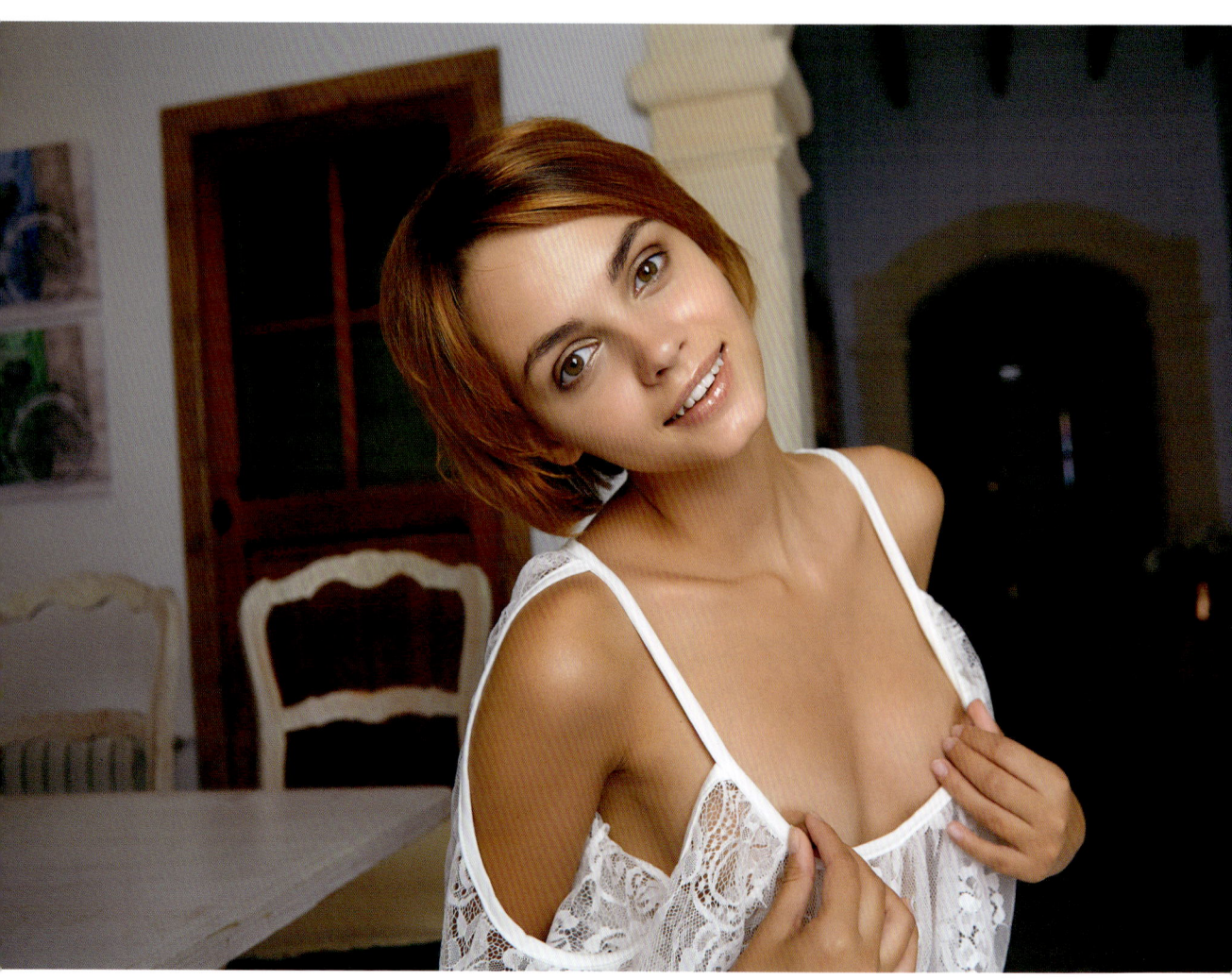

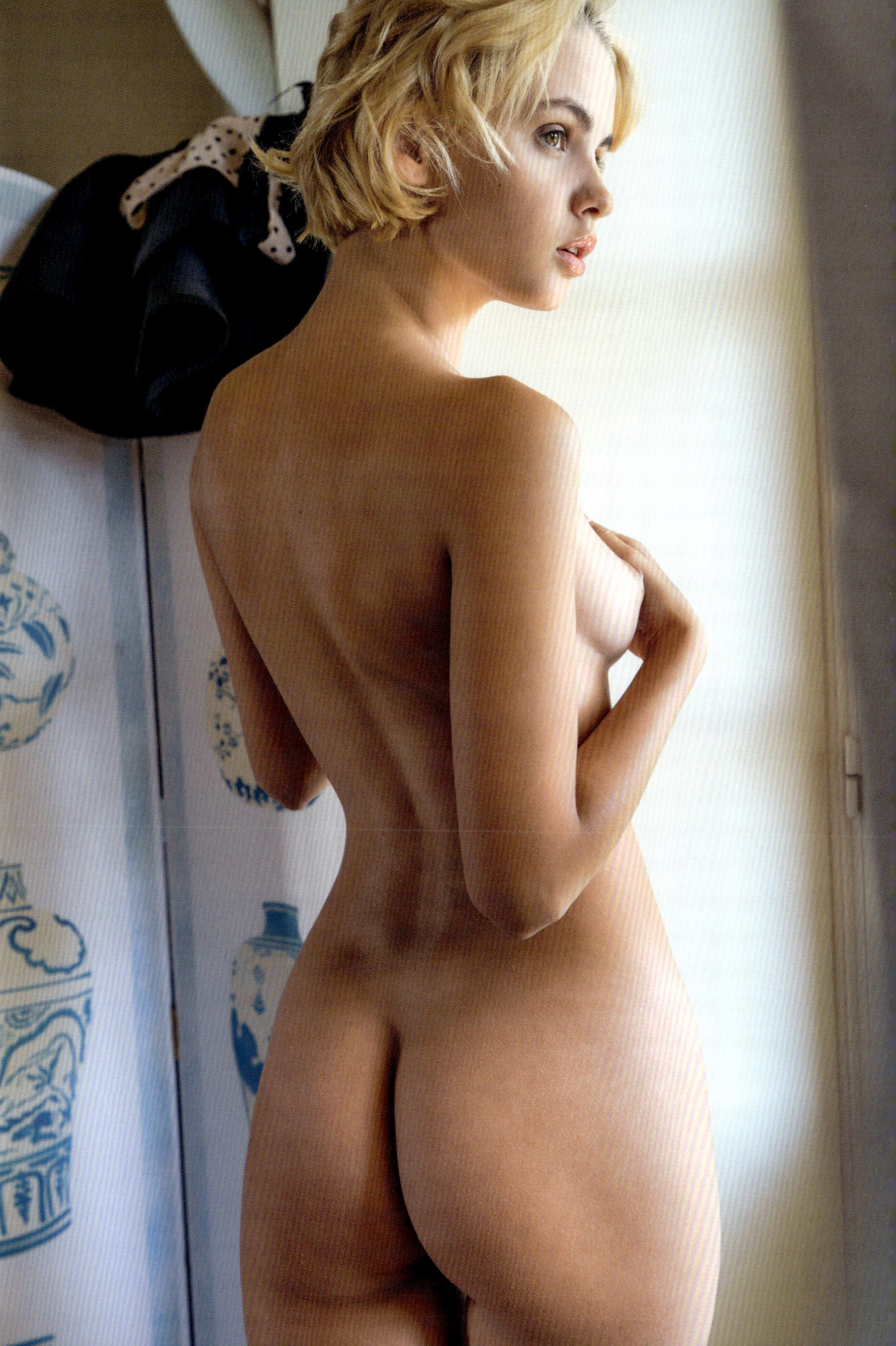

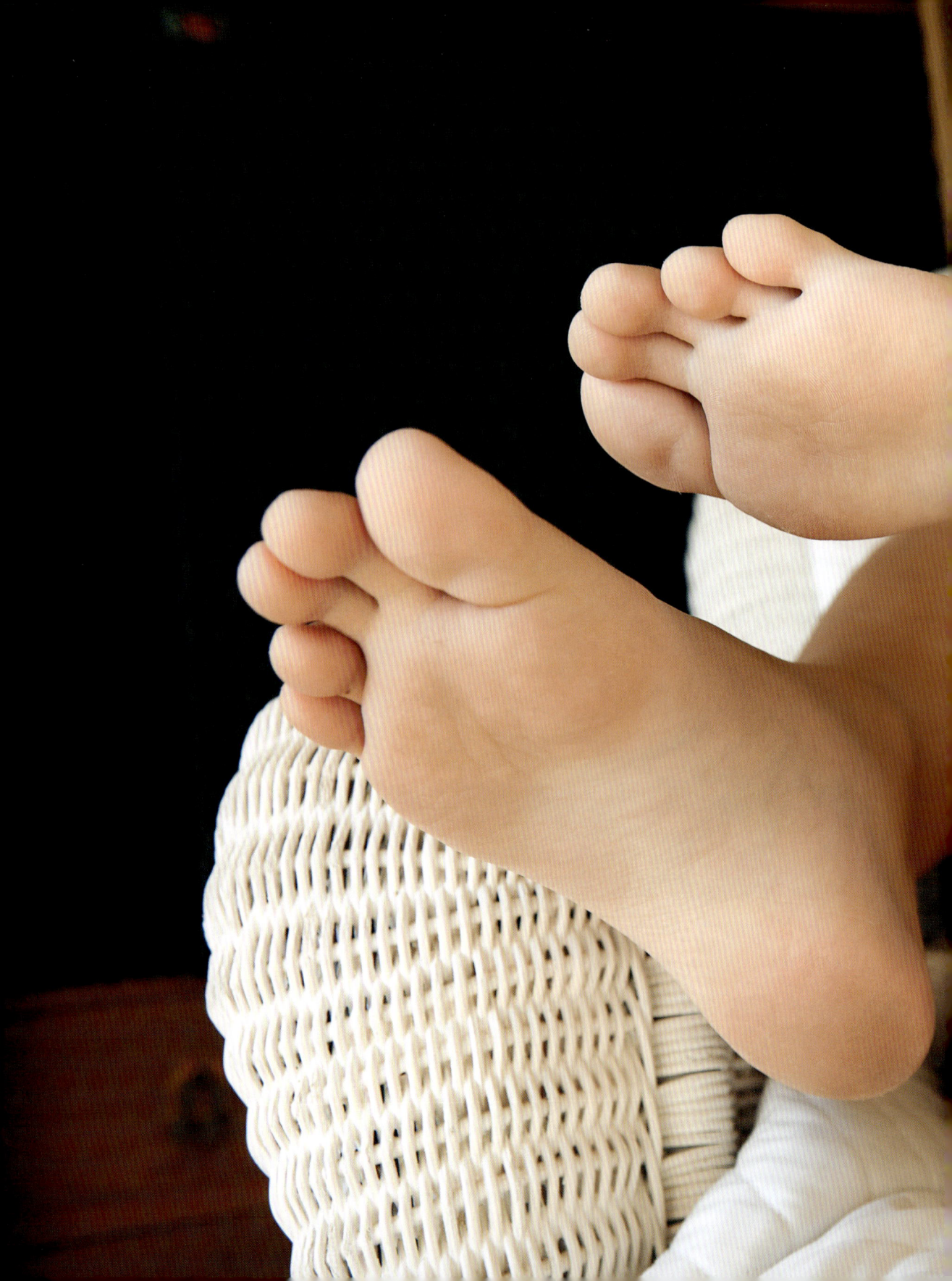

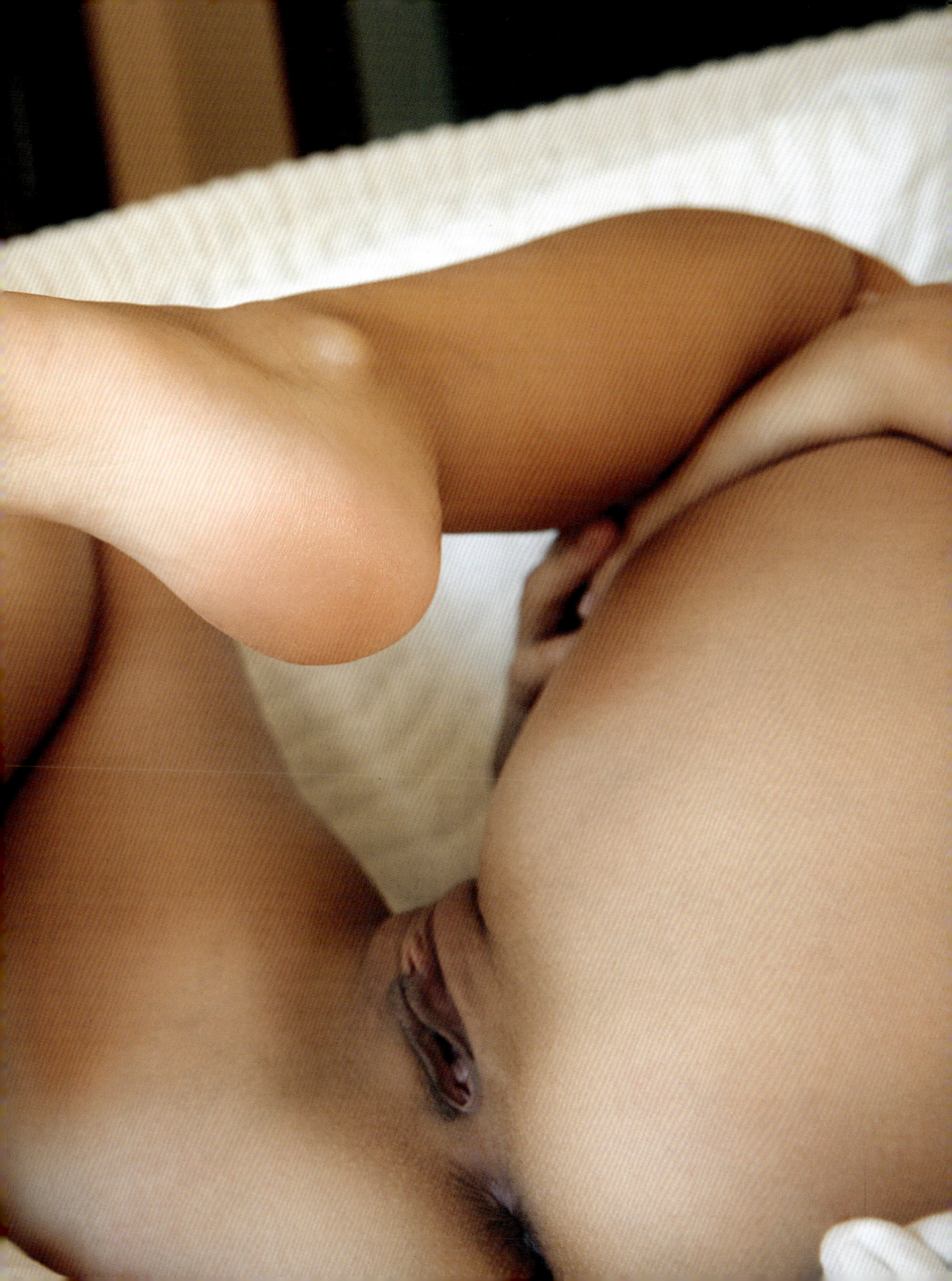

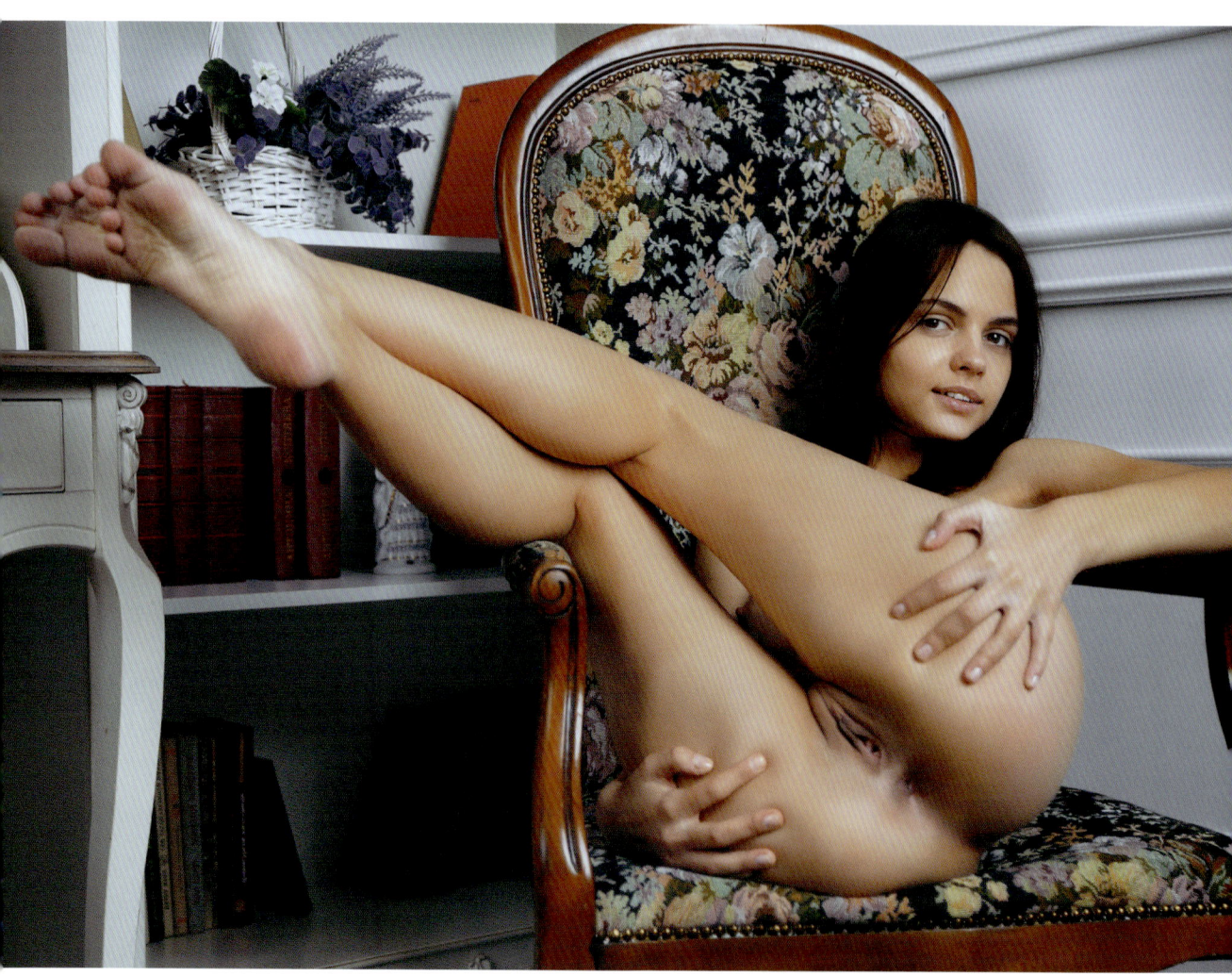

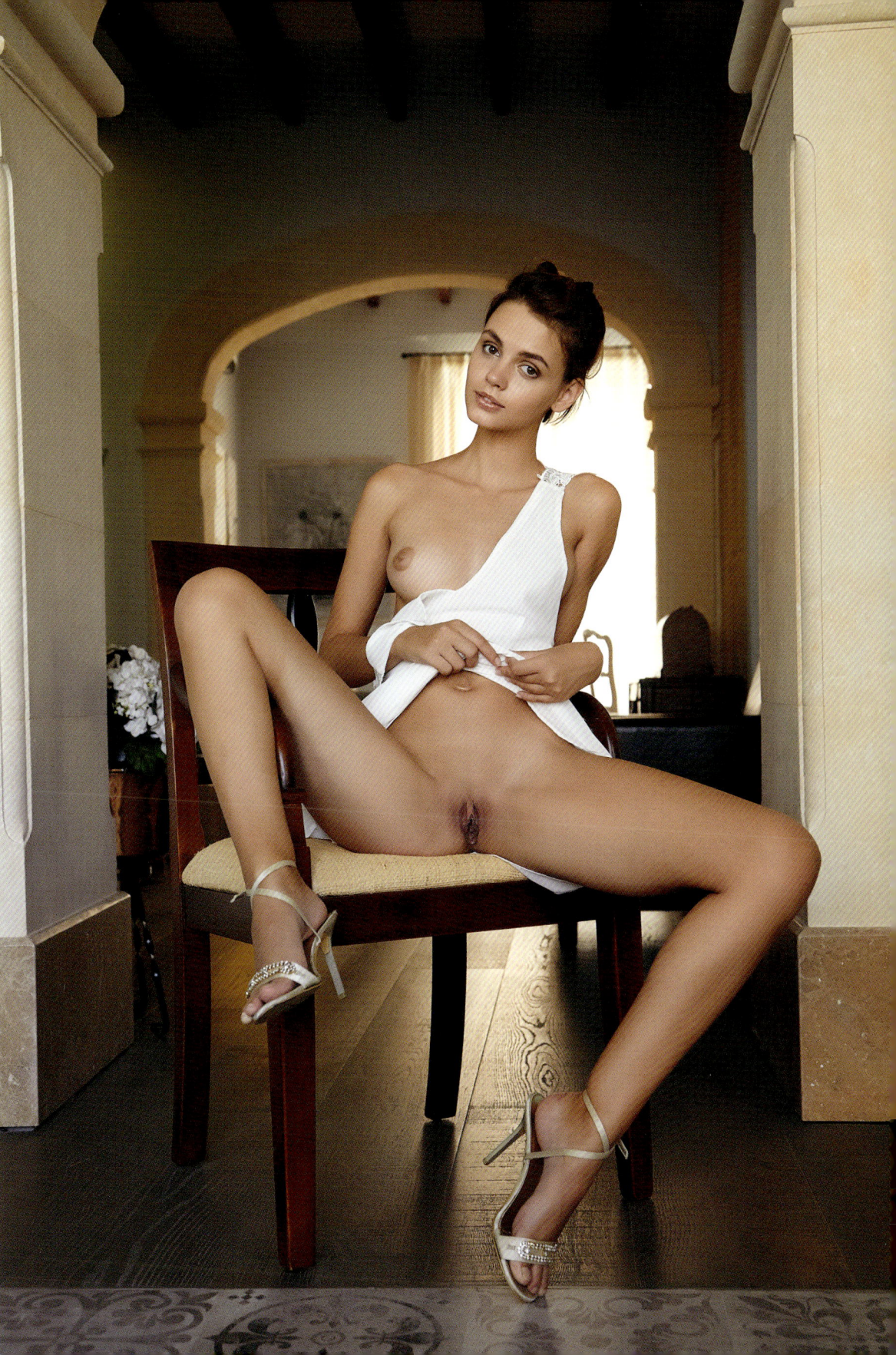

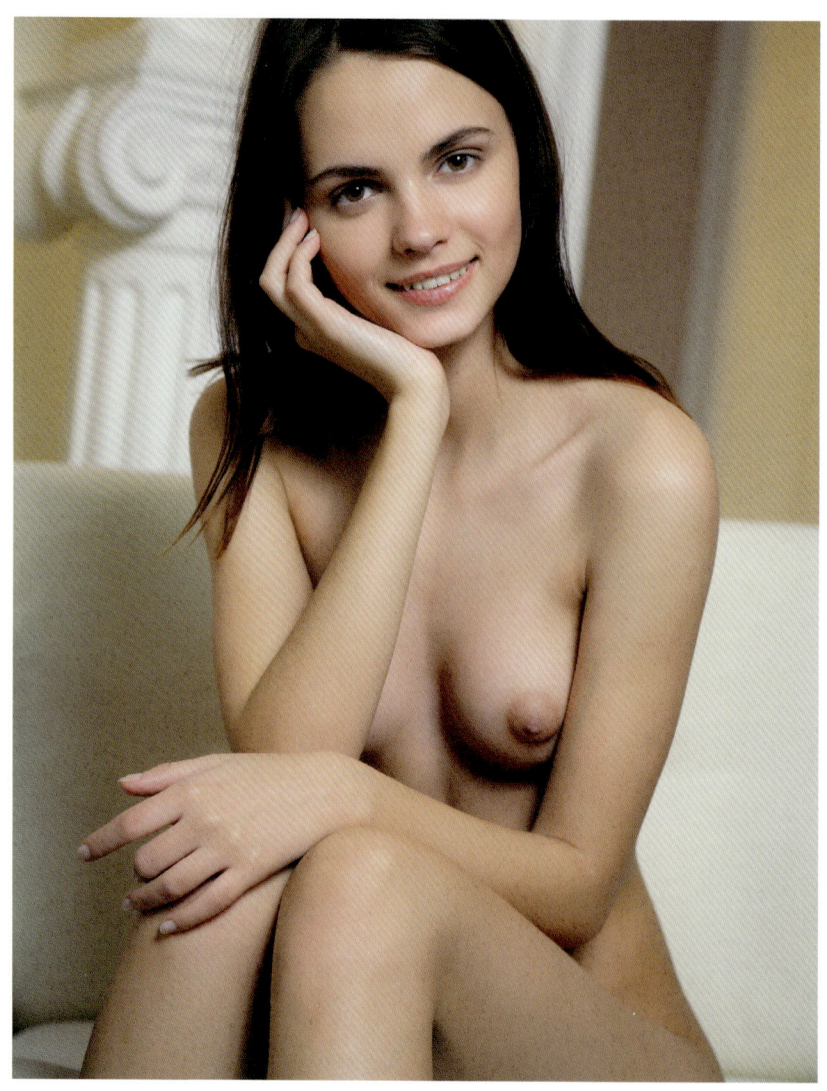

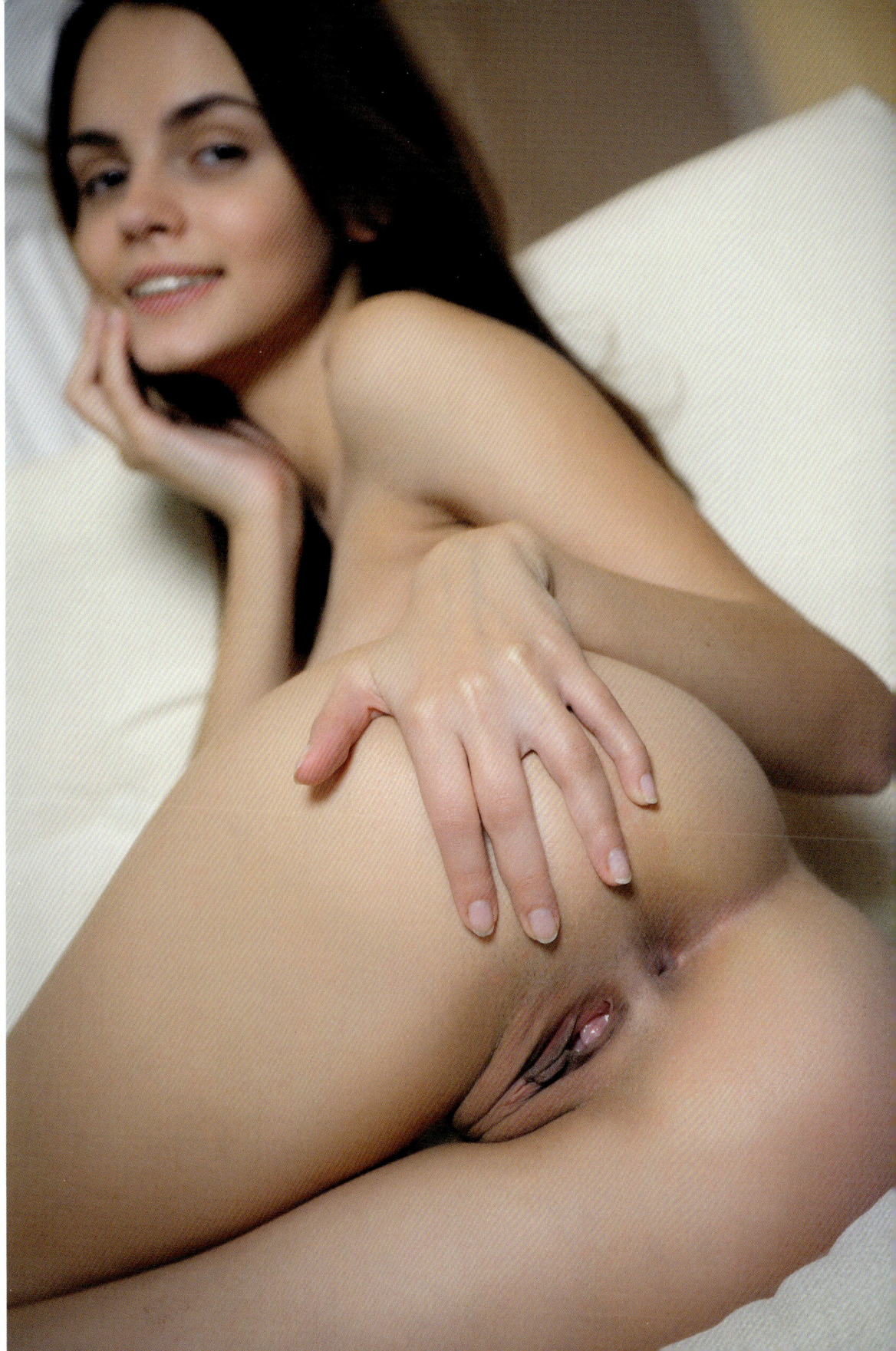

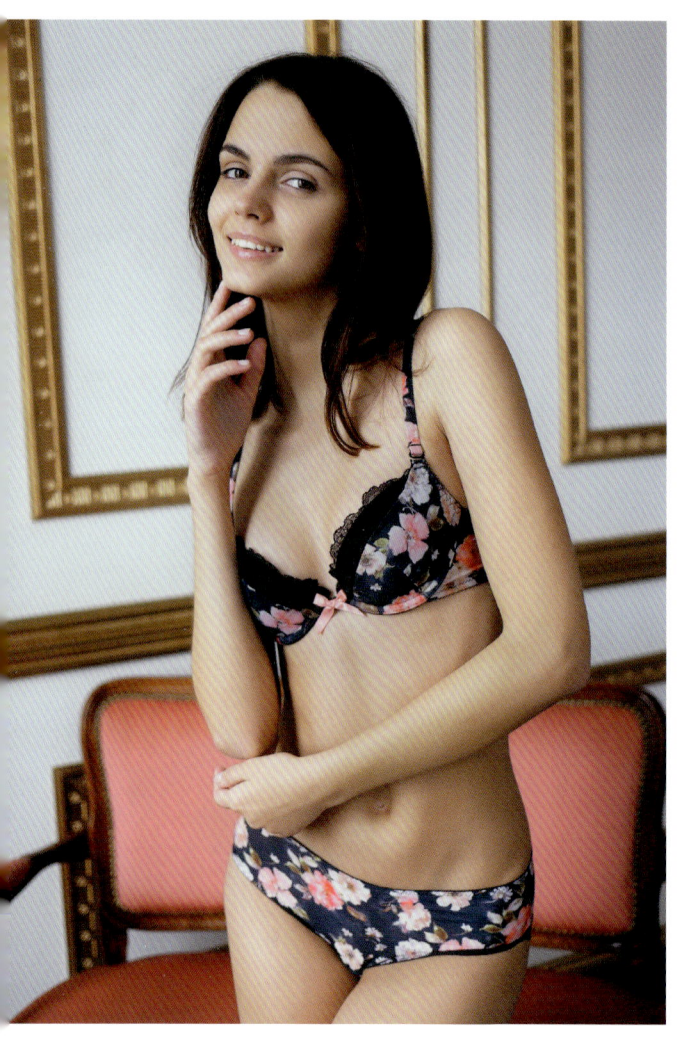
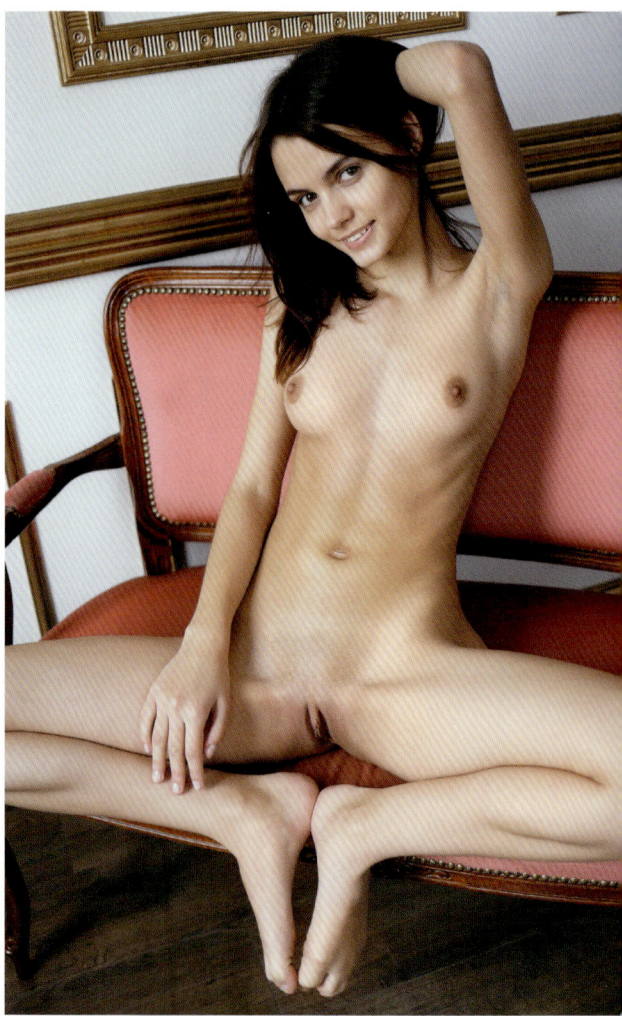

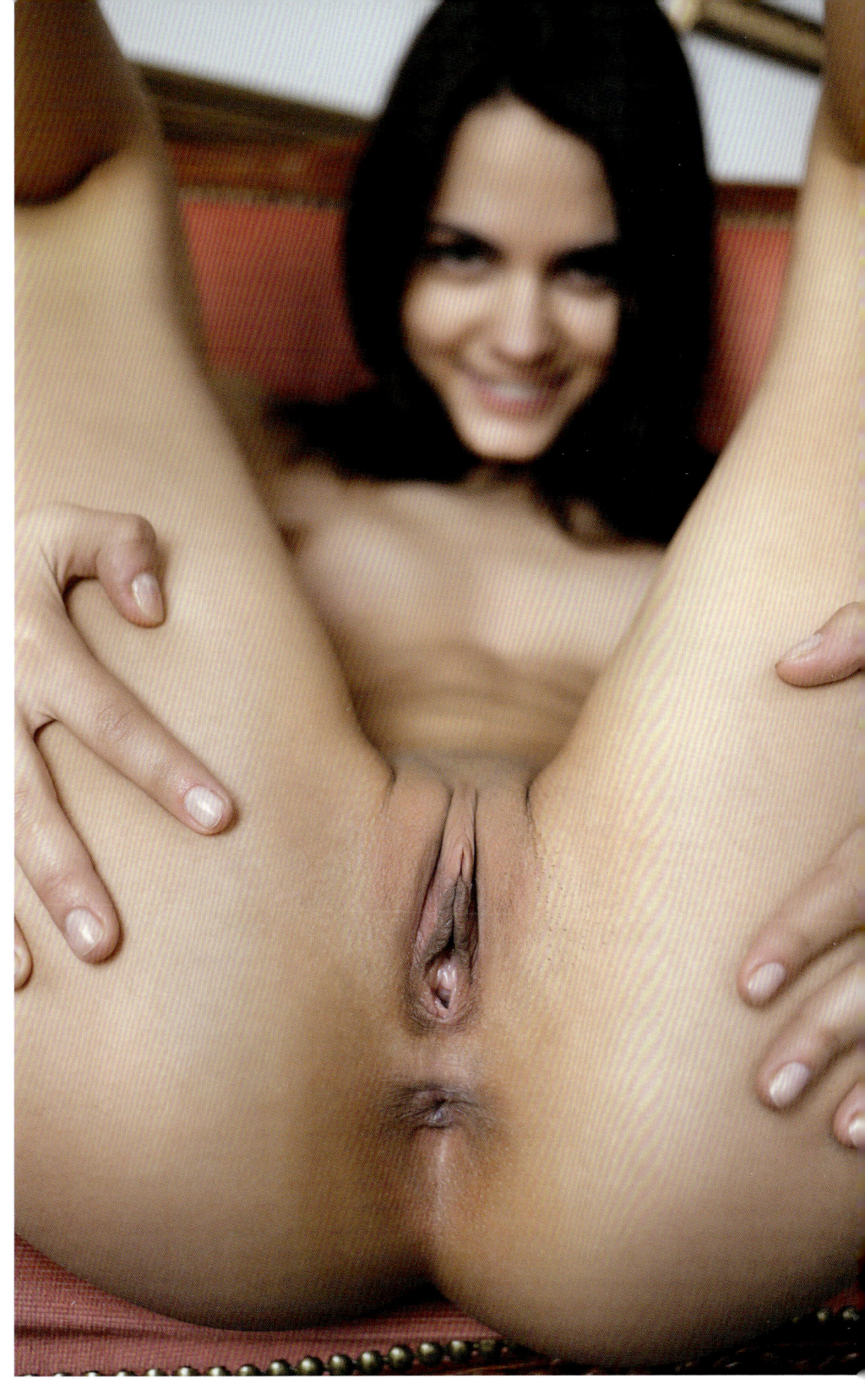

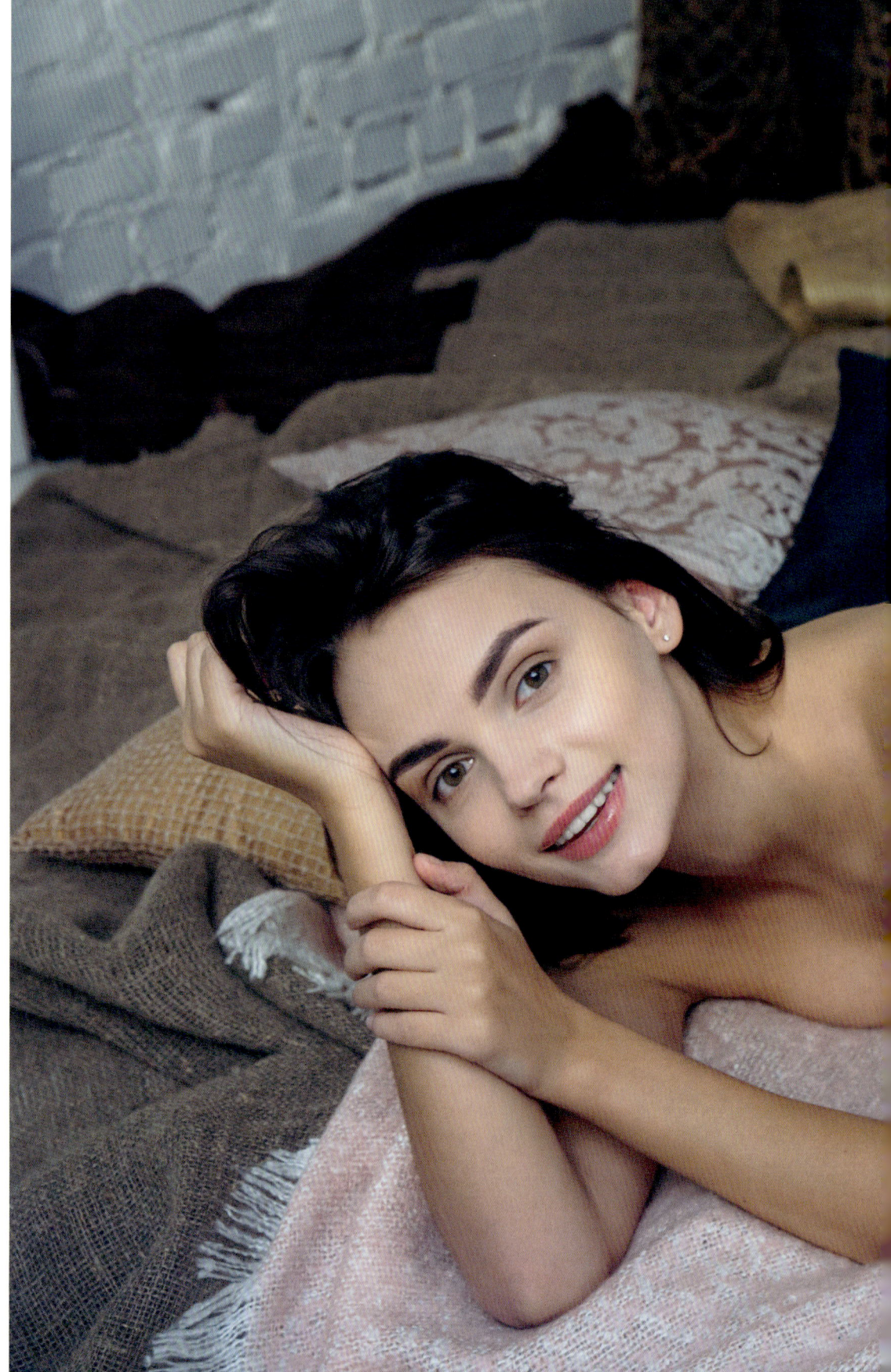

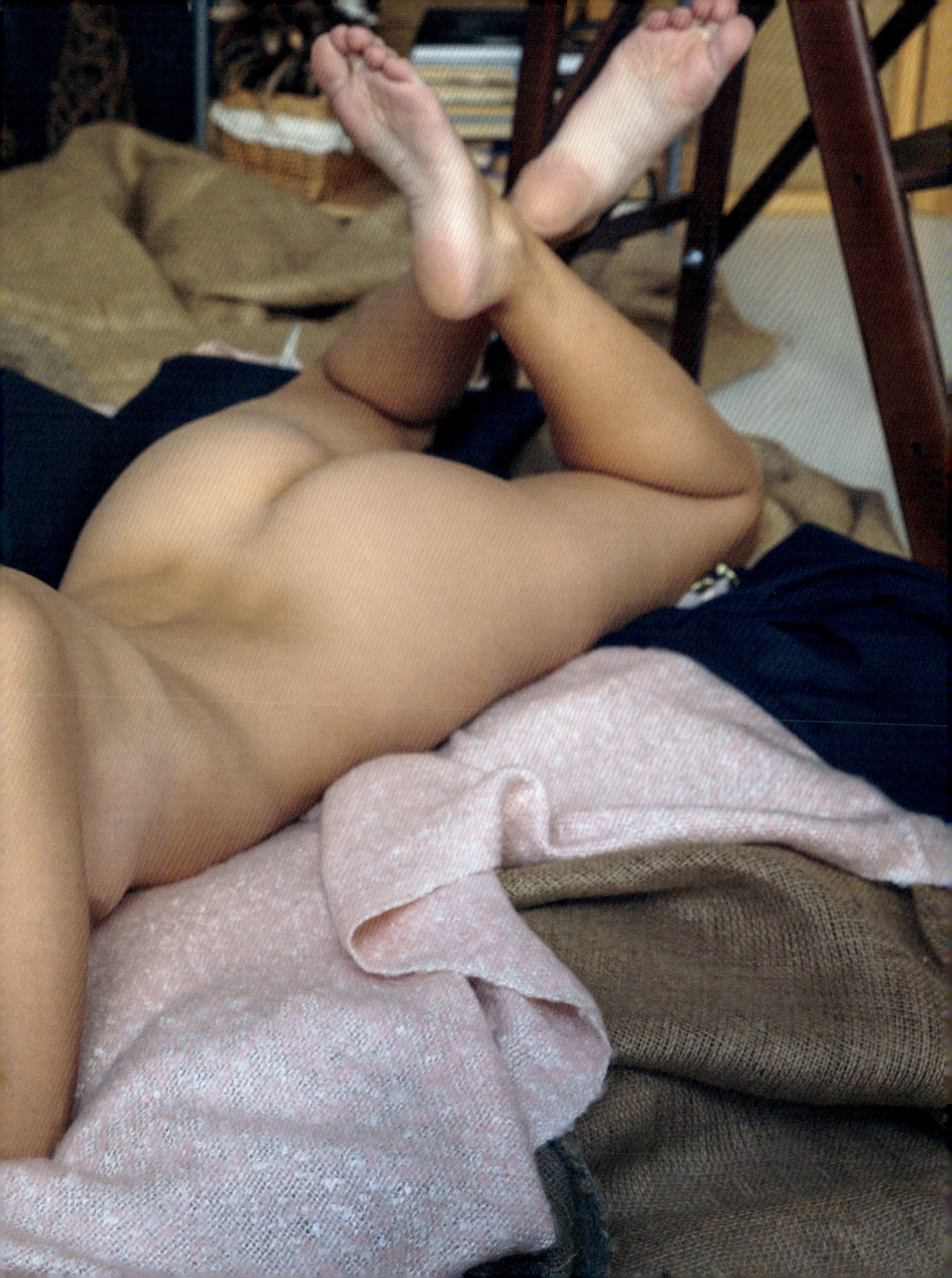

COLLECT THEM ALL: OUR MOST BEAUTIFUL

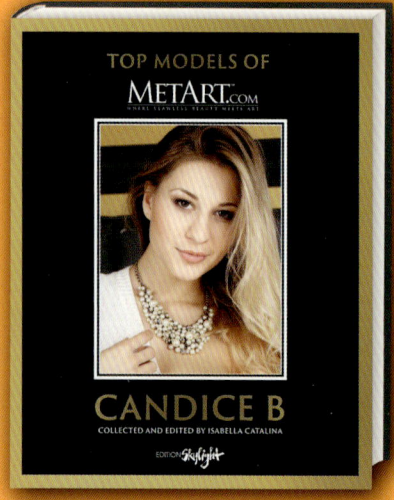
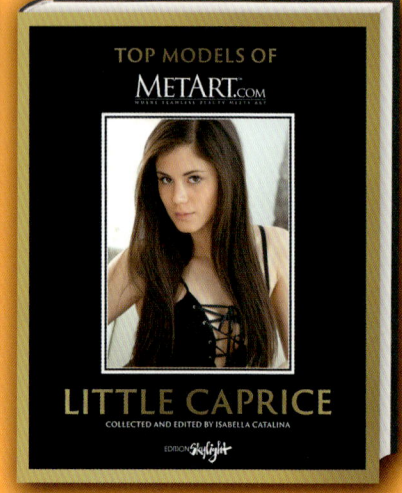
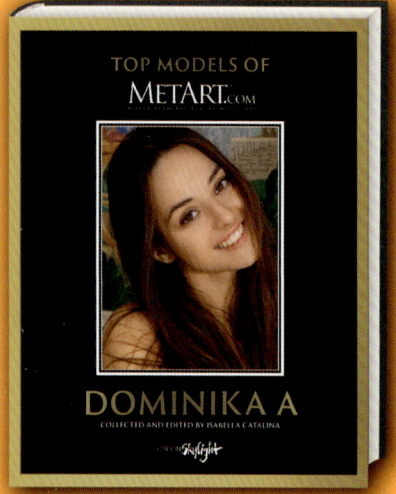
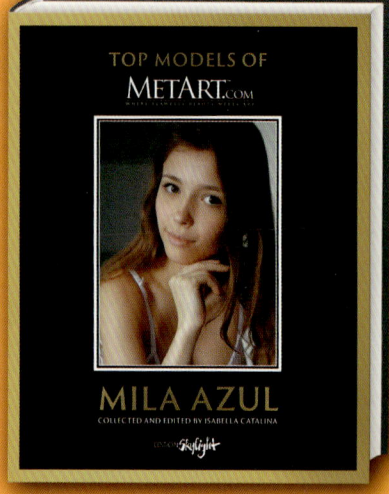
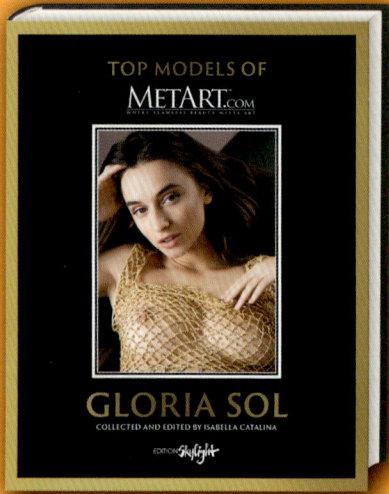